KUṆḌALINĪ YOGA

KUṆḌALINĪ YOGA

Swami Sivananda Radha

MOTILAL BANARSIDASS PUBLISHERS
PRIVATE LIMITED • DELHI

First Revised Indian Edition : Delhi, 2007
First Indian Edition : Delhi, 1992

First published in the United States in 1978
by Timeless Books, Box 3643, Spokane, WA 99220

ISBN: 81-208-0812-6 (HB)
ISBN: 81-208-1014-7 (PB)

MOTILAL BANARSIDASS
41 U.A. Bungalow Road, Jawahar Nagar, Delhi 110 007
8 Mahalaxmi Chamber, 22 Bhulabhai Desai Road, Mumbai 400 026
203 Royapettah High Road, Mylapore, Chennai 600 004
236, 9th Main III Block, Jayanagar, Bangalore 560 011
Sanas Plaza, 1302 Baji Rao Road, Pune 411 002
8 Camac Street, Kolkata 700 017
Ashok Rajpath, Patna 800 004
Chowk, Varanasi 221 001

PRINTED IN INDIA
BY JAINENDRA PRAKASH JAIN AT SHRI JAINENDRA PRESS,
A-45 NARAINA, PHASE-I, NEW DELHI 110 028
AND PUBLISHED BY NARENDRA PRAKASH JAIN FOR
MOTILAL BANARSIDASS PUBLISHERS PRIVATE LIMITED,
BUNGALOW ROAD, DELHI 110 007

DEDICATION

To all Gurus who have prepared the Path, especially to Swami Sivananda Sarasvati of Rishikesh, India, whose inspiration resulted in the birth of my spiritual life, and to my Tibetan Guru, who taught me the "laying of the foundation."

TABLE OF CONTENTS

INTRODUCTION

Swami Radha is my guru. Through the stories she told me, I learned how life can be transformed and made purposeful through Kuṇḍalinī Yoga. She was a wonderful storyteller, but always the stories reflected the wisdom she had gained from using the Kuṇḍalinī system as a structure for self-examination. For me, her stories had a higher purpose of challenging the conventional ideas and concepts of my upbringing, which I had never questioned. At the same time they inspired me to think about alternative ways of responding. Because she used the Kuṇḍalinī system to make sense of her life, I was inspired to do the same for myself.

At the time of our first meeting I saw myself as a guarded, cautious person, not one to open his heart to just anyone, and so I was surprised, even a little shocked, by the warmth and honesty I felt during our exchanges. Today I can see that I was unconsciously responding to her Light. After many years of working with the Kuṇḍalinī system, I also understand that speech based on personal experience can be trusted. In workshops and in less formal settings, when Swami Radha asked me questions about my life, no matter how personal they might appear, I could sense that they came from a place of deep caring that was inherently trustworthy. I trusted because I knew from listening to her that she had looked at the same issues in her life and had learned from them. Simple, yet profoundly precious. She had the power of one who is very aware over one who is not, and yet she exercised that power with the care and respect of a loving mother toward her child. Her guru, Swami Sivananda, had said to her, "Be a spiritual mother to all. The mother has all the milk the baby will need, before the baby is born." And that was my experience.

Swami Radha often spoke of the brief and intense time she had with her guru, and of her own introduction to Kuṇḍalinī Yoga over fifty years ago. Because of visa restrictions, she had just six months in India. Her guru could give her only a taste – a fleeting glimpse – of the yoga system that was to become the foundation of her teaching in the West. That she has done so much with that tenuous beginning is proof that Swami Sivananda knew what he was doing when he asked her to return to the West and update the ancient teachings of yoga. In her hands, he knew that the teachings would be safe.

In the spring of 1956, a few weeks after her initiation into sanyas, she left India and returned to Canada to begin her work. As soon as she could, she ordered the complete sixteen-volume set of Sir John Woodroffe's classic translation of the Kuṇḍalinī Sastra from the publisher in Bombay, and had the books shipped home to Montreal. Titles like *The Serpent Power, Shakti and Shakta, Garland of Letters* and *Ananda Lahari* would become a constant source of daily reflection in the years ahead.

Swami Sivananda had demanded a lot of her. What would it mean to truly update the teachings? She knew it wasn't just a question of transposing the language of one spiritual tradition to another. To be meaningful and lasting, the teachings would have to be based on personal experience. She started with the spiritual practices she had been given in India – the Divine Light Invocation, the Mantra, Haṭha Yoga, plus she developed the meditations and exercises that accompany each cakra in this book – and she worked steadily with them until she knew their power as it applied to her life. She practiced the Divine Light Invocation for two years, for example, before she felt ready to teach the practice to others. Working with translated texts of the ancient Kuṇḍalinī Sāstra, she was amazed to discover that speech was originally called the goddess, the Devī, the power manifest. After chanting the mantra for five hours a day for two years, she could speak of this power of speech from her own experience.

Whenever time allowed, she turned to the verses and scriptural translations to see how they could relate to her life. Through this intense period of study and practice, the hidden, esoteric teachings of the Kuṇḍalinī system began to reveal themselves. Today, going to her library and picking out any one of these sixteen volumes, I cannot help but feel something of her presence through the quiet wisdom that vibrates in the texture and beautiful language of these old texts. Little bits of yellowing paper, each with a key word or two, or a comment in her handwriting, are still in place marking passages that were particularly important to her. The knowledge gained from her work came together in the first edition of *Kundalini Yoga for the West* in 1978, over twenty years after her return from India.

In the early 1990s, Swami Radhananda and I started a weekly reflection on the mantras and verses from *The Serpent Power*, one of these old texts. We decided to do the reflections in a manner similar to the way we imagined she had done them. One of us would read the verse aloud and then we would chant a mantra for a few minutes, sit quietly and watch the thoughts and feelings arising in the mind. When we wrote down our thoughts, it was like creating our own personal commentary. But there was something more. Almost immediately a whole new world began to open up to me. Through the voice of Śakti, the feminine intelligence, the verses came to life and spoke directly to what was happening in my life. To my delight and surprise I found Her at home right in my own heart, and the discovery was exhilarating. When Swami Radha heard what we were doing, she was thrilled. "That's how you discover the deeper meaning," she said. "Keep going and you'll get there." I think for the first time I had an insight into the spiritual dimensions of this fascinating yoga. But it had to happen in its own time, and only after I had built an ethical foundation based on self-knowledge. Swami Radha calls this process character building. *Kundalini Yoga for the West* provided me with a structure for this personal work.

Awareness increases power and power has to be handled responsibly. Having taught many classes in Kuṇḍalinī Yoga, I often see myself in the experiences of those taking the class. This can be painful but it is also the beginning of healing. Appearances create the illusion of separation but awareness dissolves the illusion bit by bit until finally there is a basis for true compassion. I can see why an ethical foundation is so important and why the reflective techniques that I've learned must be kept up. After more than twenty years, I continue to discover more about myself through weekly reflections in my Kuṇḍalinī group.

In the introduction to the first edition of *Kundalini Yoga for the West,* Stanley Krippner remarked that the book was destined to become a classic in the field of yoga. Now, twenty-five years after its original printing, that prediction has clearly been fulfilled. For a whole generation of yoga practitioners, *Kundalini Yoga for the West* has become a deeply personal and meaningful guide for living their lives. Swami Radha describes a path that makes sense to the Western mind without compromising the inspiration and joy that come through personal discovery. She has created a precise blueprint for building the foundation to a practical spiritual life, and she has shown the way. The rest is up to us.

Swami Gopalananda
Yasodhara Ashram

HOW TO USE THIS BOOK

Swami Radha describes the Kuṇḍalinī system as a map to higher consciousness. In *Kundalini Yoga for the West,* she has clearly laid out this map but leaves it up to each one of us whether or not we want to take this journey and what our approach will be.

We each have our own unique way of learning, so how we approach *Kundalini Yoga for the West* will tell us something about ourselves. The questions Swami Radha asks in the first chapter are a good starting point: What is this process of learning? Do I want to learn? And what does it mean to be an aspirant? Record your reflections. They will prove invaluable as a way of seeing changes in yourself over time.

Yoga means to think intuitively, to investigate and to inquire. *Kundalini Yoga for the West* offers a wealth of questions and exercises that require thought and practice in order to realize their benefit. Much of what is offered is a process of clarifying your own thinking in order to dispel past conditioning and to find out where you stand. This process of clarification gradually will lead to the awareness that the mind has an awesome power. As you continue to reflect and practice, you will be able to see your own evolution of consciousness built on personal understanding.

One recommended approach with *Kundalini Yoga for the West* is to work in a group. Everyone can do their own thinking on the questions related to each cakra, writing down their understanding and reading their reflections to the others. In this way you can expand your awareness by hearing a variety of perceptions on the same topic – realizing your uniqueness and also your interconnectedness.

Each cakra of the Kuṇḍalinī system is related to an element, a level of consciousness and a sense perception. You can choose to focus on any of these areas. For example, work through the exercises in all the cakras on the senses, or on speech, mind or sex.

The color cakra plates are a visual representation of the Kuṇḍalinī system. These images are like a mirror. What are you drawn to? Can you see the images as symbolic aspects of yourself? The gods and goddesses represent the intelligence of the cakra. Looking at them, can you recognize the tools they hold as effective means for dealing with the issues arising at this point in your life? When you look at the whole system, ask how it relates to you. What does it mean that the cakras are represented symbolically within the human body, and particularly within the spine?

Each cakra also has a mantra, which is presented at the beginning of each chapter. These mantras, like the visual images, are seeds containing the essence of the cakra. They may seem esoteric or foreign at first, but by reading and reflecting on them you may be surprised at how they resonate and generate insights.

Kundalini Yoga for the West offers an abundance of spiritual practices. You can bring practices such as mantra and the Divine Light Invocation into every group or personal reflection to help clear the mind and encourage receptivity to your own inner wisdom.

One of the mind's most intriguing qualities is intelligence. What are the undiscovered possibilities of your mind? By using the techniques for self-discovery in *Kundalini Yoga for the West*, you will develop a foundation of understanding and awareness from which to grow. With sincerity and perseverance, you can liberate yourself from the limitations that now hold you back. This is the purpose of the path of Kuṇḍalinī. This is the path that leads to freedom.

Swami Radhananda
President, Yasodhara Ashram

A WORD FROM THE AUTHOR

The idea of writing a book on Kuṇḍalinī Yoga, when first suggested by my students, did not appeal to me at all. Yet as students took notes and taped instructions, it occurred to me that this type of groundwork, put together into a book, might indeed be helpful. Scholarly works, translations of the sacred texts (and we are most grateful to the scholars who have undertaken the formidable task of translating old scriptures) are necessary for study, but only after a foundation has been laid.

Modern men and women are under tremendous pressures today, perhaps greater than at any other time in history. Whatever the lifestyle, one seems to move too fast to digest the experiences that take place during each day. The pressure felt is not exclusively because of work, although this may be part of it, but because of the enormous amount of material that has to be assimilated by an individual to survive in a highly competitive environment. The complexity of life has become such that one becomes either panicky or lethargic. In the latter case, the attitude of "It doesn't matter anyway" may act as a key sentence in the mind and, through its unaware repetition, may achieve an almost hypnotic effect. Once settled in the mind, it is kept alive by emotions that can be both desperate and depressive. If violence is not one's nature, resignation to life seems the only way. The natural life rhythm simply cannot absorb the constant impact of news, television and urban living, combined with the many power struggles that are outside the domain of an individual's control. "Live NOW" becomes the motto. However, this is an unfortunate reaction, leading one ever faster down the road to disaster, encouraging self-indulgence and excesses on many levels.

Modern technology, despite the numerous and superficially impressive advances, is rather a punishment in disguise, increasing the burden for the average individual. With the massive bombardment of the senses that supposedly brings relaxation, relief and pleasure, men and women are driven away from their inner being. The true source of power and energy renewal is buried to such a degree that help is needed to rediscover it. There is no point in an individual expecting this help from technology and the manipulators of power. A totally new approach has to be worked out in order for life to have any meaning besides the dollar and what it stands for.

The sense of the inner self, of that knowing from within, is the only secure foundation on which to build one's life. The need to come back to this inner core is great, and it is my hope that help will be found to make that return through the material in this book.

I have attempted to steer a middle course (not that of the full renunciate) by presenting as clear an account as possible of what Kuṇḍalinī is, along with exercises that will help interested individuals in their development. It is along the lines of what my own teacher called "laying the foundation," as it will prepare one to move further along the path of Kuṇḍalinī. For centuries, Kuṇḍalinī was veiled in mystery because it was only related from the guru to a disciple who had to prove himself or herself in many ways. Since the invention of print, many previously handwritten manuscripts have been translated and have become available to the public. People with little or no background and therefore limited understanding were attracted to such publications. The mind, ever ready to create new and colorful fabrics, grasps this opportunity to interpret according to its fancy. When this is done with something as powerful as Kuṇḍalinī energy, it can lead to all sorts of disorders.

Kuṇḍalinī energy manifests itself in as many ways as the sun has rays. In most people the energy is latent. Like electricity, it is neutral. The gurus stress the need to gain control of any kind of power. To illustrate this point, we could compare such control to an electric-light dimmer, which, with each turn of the dial, gradually releases more power and so increases the light. With any kind of energy – anger, for example, which can express great power – control is essential. For those who have laid the foundation by learning self-mastery, the Kuṇḍalinī energy, when understood, can be controlled at will. The foundation must be built slowly and carefully so that this ability to control can be developed. The process of evolution, of which men and women are a part, forces them to develop physically and mentally so that higher levels of consciousness can fully unfold. The choice for both sexes is to cooperate with the law of evolution or to be a victim of it. It is essential to do the groundwork so that the person can handle the energy when it does begin to stir. It seldom happens suddenly. The aim is Liberation in all areas, wherever limitation may exist.

The first stage in Kuṇḍalinī Yoga is becoming aware. It presents a well laid-out plan that encompasses more and more aspects of one's life. Like concentric circles, it is ever expanding. Once the principal idea that moves like a red thread through the levels of consciousness is understood, a marvelous way of life is opened to the individual. There is a vast potential that lies within each of us

– the potential of energy, power, heightened perception and awareness. Evolution for humans must now refer to evolution of consciousness, and Kuṇḍalinī offers a blueprint of the vast mine to be tapped.

My own acquaintance with Kuṇḍalinī Yoga came through direct teaching while I was in India. The difference in cultural background proved often to be perplexing, leading to confusion and misinterpretations. But my desire to learn and to know was so great that this may have created by itself a sensitivity, helping me to understand what was presented to me, helping me to absorb what was given on each occasion, even though these "seeds" took their own time to germinate.

Even ordinary changes in life are often resisted because of the uncertainty of the unknown. This insecurity is due to the intellect's putting itself on the throne of omniscience and dismissing what it does not know as nonexistent. When the unknown is encountered, the intellect, together with the emotions, puts up a struggle to eliminate it or explain it away. Because of this human attitude, we know little about ourselves and are so timid about finding out that only a very few courageous individuals can free themselves from this limitation. The progress of human life is very slow. Those who dare to explore our possible powers tend to keep the secrets to themselves.

We can use our intellect differently, as my teacher pointed out to me. He declared that a person of high intellect was one who could learn from the mistakes of others, without having to repeat them. He also said, "All suffering is self-created because of ignorance. Remove ignorance and there will be no suffering." The Kuṇḍalinī energy, properly handled and controlled, can become a powerful tool in one's life. It makes its presence felt most of the time accidentally or only in a limited way as clairvoyance, clairaudience or personal magnetism.

Many exercises have been given, some of them in a form that the aspirant may consider "skimpy" or not clearly defined. The reason for the lack of definition is to exert little influence and so allow the aspirant as much freedom and autonomy as possible. The Eastern teacher will not take the joy of discovery from the student and I have followed this tradition.

In summary, the purpose of this book is to give the tools by which those who wish to cooperate with the process of evolution can do so. There is no mystification about the awakening of Kuṇḍalinī, yet this process leads to the mystical experience.

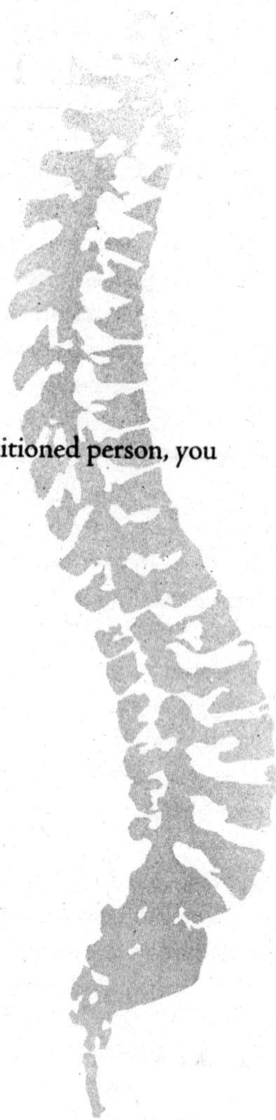

From being a sleepwalker, a hypnotized or conditioned person, you gradually become a person who is aware.

1. THE ASPIRANT

THE ASPIRANT

Self-development in yoga may, in the initial stages, seem to have much in common with the psychological approaches of the human growth movement. However, the goals are fundamentally different. The person who undertakes human growth therapy works toward self-acceptance, efficient functioning in everyday life and mature relationships not based on emotional needs. But the spiritual aspirant, man or woman, looks at this development from a different perspective. There is already an innate perception, however vague, that there is more to life than having a family, friends, reasonable success – "the good life." For such a person, the goal is liberation from all limitations, realizing all human potential and, finally, the Self.

Anyone entering the path of Kuṇḍalinī Yoga must clarify the reasons and motivation for considering such an undertaking. Any building, be it a storeroom, a tiny house or a big mansion, needs a foundation. The type of foundation reflects the purpose of the building to be constructed. Similarly, the foundation of a spiritual life indicates the perception of the purpose of life, and the way of life chosen will reflect this purpose. During the time the foundation is laid, the aspirant will need special tools to help in this development. Yogic exercises and spiritual practice provide these tools.

The first question to be asked is: "What is the purpose of my life? What makes my life worth living?" This is the beginning of self-inquiry, and in the pages that follow you will frequently be asked, "What do you mean by such words as consciousness, mind, ego?" "What are their characteristics? Do you use these words synonymously, or is there a difference?" Without such self-inquiry, you are subject to the authority and opinions of others – parents, friends, the mass media, and so on.

We must investigate all of our concepts and ideas, anything we have accepted blindly, without question. Such unquestioning acceptance of authority is tantamount to allowing ourselves to be hypnotized, programmed, conditioned. We must ask, "What is hypnosis? Where (in what areas of my life) am I hypnotized?" You may find that you are indeed being hypnotized and that in your early years you were programmed by the ideas and, in some cases, the misconceptions of the adults around you. Perhaps you were told, "You can't play outside if it's raining because you will catch a cold." Years later, you may still catch cold on a rainy day. We condition ourselves with such ideas as, "I only slept for four hours last night so I will be tired by this afternoon." We tell ourselves, "I hate getting up in the morning," but do we really mean, "I am unwilling to face the daily problems"?

The words "hypnosis," "conditioning," "programming" need to be very carefully investigated in the light of your own experience and understanding. Not what the book says. Not what the hypnotist, teacher or television says. What do you mean by them?

In the course of spiritual growth, all of our concepts, ideas and beliefs have to be investigated and re-evaluated over and over again. What you are thinking now may hold no value in three months or three years. You will have grown, your awareness will have increased and your level of understanding will have risen. From being a sleepwalker, a hypnotized or conditioned person, you gradually become a person who is aware. The process of waking up from ignorance and delusion, of becoming free from as many limitations as possible, and eventually of reaching the goal of Cosmic Consciousness – this is the purpose of the path of Kuṇḍalinī.

There are a number of pitfalls against which the aspirant must be on guard. The first is the habit of making assumptions. "I assume" means "I really don't know," and all discussions that are based only on assumption are futile and useless.

The assumption that life must always be exciting can lead the aspirant to another pitfall: seeking to develop psychic powers. These powers are not in themselves harmful or a hindrance to further development. It is rather the self-indulgence, the need for continuous excitement that will finally lead to downfall on the spiritual path as one loses sight of the goal in the search for entertainment. This attitude will prevent the development of inner peace and harmony and the achievement of depth and quality in human relationships or personal experience. To live between boredom and excitement is to be caught on a teeter-totter, having little control of your destiny, subject to the vicissitudes of life. The purpose of Kuṇḍalinī Yoga is to become aware and to know yourself. This is the path that leads to freedom.

Another pitfall for the aspirant is to seek a guru on the basis of a display of psychic powers. These are in no way evidence of a high level of spirituality. They may be very useful, and many who have developed these powers have done good work (in such cases as the mysterious disappearance of people or objects). But others have developed them to promote their self-importance and personal gain. Psychic ability is no proof of being a great guru, yogi or master, or even of being spiritual.

Surrender and humility are the most important requirements for practicing Kuṇḍalinī Yoga. When all the exercises have been done and a certain degree of self-mastery, concentration, meditation and contemplation has been achieved, you may go in search of your guru. The aspirant may ask, why not now, at this stage? Because the Teachings take for granted that this foundation of self-discipline has already been laid. No one can be taught to write poetry when the alphabet has not yet been learned.

Awareness will come in degrees and at one point in the process of development a guru will be necessary. You would not expect to become a qualified doctor solely through studying medicine theoretically. Reading about surgical procedures would not give one the courage to perform an operation. Treatment or surgery on the mind demands a spiritual teacher, for in both cases practical guidance is needed. From an Eastern point of view, all we learn in school is only information. Knowledge is gained from personal experience and reflection.

Many Westerners find it difficult to put their faith in something from which there is no tangible return. The fear of putting years of effort into what could prove to be an illusion is understandable. The proof that this arduous task of self-development is worth all the effort lies in the emergence of self-mastery in your life. The self-control achieved by the exercises is itself a power. Increased concentration, control of emotions, growing awareness, loss of fear, growing courage, an inner knowing and security all pave the road to realization and give proof to the aspirant that the road is indeed real.

So any potential aspirant, after much thought on the subject of Kuṇḍalinī, must ask some pertinent questions: What is really involved? What is this process of learning? Do I want to learn? What can I gain from it? What are the obstacles to learning? Can they be overcome? How? What does it mean to be an aspirant? What is my motive for interest in the spiritual life?

The practice of Kuṇḍalinī Yoga is deeply involving. Mere dabbling is dangerous; half-knowledge is worse than no knowledge at all. No progress is possible through reading the sacred texts and intellectualizing about their contents. Many people are victims of their own self-deception, judging themselves to be good people and assuming that they have faith. How the knowledge gained is applied to your life is the essential determining factor. Sincerity is the keynote. The process of learning is a continuous one – as with the concert pianist, practice never stops. "Do I want to learn?" is then an important decision that must be supported by the will – it is indeed a decision of will. In contrast to will, there is self-will, which creates obstacles – intellectualizations and justifications – that divert the aspirant from the path. Self-discipline, enforced by the will, must be exercised to overcome these obstacles. Each victory makes one stronger.

Where does this leave the aspirant who is married, who may have an earnest yearning toward expanded consciousness? My Guru, Swami Sivananda (of Rishikesh), would always suggest that family life was an excellent opportunity to practice selfless service, to develop consideration, love, patience and understanding, and to expand that kindness to others who are not of one's kin; to consider oneself to be God's caretaker of the family and those in need, and to love without attachment. This, he would say, is the best preparation for the time when spiritual practice can be pursued with all the intensity of which one is capable. Since one cannot serve two masters, it may be better to accept that limitation while it exists and spend that time in self-development.

The aspirant must be prepared to face the problem of "What will other people think?" There may be accusations: "Aren't you being selfish? Isn't this just another ego trip? What a terrible thing to do to your family!" Some academic careers may take twelve years' training – which may not make one a better person, or any wiser as far as personal life is concerned. Yet this "selfish" period, devoted to acquiring knowledge and developing skills in a particular field, is never questioned. But, when it comes to self-development to become a better person, to find meaning in life, the time and effort spent seem to require justification.

People once considered friends may turn cold. They feel challenged and, not prepared to accept the challenge, they turn away. Suddenly the path seems very lonely. There is no one to turn to, no shoulder to lean on. The Light that you are following seems less visible. However, at the same time another phase becomes apparent. A sense of freedom from the tyranny of social obligation, from continually struggling to meet other people's expectations, is experienced. It is like a breath of fresh air!

The aspirant will, every now and then, be assailed by doubt. The question must be asked, "Do I doubt so that I don't have to act, so that I can keep a back door open through which I can escape?" or "Do I doubt because I have an intuitive perception that this doubt could expand my present limited ideas?"

The first kind of doubt is an obstacle created by self-will. The second is a necessary step in the process of development. Be patient. Any discovery by yourself, however small, becomes a knowing within that provides another stone for a foundation of stability and security. Observation and awareness develop in an aspirant in proportion to the desire to know oneself, by the courage to accept that which is observed and, finally, by the application of the will to make the necessary changes.

Worship seems to have lost its place in modern life. Yet there is in every man and woman, coming to the foreground in precious moments, the value, the greatness and the rightness to worship that which is a great inspiration. Somewhere within everyone there is the knowing of a greater power, and it is this inner knowing that generates within us the urge to worship. When we recognize that we are a bridge between two worlds, the mental-physical-material on the one hand and the spiritual on the other, and when we walk over this bridge, there is suddenly a profound humility as we realize the great and awesome Power.

The aspirant must decide if he or she is prepared to embark upon this road, prepared to do the work and make the sacrifices. Let there be no mistake, the "Pearl of Great Price" exacts its price.

The purpose and meaning of life can be found within the mystical meanings of the Haṭha Yoga āsanas.

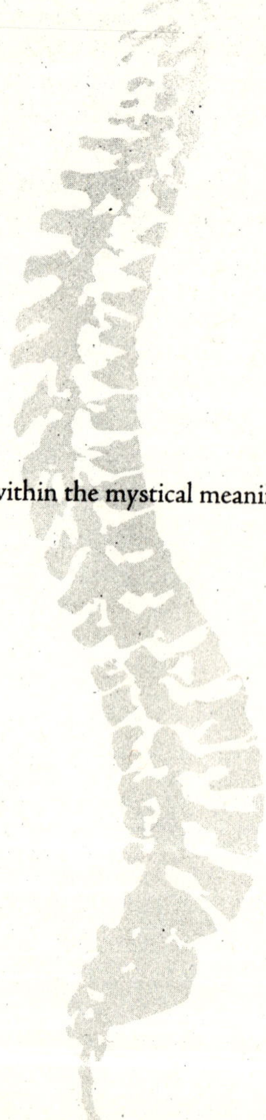

2. MYSTICAL ASPECTS OF HAṬHA YOGA

MYSTICAL ASPECTS OF HAṬHA YOGA

Balancing polarities

Haṭha Yoga is one aspect of Kuṇḍalinī Yoga and plays an important part in the development of the aspirant. The scriptural interpretation of the word haṭha expresses the polarity in which all beings function. Ha is said to be the positive or active principle of existence, symbolized by the sun, heat, light and creativity. Ṭha is correspondingly the negative or reflective principle, symbolized by the moon, cold, darkness and receptivity. The performance in slow motion of the gentle, graceful movements of Haṭha Yoga and the reflective holding of various āsanas allow body, mind and spirit to come into harmony through the balance of these two basic energies. The constant disciplined practice of breathing exercises, postures and relaxation subtly transforms the body into a vital spiritual tool through which levels of intuitive understanding are reached, and the mystical aspects of Haṭha Yoga gradually unfold and reveal their secrets.

Health aspects

Yoga is the oldest known science of physical and mental self-development, caring for the body under the intelligent control of the mind. Thousands of years ago, the yogis recognized our basic need for discipline to counteract the physical and spiritual deterioration caused by the mere fight for survival. They were aware that when the positive and negative currents by which the human body is enlivened are in equilibrium we enjoy perfect health. Through Haṭha Yoga we can achieve absolute control over the whole body, thus improving the condition of every part and maintaining the body as a necessary and valuable tool of human evolution.

Body as a spiritual tool

The body is the instrument through which we act out our desires and exercise our will. The five senses, our organs of perception and experience of the world around us, are located in the body. The brain functions as the physical organ which the mind utilizes to interpret all these experiences. The training of body and mind through Haṭha Yoga helps to bring bodily urges, emotions and misdirected willpower under control. Haṭha Yoga in its various aspects is a means to reach a new understanding of the body and how to use it as a wonderful tool. It is the aim of the yogi and yogini to attain awareness in all areas of the body, the senses and the mind.

Many descriptions of the physical benefits of regular Haṭha Yoga practice are available to the Westerner, and some information on the psychological aspects as well. The mystical aspects, however, are largely unrecognized or misinterpreted in Western writing. In the Eastern tradition of teaching, the aspirant is not "spoon-fed" information, but rather is stimulated by the guru to be a discoverer, an adventurer, an investigator of his or her own body laboratory. Practicing yogis agree that only one āsana, the headstand, can be used as an explanation to show the mystical meanings of Haṭha Yoga. The revelation of the meaning of other āsanas is left to individual self-discovery. Why is this so important? What you find out for yourself becomes an enormous source of energy and inspires you to keep on expanding beyond your limitations, to find out more, to understand more. It is up to you to think intuitively, to investigate, to inquire, because the yogic teacher will not take the joy and pleasure of discovery from you. The less that is fed to the mind, the more insight you get by yourself. Personal insight also prevents the painful doubt, "Have I really experienced this, or have I only imagined an illusion based on what I have been told?"

Symbolic aspects

The headstand (Sālambaśirsāsana) is one of the most important āsanas. An investigation of the various aspects of this āsana reveals the depth of symbolic and mystical expression of which the disciplined body is capable.

Once you are able to perform this āsana properly and with confidence, and can maintain balance for several minutes while remaining mentally relaxed and alert, you are ready to proceed to another level of experience. In order to contact the deeper message of any āsana, you must be able to surrender self-will and cultivate the ability to listen with intuition.

Psychological aspects

Begin your investigation on the psychological level. Open your eyes and look at your familiar surroundings – obviously you see everything upside-down. Be aware of what you feel and think. When the āsana has been completed, apply your observations to another level of sight and write down your reaction to looking at life's events upside-down in your mind's eye. Now look at your most cherished beliefs. Write them down. The next step is to take the opposite viewpoint and observe what you feel. Finally, become your own opponent without becoming involved in argument and opposition with anyone else. What is gained? The answer is in the struggle alone, the expansion beyond limitations by confronting your own concepts, and the greater freedom and responsibility resulting from this expansion.

Another psychological aspect can be illustrated by comparing the erect human body to a tree. The feet, firmly placed on the ground, correspond to the roots of the tree, its foundation and source of nourishment. This might indicate that in daily life you stand firmly on the ground to meet life's demands. Your head is in space or heaven. The word "heaven" in this instance means in contact with life's energy, with a wisdom beyond the intellect.

If your mind is rooted in the earth of daily life, and there are other "trees" next to you, the roots soon intertwine in many areas, and eventually you cannot distinguish your own roots from others. Are your foundations – your concepts and beliefs – really yours, or do they just take the sap and energy from other roots? The ego pushes its roots very deep – it does not want to be uprooted at any cost.

In the headstand this tree is turned upside-down. The head is no longer in the clouds, but has become well-rooted and practical, with grounded intellectual abilities. The feet are now rooted in the Divine inspiration of heaven. Although the old hard facts no longer suffice in themselves, the grounded head has not lost its contact with heaven, for inspirational nourishment is now possible that will hold up under practical application and also increase inspirational perception.

Mystical aspects

The analogy of the human tree can be expanded in preparation for the mystical aspects of the headstand. The spine is like the trunk of the tree, along which are located the various cakras. The top of the head is the crowning blossom of this flowering tree, the thousand-petaled Lotus of the Sahasrāra Cakra. A further symbolic term – nectar and ambrosia – must also be clarified. This term stands for intuition and insight of the highest order.

During the headstand, the Mūlādhāra Cakra is in the top position. The place of passion and the emotional use of energy is like a flame. Passion's energy can be used in self-service, in escalating mind and expanding awareness. While the body is in the normal position, the Divine inspirations of nectar and ambrosia fall into the fire of passion and are burned, their benefits wasted. It must be understood that passion is not evil or bad in itself, but the intensity of passionate desire prevents perceptions of a very fine nature, as a spicy dish dulls the taste buds for appreciating a subtle, new and different taste. In the headstand position, the aspirant cannot "feed this flame" to keep it burning. Intuitive perception is no longer killed in the fire of any type of passion, but is preserved for higher spiritual development.

Prāṇic energy is part of the nectar and ambrosia manifest. During the holding of this āsana, Prāṇic energy moves around the body, invigorating it and giving it extra energy. This energy does not only flow through the levels of consciousness, but is also located in the spine and vital organs. If the aspirant always connects the holding of the āsana with a deep spiritual thought, even further energy will be generated for the purpose of spiritual growth and the expanding beyond present limitations.

The performance of āsanas can become a fantastic experience of time and space. In moving the body into a posture, you are moving through time and space. When you hold the position, you are given an opportunity to ponder the meaning of space and time and to penetrate the mystical meanings of the āsanas. "I am sitting in this position for three minutes. What is time? Who am I?" When you can disregard the daily image you see in the mirror and think of yourself beyond the body, you have taken the first step.

The human body is indeed something marvelous and wonderful. Daily we see the miracles of human form – that beautiful apparatus you call your hand or your eyes, the magic mirror of your mind, the limitless creativity of your imagination. The purpose and meaning of life can be found deep within the mystical meanings of the Haṭha Yoga āsanas.

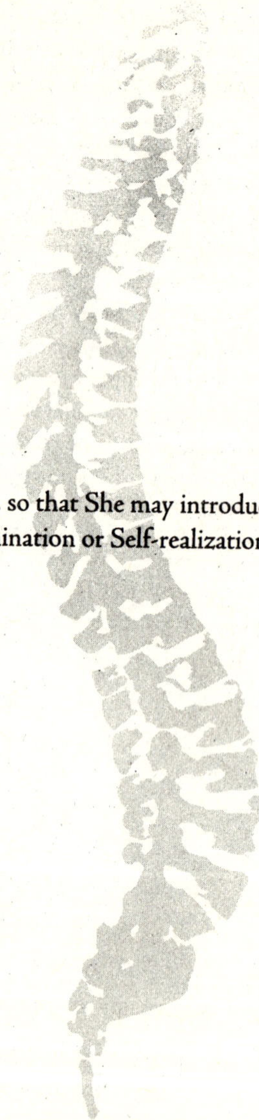

The aspirant should approach the Mother first, so that She may introduce the spiritual Child to the Father for illumination or Self-realization.

3. DIVINE MOTHER ŚAKTI

THE DEVĪ

DIVINE MOTHER ŚAKTI

Śakti Yoga Philosophy
by Swami Sivananda Saraswati of Rishikesh, India

Mother worship is the worship of God as the Divine Mother, as the power of the Lord or the Cosmic Energy. Śakti, then, is Energy. Just as one cannot separate heat from fire, so also one cannot separate Śakti from Śākta. Śakti and Śākta are one. They are inseparable.

Electricity, magnetism, force, heat, light, the five elements and their combinations are all external manifestations of Śakti. Intelligence, discrimination, psychic power and will are all Her manifestations. She keeps up the Līlā of the Lord through the three guṇas: sattva, rajas and tamas. Even lust, anger, greed, egoism and pride are also Her manifestations. Her manifestations are countless.

She lies dormant in the Mūlādhāra Cakra in the form of a serpentine power or coiled-up Energy known as the Kuṇḍalinī Śakti. She is at the center of the life of the universe. She is the primal force of life that underlies all existence. She vitalizes the body through Her Energy. She is the energy in the sun, the fragrance in the flowers, the beauty in the landscape, the Gāyatrī or the Blessed Mother in the Vedas. She is the color in the rainbow, intelligence in the mind, devotion in worship.

The worship of Divine Mother means the total acceptance of all creation. In practical terms, the need for all the "groundwork" laid out in the following chapters is to overcome any dislikes, aversions, misuse and perversions. All the obstacles of any type of rejection, for whatever reason (including the rejection of the good in oneself and instead succumbing to such negative qualities as greed), must be overcome. For the refinement of the senses, external worship, rituals and ceremonies can make a valuable contribution, particularly in keeping a check on intellectual pride.

Kuṇḍalinī is Śakti power symbolized by Divine Mother. She is pure blissful consciousness. She is the Mother of nature. It behooves, therefore, that the aspirant should approach the Mother first, so that She may introduce Her spiritual child to the Father for its illumination or Self-realization. That is the reason why the devotees have placed Rādhā, Sītā, Lakṣmī, first in the jugal names, that is, Rādhā Kṛṣṇa, Sītā Rāma, Lakṣmī Nārāyaṇa.

Devī is Śakti of Lord Śiva. She is Jaḍa-śakti and Cit-śakti. She is Icchā-śakti, Kriyā-śakti and Jñāna-śakti. She is Māyā-śakti. Śakti is Prakṛti, Māyā, Mahāmāyā, Śrī Vidyā, Śakti is Brahman itself. She is Lalitā, Kuṇḍalinī, Rājeśvarī and Tripurasundarī, Satī, Pārvatī. Satī manifested to Lord Śiva in the ten forms as the Dāsa Mahāvidyā, namely, Kālī, Bagalmukhī, Chinnamastā, Bhuvaneśvarī, Mātaṅgī, Śoḍśī, Dhūmavatī, Tripurasundarī, Tārā and Bhairavī.

Worship of Śakti or Śaktism is one of the oldest and most widespread religions in the world. Everybody in this world wants power, loves to possess power. People are elated by power. They want to domineer over others through power. War is the outcome of greed for power. Scientists are followers of Śaktism. Those who wish to develop willpower and a charming personality are followers of Śaktism. In reality, every person in this world is a follower of Śaktism.

Śakti is always with Śiva. They are inseparable like fire and heat. Śakti evolves Nāda and Nāda-bindu. The world is a manifestation of Śakti. Śuddhamāyā, Prakṛti, Nāda, Bindu and the rest are only names for different aspects of Śakti.

The countless universes are only dust of Divine Mother's holy feet. Her glory is ineffable. Her splendor is indescribable. Her greatness is unfathomable. She showers Her grace on Her sincere devotees. She leads the individual soul from cakra to cakra, from plane to plane and unifies the aspirant with Lord Śiva in the Sahasrāra.

The body is Śakti. The needs of the body are the needs of Śakti. When we enjoy, it is Śakti who enjoys through us. Our ears, eyes, hands and feet are Hers. She sees through our eyes, works through our hands, and hears through our ears. Body, mind, Prāṇa, egoism, intellect, organs and all the other functions are Her manifestations.

Śaktism speaks of the personal and the impersonal aspects of the Godhead. Brahmā is Niṣkala (without Prakṛti) and Sakala (with Prakṛti). The Vedāntin speaks of Nirupadhika Brahman (pure Nirguṇa, Brahmā without Māyā) and Sopadhika Brahmā (with Upadhi or Māyā) or Saguṇa-Brahmā. It is all the same. Only the names are different. It is a play of words, intellectual gymnastics. In reality the essence is one. Clay only is the truth. All modifications such as pot, etc., are in name only. Nirguṇa-Brahmā Śakti is potential whereas Saguṇa-Brahmā is kinetic or dynamic.

The basis of Śaktism is the Veda. Śaktism upholds that the only source and authority (Pramāṇa) regarding transcendental or super-sensual matters such as the nature of Brahman, etc., is Veda. Śaktism is only Vedānta. The Śaktas have the same spiritual experience as the Vedāntins.

Divine Mother is everywhere triple. She is endowed with the three guṇas: sattva, rajas, tamas. She manifests as will (Icchā-śakti), action (Kriyā-śakti) and knowledge (Jñāna-śakti). She is Brahma-śakti (Sarasvatī) in conjunction with Brahmā; Viṣṇu-śakti (Lakṣmī) in conjunction with Lord Viṣṇu; Śiva-śakti (Gaurī) in conjunction with Lord Śiva. Hence She is called Tripurasundarī.

The abode of Tripurasundarī, the Divine Mother, is called Śrī Nagara. This magnificent abode is surrounded by twenty-five ramparts that represent the twenty-five Tattvas (principles or qualities). The resplendent Cintāmaṇi palace is in the middle. The Divine Mother sits in the Bindu Pīṭha in Śrī Cakra in that wonderful palace. There is a similar abode for Her in our bodies also. The whole world is Her body. Mountains are Her bones. Rivers are Her veins. Ocean is Her bladder. Sun and moon are Her eyes. Wind is Her breath. Agni is Her mouth.

The Śākta enjoys Bhukti (enjoyment of the world) and Mukti (liberation from all worlds). Śiva is an embodiment of Bliss and Knowledge. Śiva Himself appears in the form of man with a life containing a mixture of pleasure and pain. If you remember this point always, all dualism, all hatred, jealousy and pride will vanish. You must consider every human function as worship or a religious act. Answering calls of nature, micturition, talking, eating, walking, seeing, hearing become worship of the Lord if you develop the right attitude. It is Śiva who works in and through us. Where then is egoism or individuality? All human actions are Divine actions. One universal life throbs in the hearts of all, sees in the eyes of all, works in the hands of all, hears in the ears of all. What a magnanimous experience it is, if one can feel this by crushing this little "I"! The old Saṃskārās, the old Vāsanās, the old habits of thinking, stand in the way of your realizing this Experience – Whole.

Aspirants think that the world is identical with the Divine Mother. They move about thinking their own form to be the form of the Divine Mother and thus behold oneness everywhere. They also feel that the Divine Mother is identical with Parabrahman.

Advanced aspirants feel, "I am the Devī and the Devī is in me." They worship themselves as Devī instead of adoring any external object. They say, "Sâhaṃ" / "I am She" (Devī, Divine Mother). Śaktism is not mere theory or philosophy. It prescribes systematic practice of yoga, regular discipline according to the temperament, capacity and degree of evolution of the seeker. It helps the aspirant to arouse the Kuṇḍalinī and unite Her with Lord Śiva and to enjoy the Supreme Bliss of Nirvikalpa Samādhī. When Kuṇḍalinī sleeps, we are awake to the world. We have objective consciousness. When She awakes, we sleep. We lose all consciousness of the world and become one with the Lord. In Samādhī the body is maintained by the nectar which flows from the union of Śiva and Śakti with Sahasrāra.

A guru is indispensable for the practice of Śakti Yoga Sādhana, to initiate the aspirant and transmit the Divine Śakti.

Sexual contact is gross Maithuna. This is due to Paśubhāva or animal disposition or brutal instinct. Mother Kuṇḍalinī Śakti unites with Lord Śiva in Sahasrāra during Nirvikalpa Samādhī. This is real Maithuna or blissful union. This is due to Divyabhāva or Divine disposition. You must rise from Paśubhāva to Divyabhāva, through satsang, service of a guru, renunciation and dispassion, discrimination, japa and meditation.

Worship of the Divine Mother with intense faith and perfect devotion and self-surrender will help you to attain Her grace. Through Her grace alone you can attain knowledge of the Imperishable.

Glory to Śrī Tripurasundarī, the World-Mother, who is also Rāja-rājeśvarī and Lalitā Devī. May Her blessings be upon you all!

Woman, the Handmaiden of Divine Mother

What is woman's place in the cosmos?
What is her true function?
How can she fulfill herself?

Woman must find her place, fulfill herself through none other. She is the handmaiden of the Great Goddess, the Divine Mother. Because of the Goddess, life renews itself.

When technological man has finished his creation, it becomes destruction. Man is focused on his principles, his order, as he sees it. It is she, the woman, who picks up the pieces to give life a new meaning.

When cultures reach a peak, subside into mediocrity or vanish, the female aspect of creation, the Goddess Śakti, starts a new cycle. Woman is Her handmaiden. She must accept the burden of renewal after destruction. Through her, the Goddess transforms the barren land into fruit-bearing growth, and the bleak world becomes once again dazzled by a million colors of Her creation. Through woman, the Great Goddess lets new life emerge and be tenderly cared for. Woman must increase her skills for the service of Divine Mother Śakti, ever keeping the gaze on Her. At one point in time, the world and all its fanciful display will vanish. Emptiness precedes fulfillment. Unless she realizes her role in this world drama and is willing to assume this responsibility, woman cannot emerge from her "second position" but, more important, she will miss the purpose of her own life.

The feminine aspect of the Divine – the Great Mother, the Goddess, the Devī, Śakti – symbolizes creation, giving birth to all that manifests. Accepting all of creation is the worship of Divine Mother.

No one – men or women – can come to the Most High unless they enter the palace of Divine Mother. In your attempt to enter the palace, Divine Mother may unexpectedly grant you boons, which you may feel you do not deserve. But she may also take away what you feel possessive about.

The masculine aspect, Śiva, is considered to be energy as such, energy unmanifest. This does not mean that the masculine is larger or more important than the feminine. Rather it indicates that you yourself have more power, more potential, more to be learned, than you can actually put into practice.

Śiva and Śakti – the energy as such and the creation of all that manifests

– dance together in a cosmic dance. Those who become aware of this dance of power and creation discover a rainbow to another dimension. Your own divinity is as intangible as the rainbow and as dazzling, as beautiful and as arresting. Just as the rainbow has no substance and is visible only under certain conditions, in the same way you cannot always see your own divinity.

At the first glimpse of this rainbow, you may suddenly discover a longing that is different from all of your other physical and emotional needs – the need to define your relationship to the universe beyond your daily experiences. Looking at distant stars and planets, you may realize the immensity of space and be overcome by this vastness.

When you can see the life-giving rays even in the most desperate human tragedies, that is the moment when you become aware that you are the handmaiden of Divine Mother. You have set spiritual activity in motion – spiritual activity beyond sexual love, beyond physical life, beyond mind. You can see the emptiness of everything that you are usually so busy with. Your relationship to the cosmos becomes the driving force and a source of energy.

Purification is needed for this power to be used for your own benefit and for the benefit of others. It is your own sincerity that protects you. Be quite clear. The responsibility is awesome.

In the Mūlādhāra of yours I worship Him who has nine natures, dancing the great Tāṇḍava, having nine sentiments, together with (His Śakti) Samaya, the quintessence of Lāsya. It is from these two, each having its own presiding form, looking in compassion on the disposition of the origination (of the world) that this world has come into existence, having you as father and mother.

MANTRA FOR THE MŪLĀDHĀRA CAKRA

4. MŪLĀDHĀRA

THE FIRST CAKRA

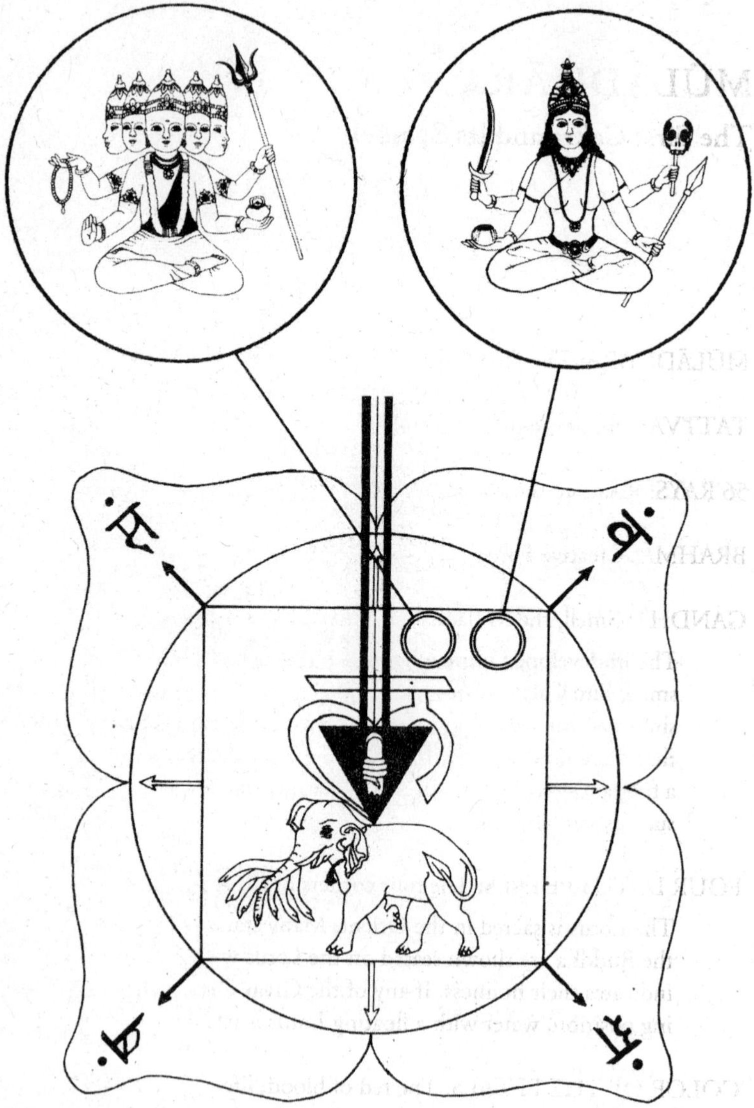

MŪLĀDHĀRA

The First Cakra and Its Symbols

MŪLĀDHĀRA: The First Cakra or Lotus

TATTVA: Differentiating faculty

56 RAYS: Relate to the Earth

BRAHMĀ: Creative Force

GANDHA: Smell, the Mūlādhāra Cakra controls this sense

The undeveloped human being is sensual, first directed to food by smell. Smell also creates sexual excitement. But if the path is followed sincerely, the sensitivity of the sense of smell can become so refined that there may be the perception of a Divine Presence by the smell of a fragrance resembling roses or violets, or the delicate scent of incense such as sandalwood.

FOUR LOTUS PETALS: The four corners of the world

The Lotus is sacred in the Orient. Many statues of Lord Kṛṣṇa, Śiva or the Buddha are shown seated on the Lotus with upturned leaves. This indicates their holiness. If any of the Great Ones is depicted in a standing position, water with a floating Lotus is usually also shown.

COLOR OF THE PETALS: The red of blood, life itself

Life has to be accepted and has to be rightly lived. Life is precious. Each life is an opportunity to develop latent potentials. One has to accept oneself and all of the human family. All forms of life are the manifestation of one Power and, therefore, reverence for all life is necessary in order to practice ahiṃsā (non-injury).

THE LETTERS ON THE PETALS: Vaṃ, Śaṃ, Ṣam, Saṃ

Before a written language was developed, speech was the means of expression and communication. Speech is our greatest performance. The spoken word has power. This power can express itself positively or negatively. The responsibility rests with the individual.

CIRCLE: Completeness or perfection

In ancient times, ideas of perfection were different from our present concept, a reflection of the difference in the mode of living. Racial and cultural backgrounds also affect the view of perfection that is held. Degrees of awareness vary in each individual and this places ideas of completeness and perfection on various levels.

YANTRA: Square, symbol of the Earth

Not only is this First Cakra the foundation of all other cakras, but it has itself a beginning. It is like building the foundation for a house. If the plans have not been well drawn, if the groundwork is sloppy and careless, the foundation will not support the structure. Similarly, our lives must have a good foundation. Careful planning is necessary. During each phase, a certain type and amount of work have to be done before the next phase can begin.

ARROWS: Directions

A specific goal may be missed entirely by running in too many directions. The five senses can push or manipulate, the physical body with its needs can make demands, the awesome power of the mind can exert its influence, all these may drive the human being in different directions. The possibilities for each aspirant, man or woman, are numerous.

YONI: Triangle, symbol for the female sex

Sex is a significant force. In the picture of the Cakra, the triangle pointing down indicates that the power comes from above. This means that the power to create a new life is not associated with the ego. The yogis of old held this same viewpoint. The energy that is manifested in the life of every human being is the responsibility of each individual. It is neutral, and it is the choice of the individual how it is used. To dissipate energy is irresponsible.

SVAYAṂBHŪ: Liṅga, symbol for the male sex

What has been said for the yoni is true also for the liṅga.

CITKALĀ: Crescent Moon, symbol for the Divine Source of all energy

Located on top of the liṅga, it represents the application of that energy on the various levels of the individual's development.

3½ COILS: Energy expressed in three different ways

Sattva is purity, rajas is activity and passion, and tamas stands for inertia and darkness. The half coil combines all three and indicates the interplay of those forces. Each aspirant must clarify what a pure mind is, what concepts are held, how these relate to life and in what areas.

AIRĀVATA: Elephant of Indra, white with seven trunks

In the beginning we are clumsy and heavy like an elephant, trampling everything underfoot; our preconceived ideas do the same thing. The seven trunks stand for the seven most powerful negative characteristics and also the most powerful positive ones. The elephant is an exceptionally strong animal. Strength is needed to overcome the difficulties encountered along the path in pursuit of the goal. Many human drives have strength, sex being one of the most powerful. The elephant is also known to be stubborn, unforgetting and revengeful. Yet the whiteness of the elephant stands for the fact that basically every human being is Divine.

ŚABDA: Sound, represents speech, the means of self-expression and communication

In the early stages of human development, the power of speech is not fully realized and, in relation to another person, we indeed blunder clumsily like an elephant in what is said and how it is said. In order to hear, we have to be silent and even all speech in the mind has to stop. The voice of conscience can only be heard when all other chatter has subsided. In moments of silence, the true śabda is heard like the humming of a bee.

BĪJA: Laṃ, the seed sound

Sometimes the Bīja is also called the Seed Mantra. It is the seed sound from which a particular energy develops. With inner visualization and contemplation of the hidden meaning, mantras lead the spirit, lost in thoughts and the pursuit of worldly things, back to pure Essence. The word "seed" indicates that there is something that can grow from it. In the seed of the oak, the acorn, the future tree is already contained.

Sound is vibration. A low key or a high key send out different rates of vibration, each one having its own effect on its surroundings. The vibrations of sound can be compared to ripples on the water that have been created by some impulse.

The experience of this Bīja, Laṃ, the seed sound of the Mūlādhāra Cakra, is only slightly perceptible and can be heard not because of intensely hard work, but rather because of sincerity, dedication, humility and surrender.

PIṄGALĀ: The Nāḍī on the right side of the body

Nāḍīs have been interpreted as psychic nerves in the subtle body. They have been compared by Indian medical doctors to the vagus nerves in the human body, which control the voluntary and involuntary nervous systems. While such an interpretation is not absolutely correct, it still can be used as a stepping-stone to a more subtle understanding, which comes with the practice of Haṭha Yoga. Ha is connected with Piṅgalā and means hot, sun, activity.

ĪḌĀ: The Nāḍī on the left side of the body

Ṭha is connected with Īḍā and is suggestive of coolness, receptivity and, more tangibly, the moon. Hot and cool, the sun and the moon, indicate a pair of opposites. The control of all pairs of opposites in the individual has to be balanced before one attempts to raise the Kuṇḍalinī. It is because of Īḍā and Piṅgalā that Haṭha Yoga has its special significance, as they are channels for prāṇa.

SUṢUMNĀ: The main Nāḍī in the very center of the spine

It is also the seat of Oṃ. It is the passage through which the Kuṇḍalinī energy rises. The Suṣumnā connects all the cakras.

CITRIṆĪ: Three in one, inside Suṣumnā

This is especially difficult to explain, but the following illustration may help. The human being is made up of a body and a mind, and of speech, which is the expression of both. The three in one are sattva, rajas and tamas.

GOD AND HIS OBJECTS:

Child Brahmā: The male aspect of Energy unmanifest

Five faces, five dimensions including omniscience, omnipresence, omnipotence.

The intelligence on this level is symbolized by the Child Brahmā. There is Divinity in everyone, as the complete oak tree is contained in the acorn. In every human being there is that Divine spark (Self). The only difference between human beings is in the degree of awareness of that potential, the awareness that it can be developed. Again, there are many levels on which intelligence can be applied or ignored. The Child Brahmā is holding objects in His hands and granting boons. These objects illustrate methods and exercises by which the aspirant can develop.

Daṇḍa: Staff

The staff is symbolic for the spine supporting the body. Since our emergence from the animal kingdom, we have walked erect. The levels of consciousness are in the spine where the life force is dominant. The base of the spine is the place where the Kuṇḍalinī energy is located.

Kamaṇḍalu: Gourd

The kamaṇḍalu is a container usually made from a gourd or a coconut shell for the purpose of holding water. The yogi or yoginī keeps the kamaṇḍalu close in order to quench thirst and to maintain a proper liquid level in the body.

Rudrākṣamālā: Rosary

A mālā can be compared to a rosary but it has twice as many beads, 108. This is considered a holy number because that is the number of Divine Mother's names. Dried rudrākṣa seeds are often used to string a mālā. They have five divisions, which indicate the five faces of the

Child Brahmā and the latent potential within each individual. The mālā is used to assist in counting the repetitions of the name of a Divine aspect such as Śiva or the Divine Mother Śakti. The purpose of such repetition, as in the chanting of all mantras, is to control the constant conversations that go on in the mind, which the yogi calls mental background noises.

Abhayamudrā: Gesture Dispelling Fear

With the lower right hand the Child Brahmā makes this gesture, meaning that all fear will be dispelled when there is sincerity, right intent and humility.

GODDESS AND HER OBJECTS:

Ḍākinī: The female aspect of Energy manifest

The intelligence on this level is symbolized by the Ḍākinī.

Śūla: Spear

On the primitive level, the spear has been used to hunt animals. Animals are symbols of various characteristics in the human being. The elephant stands for strength, the tiger for killing, the mouse for timidity, and so on. When skill has been achieved, the spear will hit the target. The question that the aspirant should ask is, "What is the target in my life? Do I live by awareness or, like an animal, by instincts?"

Khaṭvāṅga: Staff with skull on top

This is symbolic of a pure or empty mind, one that is free from preconceived ideas that block the way for new perceptions, particularly Divine insight, that is, insight by intuition during meditation, reflection or quietness. In contrast to the preconceived idea stands true knowledge, which is knowing from personal experience. Information is often mistaken for knowledge. The skull is mounted on a staff (the spine). The Energy, then, can rise in the Sahasrāra. The flow of the Divine Energy through the staff or spine into the empty skull, the mind free of preconceived ideas, is an experience that shakes one's whole foundation. If the Divine nectar received in those indescribable moments falls into the fire of passion (there are many passions besides sex), like water it steams off and is lost, because the aspirant, caught up in the illusion of worldly affairs, might recognize too late what has taken place.

Khaḍga: Sword

The khaḍga is symbolic for discrimination, without which numerous mistakes can be made. The practice of discrimination helps to develop a good mind that can reason effectively. Discrimination has to be applied right from the beginning of one's path, at the onset of the spiritual life. The essential and nonessential must be recognized and sorted out. When the strong tool of discrimination is used during the time of reflection, mistakes are cut down very quickly, emotional or mental pain is minimized and mechanical habits are controlled. Life becomes enjoyable in a very positive and good sense.

Caṣaka: Drinking Cup

When filled with wine, the wine is symbolic for Spirit and the aspirant may become intoxicated with drinking this Spirit. One is urged to drink slowly and steadily in small sips with awareness and discrimination to understand and assimilate the Divine nectar and ambrosia with intuitive thinking and feeling.

When the caṣaka is filled with water, it symbolizes the water of life. By thought association, one can consider quenching one's thirst with this pure water of Divine Wisdom.

The Goddess of Speech – Śakti

The Devī, the Goddess of Speech present in each cakra, has to be recognized as an integral part in the process of development.

Power of speech

The great significance of speech, personalized and deified, can perhaps only be understood if it is borne in mind that the ancient poets of the mantras and the Vedas handed down their wisdom by word of mouth. The spoken word, trusted to memory, can float away into the distance of time because of its intangible nature. This points to the incredible power of memory of these ancient ṛṣis and their devotees that they were able to preserve perfectly the ancient scriptures.

Each letter of the Sanskrit alphabet is on a petal of the sacred Lotus. This is to signify that every word or sound has power. This power is not only connected to the emotions and mental activities, but also to a Spirit of the highest order. It can, therefore, lift us to heights we ordinarily do not even anticipate. Speech has two aspects – the audible and the inaudible. Inaudible speech differs from mere talking in one's head; it is an ethereal intuitive perception. It could also be called the Language of the Heart.

The power in a word or sound is Śakti, therefore, She is called the Divine Mother in the Mūlādhāra Cakra. She is the Goddess of Speech. On the petals of the First Cakra appear the first four letters. Because the path of Kuṇḍalinī is a path of evolution, it becomes evident that with each cakra there is an increased perception of power manifest producing all forthcoming letters.

Refinement of speech

The mere naming of things has been humankind's privilege, of which we make wide use until awareness of the true power of language is realized. Speech has to be refined. We must become aware of our speech. Coarse language is termed "wrong conduct" for all aspirants of any path. Sensitivity is only gained by refinement and cultivation. As a plant is cultivated, so humans must cultivate themselves to become more sensitive in a positive way. In many scriptural texts, commands or utterances can be found that seem to have the recognition of the power of the word. Its refinement and careful cultivation are reflected not only in the sacred texts, but also in the poetry of many nations. Poets, like prophets, are often ahead of their time. Some poetry has an almost prophetic nature.

Power of mind

The ṛṣis, being highly developed seers, were the poets of the ancient writings. They perceived "Divine insight" by an indescribable intuition and power of mind. The power of mind is needed to transmit what has been intuitively perceived into speech. The seers knew of these powers of mind and sound by experience, and they understood the force inherent in the mind and its desire to create. The purpose of the ṛṣis was, by their higher perceptions, to guide humankind. When we speak of powers today, it is often assumed that such powers are meant for the control of others. But the ṛṣis knew that their powers were intended to be used in the service of others.

The powers of the seers of old were achieved by persistent practice. As discipline, even in the East, slowly declined, those towering ṛṣis seemed to vanish. Their stories appear to have no more relevance, as it is inconceivable to the modern person that anyone could have such an awesome memory and such intense concentration.

Mantra

Mantras are words of power and include sacred texts like the Vedas and Upaniṣads, formulations in praise of aspects of the Divine. On a basic level, the mantra is used as an incantation similar to those of some Christian churches. At a higher level, when it has become Mantra Yoga, the mantra is practiced for single-pointedness of mind. On a still higher level, it activates and amplifies latent forces that are within every human being and which then can be termed cosmic forces.

To speak these words or sounds of power is to acquire the power in them and to come in contact with the source of sound and thought, the "root" of the mantra. The ṛṣi or seer who became the receptacle of the mantra had achieved that state of mind. The sincere aspirant seeks the accomplishments of the ṛṣis and wishes to become such a receptacle also.

Pure mind

The empty skull (void) is too awesome for the average being to conceive. The mind resists a vacuum and does its best to fill it with its own creations. So it is a constant battle to keep the mind still, in its natural state of calm (pure mind). Finally, when the mental processes have exhausted themselves through the chanting of a mantra, the mind becomes open to very subtle intuitive perceptions. At a certain point, it would not be an exaggeration to say that some of these perceptions are emanations from a source that is outside the human mind. Where and what this source is cannot be determined to the satisfaction of those who seek proof for everything. The source of a creative genius of the nature of a ṛṣi, a Johann Sebastian Bach or a Leonardo da Vinci cannot as yet be established by scientific means.

Just as on a particular level there can be a meeting of like minds, it would not be unreasonable to contemplate that one can come in contact with that vortex of energy that was at some time in a physical body, a ṛṣi or seer, who would help, guide and sustain the devotee to be persistent in the practice of mantra.

Speech: Exercises

Speech is our most constant expression, our greatest performance and the barometer of our emotions. Between the cry for help and the cry of joy, there is a whole range of sounds expressing minute degrees of emotion. The foremost tool for self-expression is the human voice. Control of speech is a necessity and the practice itself is of great significance because of restlessness and the tendency of most of us to indulge in talking, using words either with or without sense. The urge to talk may originate from the fear of silence or loneliness, or the pride of wanting to show off what we know, or the need to put in our "two cents' worth." Even giving advice can be more a case of a desire for self-expression than concern for the one who is seeking help.

Awareness of speech is essential in order to discover these urges.

1. Keep a ring or small coin in your mouth to give just enough time to ask yourself why you need to say something and what it is you want to say, since the coin has to be tucked under the tongue or in the cheek before you can say anything.

2. Talking can be evidence of the desire to be noticed, or to defend your actions. Fear can be the motivation for the need to talk, perhaps to quiet the still, small voice within. "I don't have to listen if I keep on talking." The manifestation of the human voice can be a curse as well as a blessing.

Ask yourself: What is behind your urge to keep talking?

- self-justification?
- killing time?
- self-importance?
- so that you won't have to listen . . . to others, to your inner Self?
- desire to talk about yourself?
- mistaken belief that you are sharing, when you are really only trying to collect pity from others?

3. Notice how you use terms connected with speech and the organs of speech: double-tongued, tongue-tied, getting your teeth into something, being in the grip of the need for self-expression through talking, opening up lanes of communication. Add your own.

4. The tone of voice can express a whole range of emotions – joy, happiness, laughter, doubt, irony, arrogance. A quiet, low voice makes everybody listen. (This is a trick often used by politicians when they want to be heard.)

5. Difficulties in self-expression may be caused by shyness (Why is one shy? Is it perhaps the reflection of an inverted ego?), or the result of speaking before thinking. (Students often remark, "I don't know what I am going to say until I hear myself saying it." It might be necessary to find out what is behind such a remark.)

6. It is advisable to practice silence (mauna). Mahatma Gandhi has set a wonderful example by observing silence on a particular day for certain hours. No one could persuade him to break his mauna. The highest dignitaries had to wait to speak to him. Mahatma Gandhi knew the significance of the control of speech for himself and the reflection of this on others. The aspirant must choose a time when the temptation to talk is greatest. The continuous need to express oneself has no validity in the life of an aspirant. All urges must come under control and all excuses must be dropped. The hours, the length of time, must be determined beforehand to enforce discipline and a record kept of the results.

Refined speech is song, sung in glorification of a power greater than our own.

Thoughts on Smell

Each cakra controls one of the five senses. The Mūlādhāra Cakra controls smell. In many people this sense is quite undeveloped, while in others it is very keen. There are, of course, various degrees in between.

Levels of refinement

The three and a half coils representing the Kuṇḍalinī energy are divided into sattva – purity; rajas – activity or passion; and tamas – inertia or darkness. A person whose sense of smell is little developed has not paid enough attention to its function. Lack of concern can be called inertia or laziness. But, with even a little thought, it is obvious that the sense of smell is very important. For example, it tells when food has become rotten. It also recognizes by the aroma of good food cooking when a delicious meal is about to be served.

Smell and sex

Very often the attraction to the opposite sex takes place on the level of physical smell. The eyes may not be satisfied with what they see or the ears may not be pleased with what they hear, but smell might attract because it has a very strong connection to the powerful sexual instinct. The physical smell of some people (not only from lack of cleanliness) can create difficulties for one sensitive in this area, when it is necessary to share limited space.

Rajasic and tamasic experiences in smell are not clearly separated. The sense of smell affects an individual differently at different times.

Sattvic level: experience of a Divine presence

Padre Pio, a Franciscan monk of Italy, who was one of the few men bearing all five stigmata (marks of Jesus) on his body, had the ability of bilocation (being in two places at once). His presence was recognized by his disciples through the smell of roses and violets. There have been hundreds of such reports from Catholics and non-Catholics alike. Devotees of Lord Śiva have experienced His presence by a very delicate fragrance of sandalwood. Often a group of people who pray and meditate together can, at the moment of having transcended personality aspects, experience some very beautiful scents. These may not seem to belong to any particular flower, but those present will experience, through their sensitivity of smell, an elevated state. To some there may be a distinct feeling or knowing of Divine presence.

Smell: Exercises

I smell. The act of smelling. What is smelled?

1. Become familiar with the difference in the smell of each fruit, each vegetable. Do not just smell food as being good or bad. Observe how much smell stimulates you in eating or drinking. Does coffee really taste as good as it smells? Can you think of a drink or a food that smells terrible but tastes wonderful, besides ripe cheese? In the reverse, what smells good but tastes terrible?

2. Check your own body at different times of the day to observe different smells. Discover the difference between the smell of the body and the smell of the breath by breathing into your hands. Also smell your clothes when you take them off. When you use creams, ointments, eau de colognes or perfumes, find out if they blend with your natural body odor. The body will give off different smells if you change your diet or if you fast. Most people give off a terrible odor when fasting. Your own breath can tell you if there is an oncoming illness. Increase your time for breathing exercises to help the body deal with and overcome the problem.

3. Blindfold your eyes and have someone arrange a number of different items for you to identify by smell. The objects must not, of course, be seen, touched or tasted. Record your guesses and include them in your exercise book for future reference in checking development. With a little practice, most people are able to name or describe accurately what is smelled.

The sattvic state of the sense of smell is achieved at a further stage of development when all senses are refined and when the mind has been given proper spiritual food.

Thoughts on Sex

The Energy is neutral

The energy of this cakra is neutral and therefore we have a great responsibility to choose how it will be used. In its most powerful form, the energy is expressed by sex. Aspirants must clarify in their own minds the meaning of sex and understand on how many levels and in how many ways this most powerful energy can be expressed in human life.

Most of the manifestations of this energy are expressed on the physical and mental levels, while the spiritual level is almost totally neglected. The aspirant must lay a good foundation in his or her life. In order to come to the basics, we have to decide what kind of person we want to be. Often the spiritual path is attempted simply for the enchantment of its differences from ordinary life, its mystical aspects, or powers to be gained. But in the same way that a person does not become a Johann Sebastian Bach without laying a solid foundation in the law of harmony, in the practice of playing an instrument, in the development of acute hearing, so one cannot become a yogi or yoginī without such groundwork.

Laying the foundation

So what kind of an aspirant do we want to be? There have to be some clear definitions about the physical level. The basic desire is to have a good healthy body and Haṭha Yoga exercises contribute to this. Proper food is necessary that will nourish the body instead of being used to indulge the emotions or for compensation. If there is a good foundation – in other words, good discipline and self-restraint – at the more advanced level of exercises there will be no problem.

Because of the overemphasis on sex in modern life, particularly in the West, it is important to give consideration to certain of its aspects. All the questions that we pose to ourselves should be expressed in the first person. We must take responsibility for our viewpoints and standards. Whatever the viewpoints of any individual, there must be no double standards – one standard for oneself and another for everyone else. ("Do as I say, not as I do.") This is destructive because double standards undermine our security and result in inner conflicts. It is necessary in the beginning of the yogic path to lay down very carefully the foundation of our life.

The aspirant should begin a process of questioning about sex.

What does sex mean to you?

Is sex a biological function over which you have no control and power, and thereby must simply obey the dark instincts of nature? Is sex meant only for procreation since, in the normal course of events, pregnancy follows? What about birth and death? Because birth is only one side of the pair of opposites, death has to be looked at also. Take time to think about birth and death, which are bound up with each other, and responsibility for the sex act will take on a new dimension.

Views on marriage, sex and partnership

With this in mind, now look at marriage. Is it just a custom, a kind of social institution? What part does sex play in your own marriage? We are not concerned with the views of anybody but the aspirant. Some very soul-searching questions have to be asked. Why did you marry the person you did? What were the reasons? What were your hopes and expectations at the beginning and what are they now? As an illustration, were the reasons for marriage physical attraction, leaving home, feeling important in a new social status, good looks, money? Did you think of a partner for life, someone you could trust, someone with character who could be truly a companion? All these viewpoints will reflect in the sexual relationship. If there is disappointment, sex will be used for punishment and reward. If there is indulgence in self-pity, sex will be used for compensation. If there have been no ideals at the start, there will be no quality in the relationship. Is divorce a solution to problems? Perhaps it is only a delay. Karma will follow you into other lives to come. A lesson not learned in this life will still wait in another.

From a yogic point of view, self-mastery, control of

basic instincts, is needed to become a fully developed human being. For one seeking higher values in life, a new aspect of love must be brought into the relationship between two people. A person with bisexual tendencies is on a teeter-totter, while homosexuality can be a lack of proper adjustment when changing sex in a new incarnation. Sex without the love aspect is only following instincts, however pleasurable they may be. The great significance of the exchange of energy between two people is seldom understood. A possible new dimension is only grasped by a full investigation of the purpose of sex.

That most precious energy that is able to bring another human being into this life must not be scattered senselessly and uselessly. Those who defend sex for pleasure do not realize the consequences on different levels. Children born "by accident" or to be a material asset to their parents, and who are not wanted for themselves, grow up without the dignity and love that is the right of every human being. In the same way that we have to know human laws, so it is our responsibility to study Divine Law. Ignorance is no protection.

For loving parents, even a few steps on the path of yoga will be of benefit and they may become gurus for their children. They can know the Divine Law because of their own practice and study.

Spiritual marriage

There is the possibility of a truly spiritual marriage between two people who are highly developed and close to the same level. In such a spiritual marriage, sex would be neither demand nor duty, but communication with a true understanding of love.

There are too many people who seem to be in love with "the idea of love." Does this mean that they are capable of truly loving and truly giving? All the good intentions may be there, but, as in any stage of development, it is easy to deceive oneself. Awareness is the vital ingredient for all personal development.

It is quite possible that on a higher level, in a spiritual realm, people could be soul mates. The idea of twin souls appeared early in human history, but how easily can we be mistaken? Is it perhaps an excuse to do what we want to do?

Spiritual life and the family

To strive for the Most High and yet have a family and all the responsibility that goes with it is, for the average person, almost impossible. Even in other aspects of life, in careers of men and women, it has been shown that it is barely possible to handle both jobs with equal attention and quality. If, in a marriage, one partner is wholly dedicated to a career and does not pay attention to the family, the marriage suffers from the neglect of that partner. If there are children, they also suffer. The marriage may even break up. However, some great yogis are known to have been married. In such cases, the one partner gladly becomes the "servant" of the other, considering it a blessing to have a companion who pursues the spiritual path.

Sex being one of the most powerful life energies, a clear understanding is essential. Independent of the course or the attitude that an individual takes toward sex, and independent of the level to which the sexual relationship can be elevated, the fact remains that sex is the beginning of birth. Sex is, in its basic function, bonding. The aspirant should consider what it means to take steps to avoid the resulting birth. In spite of efforts to avoid the consequences of sexual involvement, babies are born, unwanted byproducts of some pleasure. There is little dignity, self-assurance or self-worth for the individual who comes into the world in this way.

What is born must die. Therefore, sex, birth and death are a unit that cannot be separated.

Sex: Reflections, An Illustration

Nature maintains itself in two ways. Plants, animals and humans search for food to survive. They all have sex impulses to propagate, which keeps the species alive. Both these powerful driving forces are strongly expressed in human life. Here we deal with sex in a particular way.

Reflection will help in clarifying your own understanding. What is meant by reflection? As an example, we will look at the word "sex." The questions presented in this material are only a small beginning to help you get started exploring your own ideas.

What does sex mean to me?

- Is it a biological functioning?
- Is sex for procreation?
- In how many forms is sex practiced? Monogamy, polygamy, bisexuality, homosexuality . . .
- How do I use sex? as enjoyment? for pleasure? to have children? for compensation? as punishment, or as reward? as free sex without any responsibility?
- Sex outside marriage – is it sin?
- Is sin a cultural thing? Is it my upbringing? Is it a Christian concept? Where does sin come in with regard to sex?
- If sex is love, why so many conflicts? Why is bad language connected with it? Why the rejecting or barely accepting of the fruit of that love, children? Is love excluded from sex? Can it be included?
- Is sex an exchange of energy? Is it psychic power of some sort?
- Is a marriage spiritual without sex, or can sex be included?
- Is there such a thing as soul mates? How does one know?
- What is a mystical marriage? Is it mystical only when sex is excluded?
- Why do some people think celibacy is important? What do I think about celibacy? Would the human race not die out if all were celibates?
- Is Cosmic Consciousness only for celibates (brahmacāris)?

- Is it a matter of attachment or responsibility?
- Is sex the Kuṇḍalinī force? What is Kuṇḍalinī?

Pain: Reflections

Pain is a great teacher. This is an old saying that bears truth in all ages. But what is pain? How many different kinds of pain can we experience? The yogis claim that all pain is self-created. How can we understand this? As the word "pain" is investigated, its meaning clarified by making a list and jotting down what comes to mind – a sort of brainstorming, if you like – many ideas will come to the surface. Sometimes they are conflicting, sometimes unrelated.

Let us list key words and associations for clarification.

- Pain, physical, emotional, being humiliated, pain in pleasure, painfully low self-image, pain of being a martyr, of breaking away, attachment to pain, conflicting emotions, insecurity, guilt, being unforgiving, death, birth . . .

This is only an indication of how to clarify the meaning of words, their use and the ideas attached to them, to understand their power.

In the case of physical pain, wait before you take a "painkiller" so that you can know the limits of your endurance. Do not enjoy pain; you do not want to become a martyr or masochist. (Those deviations have no place on the spiritual path.) In some instances, the dividing line is a very fine one.

In the case of emotional pain, try to "enter" the pain, as you would enter delight. Experience the pain as deeply as possible. Then let go! After having written down everything that comes to mind about pain, we can again consider the statement of the yogis that pain is self-created.

Now keep on asking yourself questions such as these:

- Did my friend really hurt me; really want to hurt me?
- Why do I feel so hurt?
- What are the repercussions of being let down?
- Are my plans upset?
- Do I have a strong attachment to my plans?
- Do I dislike having to change any type of plans?
- Maybe I am only "inconvenienced." Am I?
- If this is the case, where is the hurt?
- Maybe I am not hurt, but angry about being inconvenienced?
- Can I hold my emotions back in the future, long enough to recognize the difference between being really hurt and just being inconvenienced?
- Can I "learn" from my "mistakes," let them fade into the past?
- Will they fade if I keep my emotional response "alive"?
- Does this mean to discriminate?

How much imagined pain do you carry around with you? Recall.

How much of your energy is locked up in it? Can you forget and forgive if you keep old (maybe imagined) hurts alive? That energy could be used more beneficially.

Thoughts on Death

Sex, birth, and death

The great effort to avoid birth is matched by equally strenuous efforts to avoid death. We are afraid to die. Why? What does death mean – our own, our loved ones'? The yogi or yoginī recognizes sex, birth and death as one unit. The aspirant needs to clarify these personal thoughts in order to determine the goal for this life.

It is not necessary to spend nights in a cemetery and to sit on a corpse to ponder the meaning of life and death, as described in some of the traditional yoga books that are now reaching the West. But it is very definitely necessary to ponder these great mysteries of human life. How else can ideals, ethics and standards be established for ourselves? The evolutionary process goes on regardless of ignorance. Suffering can be minimized by knowledge first obtained, then put into practice. Practicing what one thinks makes life worth living and gives it new meaning.

The time of our physical death may be known beforehand, by intuition or through dreams, or as a voice in meditation. If all affairs are in order, the last will made, and there is harmony with all those left behind, death has little anxiety. For the yogi or yoginī, it means passing into another realm of existence. Consciousness has many expressions and is not entirely dependent on a physical body. But a physical form will be assumed again as long as there is an intense desire that is still unfulfilled.

The Divine Light Invocation

A spiritual practice called the Divine Light Invocation, which is described in this cakra, is one of the spiritual activities that will make a distinct difference at the time of death. The term "passing into the Light" is most descriptive. When an individual has passed on into the Light, there will then be a favorable rebirth.

The sex-birth-death chain of cause and effect can be traced everywhere, in every aspect of life. To foresee or anticipate the effect is one of the methods used by some yogis and yoginīs to practice awareness, to avoid repeating mistakes. One mistake could be to have an unfavorable rebirth. Strong desires can hasten rebirth and an anxious person will accept "anything," just to get onto the train of life to keep fulfilling those very desires.

Into what circumstances does one want to be born? The Bhagavad Gita says that one could be born into the family of yogis. If we refer to the four twenty-five-year stages of āśrama, the first two are given to learning and duty (family, children), the third is learning under the guidance of a guru, and the fourth stage is to become a guru. Times have drastically changed and, while the "spirit" of the Teachings must be kept alive, their application has to be adapted to the circumstances of present-day life.

Biological ideas about evolution have their place in their own setting. The yogi or yoginī sees the individual path of evolution as a parent would see the child grow into physical and mental maturity. He or she does not limit the process of growth, but is keen to develop many potentials and rise above limitations.

Death and Deadly Games: Reflections

Death has many aspects. It is most important for the aspirant to examine all thoughts on death. To help with your reflections it might prove useful to look first outside yourself at what is happening in the world. Everywhere there is food for thought. Consider, for example, the tremendous efforts that medical science is making to preserve life, from the baby in the incubator to the old man on his deathbed. Why? In contrast to preserving life, there is the effort to prevent life, of which the "Pill" is the common example. What do you think about the Pill and its ramifications? Any newspaper we pick up today is filled with deaths, some as a result of natural disasters, but many are lives sacrificed to greed and power. How does this fit into your ideas of life and death?

Death, which you are investigating, is not only physical. There are many ways to die and administer death. It might be good to start first to look at the many deadly games that we play. Let us begin with one of the most obvious – language.

Here are a few examples. Add your own:

- I would die if . . .
- I could kill him/her because . . .
- I could kill myself for having done . . .

Then think of the deadly emotions expressed by:

- I hate that color . . .
- I hate to eat that stuff . . .
- I loathe doing this work . . .

Stop being careless in the choice of words. The power of words is such that we are indeed playing deadly games when we casually use such words. Find replacements for these needless exaggerations. Say what you really mean. Instead of "I would rather die than do such-and-such," say, "I would rather not do it." You don't hate that color, but you do have a preference for another.

Ask: "Do I want to kill that person?" Or – "Do I want to kill the frustrations I feel because I am unable to deal with a difficult individual?" And if you say, "I could kill myself," look and clarify what it is in you that you really want to kill.

When you control your emotions, do you "kill" love?

- Or is it only the habitual reactions and possessiveness that are gone?
- Perhaps, by this very control, love is now really alive?

Do you have a soul?

- Is your soul/Self alive or dead?
- Or undiscovered yet?

Philosophical ideas of death need to be investigated also and not used as excuses for deadly games. Ideas may be sustained because of a strong emotional investment, powerful enough to bypass the most important point: that one must accept responsibility for the actual consequences when such ideas materialize. The reality of any philosophical idea has to be examined carefully.

Ask yourself: What is real?

Competition and violence are links in the chain connected to killing physically and non-physically. In competition for power, riots or revolutions may take place, resulting in the killing of innocent people. In competing for a business position, people may "kill" the reputation of their competitor.

How many ways can one kill?

- body, joy, peace, protest, business, reputation, opposition, laws, expectations, hopes, honesty, ambition, innocence, goodwill . . .

What part is played by the power of the mind?

- imagination, emotion, personal will, awareness of consequences, responsibility, escape, projection of oneself, self-importance, revenge, hate . . .

What is the emotional pitch of a killer?

- Has the killer reached the culmination of all emotion?
- What is the emotional state of the victim?

Sacrifice, martyrdom and suicide have many roots. As mentioned earlier, the choice of language used gives hints of what is in the recesses of the mind. Assassinations often have their roots in a sick kind of self-glorification. A person may begin by indulging in self-pity and be led by stages to become an assassin, believing himself to be striking a blow against injustice or cruelty. Vanity, self-importance and imagination may also play a part.

Some thoughts are like weeds, running wild in the mind. Some thoughts are flowers, turning to the Light.

- Which are growing in your mental garden?
- Which do you want to grow?
- What roots have to be pulled out? have to be killed?

The garden-mind has to be cultivated with great care. Undesirable characteristics must be weeded out ruthlessly before the good is lost and another round of birth and life has to start again.

A great talent, a genius, does not appear suddenly, but comes into existence by careful cultivation, training and discipline through many lifetimes. The same Law of Karma applies to all the negative and destructive characteristics, if these have been allowed to develop in previous incarnations. The choice is the responsibility of each individual.

Why must we spend time looking at this ugly side of life when the goal is just the opposite? The yogis of old thought that there would be no appreciation for the bright sun if the night were not accepted also. By turning away and pretending the ugliness does not exist, there will be very little effort to make the Earth a place of peace and harmony. It is all too easy to postpone the work on ourselves until tomorrow. "In the next life I will do it. This time let me have fun."

- What fun?
- Can you have fun at no cost to anyone?

These are the questions that have to be asked, regardless of our level. Everything has a small beginning, but can grow out of all proportion. However, many undesirable characteristics can be nipped in the bud if searching questions are asked.

Finally:

- How well do you know yourself?
- What is your regard for life?

Competition: Reflections

In the practice of yoga, there is no competition. You start where you are.

Ask yourself:

- What does the word "competition" mean to me?
- Do I compete?
- In what areas do I compete? on the job? with my husband or wife? with my father? with a colleague? with a co-student or co-worker?
- For what do I compete? for love? for acceptance? to win? because of habit? because I was trained that way? because everybody does? because it is the only way to live? for survival, recognition, fame, self-glorification, self-importance?

These are serious questions and must be fully examined. To carry competition into the spiritual path is a disaster.

Yoga makes great demands of discipline. Any type of work that is worth doing must be done well, with perseverance and sincerity, and not for the purpose of competing. In following spiritual instructions, keeping a daily diary, chanting or reciting mantras for many hours, the level of performance must be maintained. Dabbling in spiritual practice is a deadly game because it creates karma.

Mechanicalness: Reflections

You may not have discovered how mechanical you are. Maybe in the context of yoga practice it does not even make sense. An illustration will help. After you learned to drive a car, you no longer went through the entire process of driving. You could drive "automatically." In daily life there are many examples of this. But all areas in which one is mechanically functioning, whether physically, mentally or emotionally, have to be slowly discovered. You must become aware of them.

Ask yourself:

- What does the word "mechanical" mean to me?
- What do I do mechanically? Go through the routine of the day. Think of actions such as driving, eating at particular times, sleeping a certain number of hours . . .

What are my emotional mechanical reactions?

- I always get angry when . . .
- I always get a headache when . . .
- I'm always afraid in the dark . . .
- I cannot be alone; I'm automatically afraid to be in my own company.

What are my mental mechanical reactions?

- My mind always gets restless if I am not busy
- My mind always drifts off when things get rough or boring, when I am not the center of attention.
- My mind is always too tired to concentrate.

Love: Reflections

To investigate love, you begin where you are right now by jotting down your thoughts. If thoughts don't come, ask questions such as: What is love?

– companionship, being needed, being accepted, being married, having children, emotions, responsibility, self-gratification, helping someone, loving nature (trees, flowers and animals do not talk back) . . .

The list is endless and you may continue it on your own. After you've written your initial reflections, ask yourself if you can answer what love is. Perhaps you are in love with the idea of love. This is more common than is generally suspected because of lack of thinking on a deeper level.

When you say "I love you," what exactly do you mean? I love you because:

- you accept me
- you are so friendly, nice
- you take care of me
- you are very entertaining, lots of fun
- you are rich, educated, good-looking
- you offer me security, social status

Try to eliminate all the becauses. Having done so, you may feel more honest, almost relieved, and be more modest in your statement, saying instead, "I like you (very much)." If you like a person for various reasons, you are being truthful and there is nothing wrong with this. But the word "love" has, in many a person's mind, a very clear definition with many expectations attached to it. When these are not fulfilled, the result is disappointment and pain. If you really take a good look at love and how you understand it in contrast to its true meaning, your conclusions might be something like "If I love . . . I can forgive . . . I can forget . . . I can refrain from making demands on my loved one . . . I can accept what is . . . I can renounce praise and drop expectations. This love is my sole happiness."

There is one more question left: "Which of my senses experiences love?"

Consciousness – Mind: Reflections

If you find it difficult to reflect on the subject of consciousness and mind, try some of the others first. You can, however, begin this one in the same way by just trying to find out how you use these words.

When do you speak of "consciousness" and when do you prefer "mind"?

- How do I use "consciousness"?
- How do I use "mind"?
- Do I use these words interchangeably?
- If I interchange them, when and why?
- What are the characteristics of the mind? thinking, memorizing, concentrating, observing, daydreaming, learning, imagining, procrastinating
- Are there levels of mind? How many?
- What do I mean by each level?
- What about telepathy, clairvoyance, inspiration, intuition? Do I credit mind or consciousness?
- Where does mechanicalness come in?
- Higher Self versus lower self: what does it mean to me?
- ESP, hypnosis, self-suggestion, projection, analysis

Once you understand even a little better the mysteries and functions of your mind, you will become aware that it has an awesome power.

Mind is the interpreter of all experiences.

Divine Light Invocation

It is necessary to learn to relax and also to create tension at will in order to understand both functions. The following exercises will help you get in touch with areas of tension in your body and help you learn to relax. They will also prepare you for the practice of the Divine Light Invocation.

Tensing and Relaxing

1. Stand erect and tense the feet. Feel every degree of the tension. As you release the feet, feel every degree of relaxation. Slowly tense the hands, spreading the fingers apart. Then relax them. Repeat the tensing and relaxing of the feet and hands several times. Now tense the hands and feet together. Slowly relax them together. Repeat this until it becomes easy, while keeping all other parts of the body relaxed.

2. Now tense the hands and let the tension extend into the forearms. Relax – hands first, forearms next. Tense the feet and let the tension extend into the calves. Relax – feet first, calves next. Now slowly tense the hands and forearms as you tense the feet and calves. Relax – beginning with the hands and feet, then the forearms and calves. Repeat this until it becomes easy, while keeping all other parts of the body relaxed.

3. Tense the hands, forearms, then upper arms. Slowly relax, beginning with the hands, forearms, then upper arms. Tense the feet, calves, then thighs. Slowly relax, beginning with the feet, calves, then thighs. Now practice smoothly tensing the hands and arms, feet and legs together. Then relax smoothly, always beginning with the hands and feet.

4. Tense the hands, forearms, upper arms, and now the shoulders as well. Slowly relax. Tense the feet, calves, thighs and buttocks. Relax – always in the same order in which you tensed. Now practice coordinating the tensing and relaxing of the lower and upper body together.

5. Tense just the abdomen. Relax the abdomen. Tense the neck. Relax the neck.

6. Now practice coordinating the successive tensing of the feet, calves, thighs, buttocks and abdomen with the hands, forearms, upper arms, shoulders and neck. Slowly relax, beginning with the hands and feet. Repeat this coordinated tensing and relaxing until it becomes easy: hands and feet, forearms and calves; upper arms and thighs; shoulders and buttocks; neck and abdomen. Relax in the same order. Keep your face and head relaxed at all times.

7. Now you can incorporate controlled breathing into this exercise. As you tense, beginning with the hands and feet, inhale. Hold the tension and retain the breath. As you relax, beginning with the hands and feet, exhale. Inhale and tense the whole body smoothly. Do not strain. Retain the breath and tension only as long as it feels comfortable. Relax and exhale slowly, experiencing clearly each degree of tension and relaxation.

After you have thoroughly practiced these exercises, you are ready for the actual Divine Light Invocation.

Instructions for the Divine Light Invocation

Stand erect, feet shoulder-width apart. Keep the eyes closed and focus them on the space between the eyebrows. Lift the arms above the head at the same time as you smoothly and gradually tense the whole body, while you inhale. The arms should be kept straight and the tension maintained throughout the body (fig. 1). Hold the tension and the breath. Make the following affirmation to yourself, silently and with all the concentration possible:

I am created by Divine Light.
I am sustained by Divine Light.
I am protected by Divine Light.
I am surrounded by Divine Light.
I am ever growing into Divine Light.

Slowly lower the arms as you exhale and relax. Keep your eyes closed and use your imagination to see yourself standing in a shower of brilliant white Light. See the Light pouring down upon you, flowing into the body through the top of the head, filling your entire being.

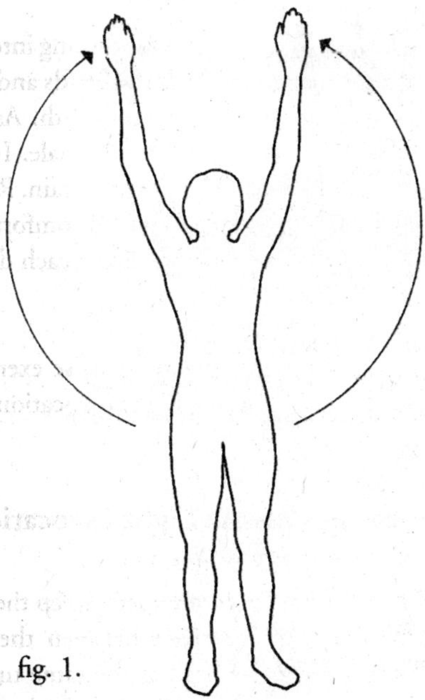

fig. 1.

Now, without raising the arms, keeping them at your side, tense the body and inhale (fig. 2). Hold the tension and the breath. Mentally repeat the Invocation.

I am created by Divine Light.
I am sustained by Divine Light.
I am protected by Divine Light.
I am surrounded by Divine Light.
I am ever growing into Divine Light.

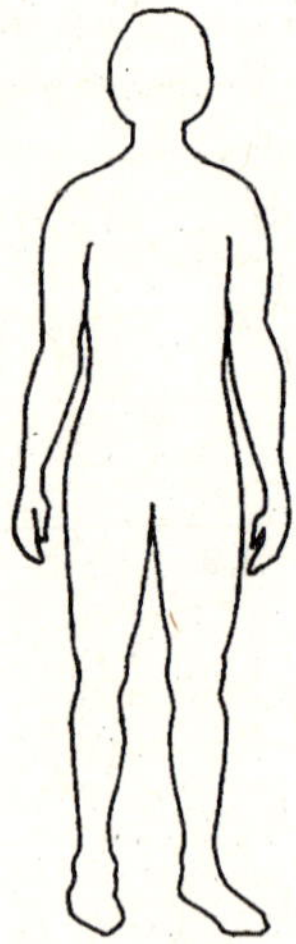

fig. 2.

Slowly exhale and relax. With the arms beside the body, concentrate on feeling a warm glow of Light suffuse your entire body, outside as well as inside. Acknowledge silently to yourself:

Every cell of this, my physical body, is filled with Divine Light. Every level of consciousness is illumined with Divine Light. Divine Light penetrates every single cell of my being, every level of consciousness. I have become a channel of pure Light. I am One with the Light.

The Divine Light Invocation is an exercise of will, as well as an act of surrender. Be receptive to the Light and accept that you are now a channel of Divine Light. Express your gratitude with deep feeling. Have the desire to share this gift with someone whom you wish to help. Turn your palms forward (fig. 3).

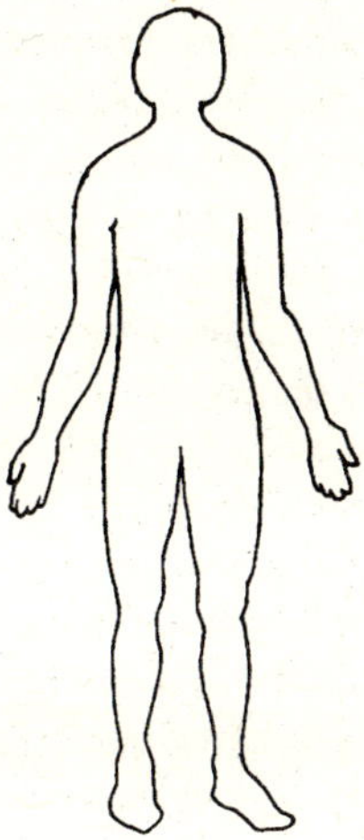

fig. 3.

You can now share the Divine Light with any friend or relative. Keep your eyes closed and visualize him or her standing before you. Mentally open the doors of your heart center and let the Light stream forth toward the feet of this person. See the Light encircling the person and spiraling upward in a clockwise direction, enveloping the body completely. See the spiral moving high up into the sky, taking his or her image along with it. Finally the person merges into the source of the Light and becomes one with the Light. You may even lift your head to follow the spiral of Light, keeping the eyes closed. When the person has passed from your view, relax and silently give thanks for having the opportunity to help someone in need. Remember, in helping others we are helping ourselves.

You are now ready to begin all over again, putting others into the Light, one by one, in the same way. As you become more familiar with the Invocation, you may take several people in a group or a family together. If you should want to help many people, you must repeat the complete Divine Light Invocation as soon as you notice that your attention begins to slacken. If you wish to help someone that you don't personally know, visualize the outline of a person in the Light. Your efforts will not be in vain. The Divine Light Invocation may be used to bless any friends or relatives who have died. When you put them into the Light, see them at their very best in the physical body before their transition. See them surrounded by and filled with Light. This will help you to release any attachment to them, and will also help them on their path on the other side.

The Divine Light Invocation may be used as a mantra also. Repeat the words of the Invocation to yourself and see yourself surrounded by Divine Light in your daily life. It will help you to keep in touch with the Light within you and to see the Light in others around you.

Before you go to sleep each night, see your body and bed surrounded by a spiral, like a cocoon of Divine Light. In this way, your physical body, which is the temple of the soul/Self, will be protected.

The Divine Light Invocation has to be meaningful. Never allow it to become a mechanical routine. When water runs through a rusty pipe, the water comes through but so does much else that is unwanted. Just as the water will finally clean out the rust, so through your efforts you will become a purer channel for the Light. As you keep practicing, the channel becomes clearer.

Perception and Use of Neutral Energy

I am created by Divine Light.
I am sustained by Divine Light.
I am protected by Divine Light.
I am surrounded by Divine Light.
I am ever growing into Divine Light.

Each aspirant has to clarify two words that are very important – POWER and ENERGY – as to their meaning and their use. A good way to expand on the meaning and use of these two words is to think how power and energy are used, and then to think of this in terms of yourself.

A further step is to use a mantra and test its power. Personal experience can verify what has been stated in this book. The possible use of power becomes clear. The practice of the Mantra of the Light alone will increase the power of concentration, something that is very beneficial in everyone's life. Success in all walks of life is the result of power of concentration. Without mental discipline, concentration will remain poor. The desire to achieve good concentration can be stimulated and sustained by choosing a particular method. The Mantra of the Light is very suitable to increase concentration because it puts the practitioner into contact with energy in a symbolic way. That will help the understanding that energy is not only neutral, but is also a tool in the hands of the user, who decides how it is going to manifest and with what repercussion – negative or beneficial.

So far the energy is basically used in sex and meant for the continuation of the species. The next step is to use the energy for creative expression. With greater awareness, it becomes obvious that the energy can be channeled or used differently, particularly by the use of the power of the imagination, as we will see in the next cakra, the Svādhiṣṭhāna.

Dance is Yoga, Yoga is Dance

The first glimpse of the dance comes to us from Lord Śiva Himself. Śiva, the Yogi of Yogis. He shows us the cosmic dance and portrays to us the unity of Being. He demonstrates that the highest being is in the complete oneness of soul and body and that this can be attained through dance. That is why dance is called yoga, not merely physical acrobatics, but yoga as a means of achieving unity in consciousness.

The Supreme Life dances. From Him vibrates the essence of all sound, of all movement, holding within itself the potency of all expression. To the accompaniment of the music of thunder Śiva dances. The cosmic rhythm of His dance draws around Him the ensouled matter that differentiates into the variety of this infinite and beautiful universe.

Śrī Kṛṣṇa, the Lord, the Paramātman, dances in Brindaban and the gopīs dance around Him in the rasa that is called the Kṛṣṇa-līlā. In the Rhythm of the Dance, the Paramātman draws to Himself the jīvas that have separated from Him. In the Rhythm of the Dance, each gopī discovers Lord Kṛṣṇa for herself. The jīva knows once again the supreme Fount of Life from which originated all that is manifest. This is the origin of dance and the originator is Bharata, the great sage. This great ṛṣi communicated the Dance of the Lord in very subtle ways understandable only to those who had refined all their sense perceptions. This is not for ordinary human beings to comprehend.

The dance, then, is an expression of the Unmanifest (avyakta) and the Manifest (vyakta). It is the Spirit of Eternity. Life is flow, is motion, is the interaction of puruṣa and prakṛti, a manifestation of the evolution of movement. Here movement is truly creative, the highest expression of the human body. It is the rhythm of the mighty spirit of the Divine. Therefore, it is possible for each mortal to follow the footsteps of the gods – each according to the measure of understanding and yet each sharing in the Divine Bliss (ānanda). The dance itself does not evolve through the effort of human beings, but through Divine inspiration from above.

The body is the spiritual tool to express the Most High. Love and devotion form the basics from which each individual proceeds. The portrayal of the finest emotions in the movement of the body are, then, truly love and devotion. In this process of refinement, Divine Grace descends. For without these qualities, the inner chord cannot vibrate in those who witness this most beautiful expression.

Art is the supreme expression of mortals and with it goes a responsibility to all human beings. In the highest form of art, the spiritual genius flowers. With this borne in mind and heart, it is easy to understand that constant refinement will benefit all of any community. Not all situations are appropriate for representation on the stage, or for the view of everyone at all times. When the genius flowers, the few who will have the privilege to be present and inspired will be lifted to great heights, desiring to attain such a state of Bliss also.

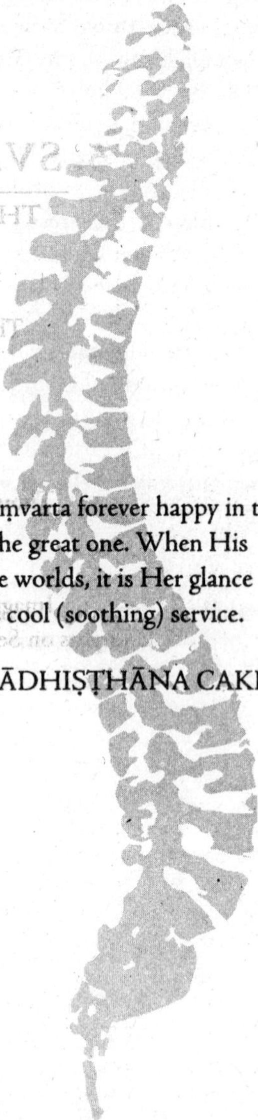

In the Svādhiṣṭhāna of yours I praise Him as Saṃvarta forever happy in the form of fire, O mother and also Samaya, the great one. When His glance filled with great anger consumes the worlds, it is Her glance dripping with compassion that makes this cool (soothing) service.

MANTRA FOR THE SVĀDHIṢṬHĀNA CAKRA

5. SVĀDHIṢṬHĀNA

THE SECOND CAKRA

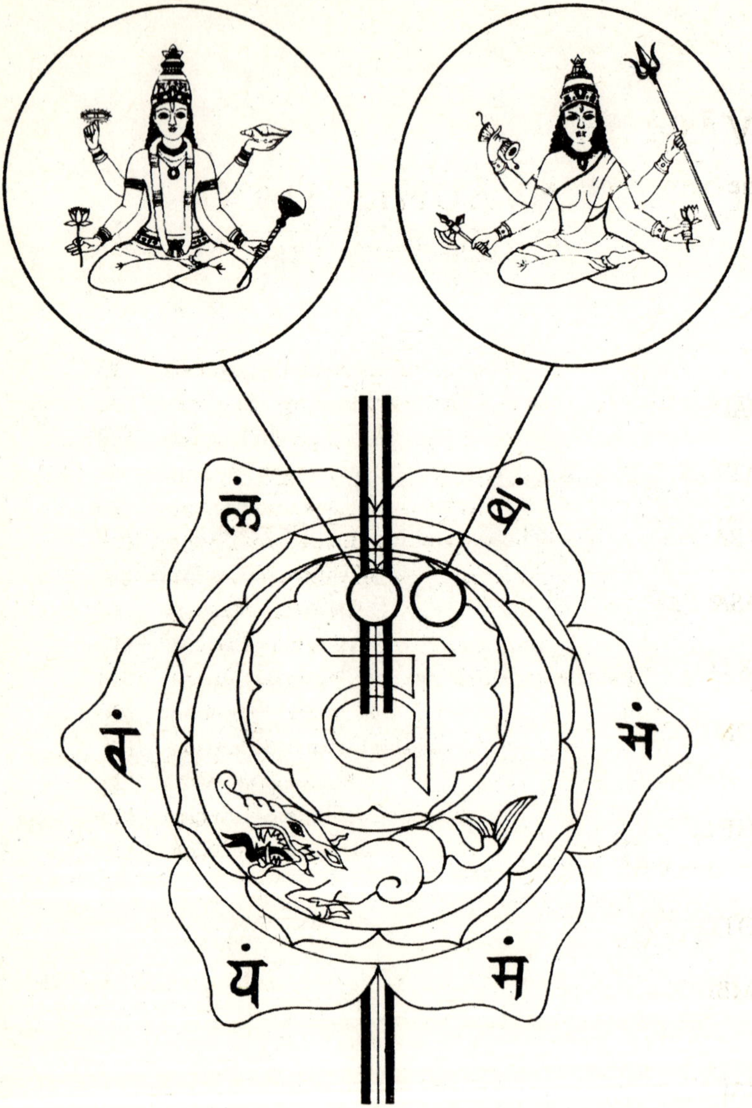
बं
भं
यं
मं

SVĀDHIṢṬHĀNA

The Second Cakra and Its Symbols

SVĀDHIṢṬHĀNA: The Second Cakra or Lotus

TATTVA: Differentiating faculty

52 RAYS: Relate to water

RASA: Taste, the Svādhiṣṭhāna Cakra controls this sense

SIX LOTUS PETALS: The Lotus is sacred

COLOR OF THE PETALS: Vermilion, the color of this Lotus indicates impulses, imagination and ideas, which are stimulating to the mind

THE LETTERS ON THE PETALS: Baṃ, Bhaṃ, Maṃ, Yaṃ, Raṃ, Laṃ Language increases.

LOTUS WITHIN THE LOTUS: The Kunda flower

AMBHOJA MAṆḌALA: Crescent Moon, it is luminous, white, cool and negative (receptive, inactive), representing water

MAKARA: Looks like a combination of an alligator and a fish

Its wide-open mouth swallows up everything without discrimination. This cakra governs imagination, which creates desire leading to gratification, particularly of pleasure.

BĪJA: Vaṃ, the Seed Sound

PIṄGALĀ: The Nāḍī on the right side of the body

ĪḌĀ: The Nāḍī on the left side of the body

SUṢUMNĀ: The central channel in the spine

CITRIṆĪ: Three in one (sattva, rajas, tamas), body, mind and speech

GOD AND HIS OBJECTS:

Viṣṇu: The male aspect of Energy unmanifest, Brahmā with Vanamālā (Hari Viṣṇu)

The intelligence on this level is symbolized by Viṣṇu, the Preserver, the second aspect of the Hindu Trinity (the two others are Brahmā, the Creator, and Śiva, the Destroyer). The aspect of preservation is extremely important to human life.

The mind expresses itself through the physical vehicle of the brain. All actions are carried out through the physical body. The body is the seat of the five senses. This particular cakra deals with taste. It is also the seat of the imagination. It is through mental and physical activity that karma is created, and the healthy and proper functioning of mind and senses is necessary to overcome karma.

The mālā is called the Vanamālā because it is made of forest flowers and it extends down to the knees, as a garland of flowers of all seasons. The Vanamālā is also called the celestial garland. The use of the mālā is the same as explained in the Mūlādhāra Cakra.

Śaṅkha: Conch Shell

Listening to the conch shell and hearing the sound are only possible if one keeps silence. This type of listening demands attention. The soft sound of the conch shell must not be drowned out by the talkative activity in the mind. For most aspirants who begin to practice yoga, it will be necessary to practice listening to different sounds such as bells and music in the beginning. Later this must be extended to listening carefully and with attention to another person. The aspirant must also learn to hear what is said. See the speech exercises.

Cakra: Disk

When the disk is thrown at a target, the aim must be true so that it hits the center. Controlled movements of the body and perfect attention are necessary. The disk symbolizes the mind; concentration has to be achieved. See the Watching the Mind exercises at the end of the chapter.

Gaḍā: Mace or War Club

This is an object with which to kill or to subdue. The many personality aspects and their egos need to be subdued. See the exercises on self-image and personality aspects at the end of the chapter.

Padma: Lotus

The Lotus is symbolic of sacredness, of the spiritual goal. The Lotus floats on the surface of the water of the mind and yet it is connected to the bulb from which it grew, which is rooted in the mud. These two different aspects of the Lotus are expressed in the double Lotus or Kunda flower. One is below and one is above the surface of the water. The spiritual goal is open to all, be they of high birth or of humble origin in life. The Divine spark is within each, but the degree of awareness varies. Effort must be made to see that Divine spark in all encounters with others.

GODDESS AND HER OBJECTS:

Śakti Rākinī: The female aspect of Energy manifest

The intelligence on this level is symbolized by Śakti Rākinī. The Goddess, being the creative aspect, is of blue color. Her three eyes are red and Her teeth protrude, giving Her a fierce appearance. This symbolic picture tells the aspirant that uncontrolled and uncultivated imagination is, indeed, a great danger. To be in the grip (protruding teeth) of this powerful aspect of the mind can make one lose one's mind. See the section on imagination.

Śūla: Trident

A trident is a stick that is divided into three parts on the top. This indicates the oneness of body, mind and speech. Observation has to be exercised to become aware of the interplay of forces among body, mind and speech, while the stick represents the spine in which Kuṇḍalinī is active.

Padma: Lotus

The sacredness of the Lotus is expressed in the mudrā of the hand or in the Padmāsana of Haṭha Yoga, and in the thousand-petaled Lotus on top of the head. The guiding thought of the Lotus as a symbol is toward purity of the mind because the Lotus flower, while growing in muddy waters, is not stained. In the same way, the Self, while undergoing various experiences, is uncontaminated.

Ḍamaru: Drum

The vibrations of the drum are the easiest to recognize in the body as they stir up emotions and sexual feelings. The repetition of a rhythm stimulates responses in the body that can cover a wide range of emotions. All such responses have to be controlled and refined.

The drum is also a symbol of the time element. It takes a certain length of time before a person hears the drum, or until a whole group hears the drum, depending on the distance and the loudness. The aspirant is advised to be extremely careful because resistance to temptation can be worn down. Continuous exposure to words and to temptations makes it a matter of time until the physical body will respond to the rhythm and be stimulated into desires that have not been intentionally anticipated.

We must also consider that the drum is symbolic of the continuous hum in the head, the mind ever active, the mental talk. Remember that we can talk ourselves into and out of anything. It is very important to be aware of this and use this ability to our advantage.

However, a good drummer can be a virtuoso and demonstrate that this ancient instrument is able to produce inspirational sounds and vibrations.

Ṭaṅka: Battle-ax

The battle-ax is symbolic of the uphill battle of life. In The Bhagavad Gita, Lord Kṛṣṇa enticed Arjuna to fight. Daily life is a constant battle. Instincts, mechanical reactions, impulses, false pride, false modesty, selfishness, self-importance, self-pity – the aspirant has to fight and balance all these negative characteristics with positive characteristics in order to overcome their destructive and painful influence. Life can then take on greater quality – depth, peace, joy and harmony.

The Goddess of Speech – Śakti

The Devī of Speech symbolizes the first level of self-expression and here in the Svādhiṣṭhāna or Second Cakra increased refinement is already coupled with greater awareness. Awareness, when seen as a characteristic of consciousness (rising) expanding to other levels of understanding, makes the idea of hierarchy of these levels more easily comprehensible. In "higher expression," language moves to a level where even the meanings of words are expanded and words are used to express meanings that cannot be defined. A term like manasic level is then not accurately interpreted as mental level, nor mantra as prayer. The language of the Gods as contrasted to "ordinary language" has to be penetrated by happy listening – intuitive listening.

The same degree of intuitive perception has to be developed in listening as in speaking. This means listening within. When one listens, all mental talk has to cease – this is the true meditation state reached in true meditation. This is not to be confused with what we in the West term a state of trance, into which it is possible to slip at a certain stage of intense concentration. In meditation the mind is meant to be absolutely alert, even while it is occupied with something else. It is like a lover sitting on a bench in the park reading a book and understanding what is read, but at the same time having an inner alertness for the arrival of the beloved because the beloved is expected to come. The listening is somehow intuitively tuned in to recognizing the footsteps or the rustling of clothes, something that will announce the presence of the beloved. Immediately this is heard, the lover who waits is alert and ready to receive the beloved.

In the trance state, however, the alertness is not there and the person in trance does not perceive what the person in the true meditative state does. The lover can be so absorbed in the book that the beloved can stand in front and not be noticed. When the suggestion is given to recite or chant a mantra (it can be said that this is cultured speech and a way to cultivate the voice), it is not meant to be a trigger into a state of trance.

This little illustration is a method by which the unexplainable can be grasped. It indicates that the meaning of each word is stepped up to a much higher level than that which the word has in "ordinary" speech. It is up to the aspirant to cultivate perception and then to express it in a more refined way. This process should never really stop. As the intuition develops, it becomes the source of extraordinary awareness. For instance, in the beginning of musical training we learn the rhythm of a song by counting. Not so on the path of yoga. Intuitive listening is necessary to perceive the rhythm and to tune in to the teachings or to the guru. It is not a blind following, it is a slow perceiving and understanding of the why and how. When it is blind acceptance, development is so slow as to be imperceptible.

Every guru or teacher has disciples who have greater limitations than others. But it is only a question of time, patience and persistence for them to expand beyond their limitations and to become more aware and perceptive. The path is open to everyone. Only pride, the ego, greediness and self-importance prevent the aspirant from listening intuitively. Therefore the will must be applied and a clear decision made to put all else aside so that there is nothing left but full attention, listening with intuition, and surrender. When the interplay of forces between intuition and awareness has developed, listening ability will increase. The aspirant then stands on firm ground. From this direct personal experience, knowledge is gained.

Sound and its resonance are inseparable and occur in ordinary speech or song. They can give birth to powerful emotional responses. The average person misses on the very subtle level the power of sound and its resonance. The gross is not a receptacle of the subtle.

Because of our habit of naming a thing and thereby

assuming that we know something about it, we find in all cultures that God has uncountable names. Each name has an inherent power because the name was created by the desire to make an immeasurable energy personal, to make it meaningful. The practicing yogi or yoginī tries to pull all these names together into one sound, Oṃ, which then takes on a specific characteristic and is called prāṇava. The personified name gives contact on a personal level with the Divine.

Speech: Exercises

The conch shell (śaṅkha) comes from the sea (water). When put to the ear, its sound comes in steady soft waves. Listening to the conch shell is like listening to the still, small voice within. The mind must be still to be able to hear this soft sound/voice. The mental background noises of the mind are produced by the emotional waves arising from uncultivated or selfish imagination.

1. This symbol tells the aspirant what action must be taken in order to hear this soft sound. If you have an opportunity to pick up a conch shell and to listen to it, you will observe many important details in this process:
   - intent, expectation, hearing something delicate, maybe even holding the breath or making a gesture with the hand saying "silence please," or assuming a certain bodily position.

2. A sentence expresses the meaning of words, conveys the message. A word by itself is a symbol of one or several ideas. As in mantras, a combination of words put together, or a single but very long word, can give a complete message. It is not usually recognized that behind each word there is a range of ideas and that the listener has the freedom of choice to pick the most acceptable.

The word is the pronouncing of a thought, making thought audible. Sometimes the thought may be away in the distance and slowly come into focus by pronouncing it.

Ask yourself:

- Where do thoughts come from?
- What is that invisible source that provides the power to manifest sound in speech?
- What happens when the spoken word becomes the written?

A spoken word can condemn a man to death or save a life. Ask yourself:

- How is this power used in my own life?
- What actually happens when a word is spoken?
- What are the mechanics?
- What part does breath play?
- How does different breathing affect the brain?
- What is the difference in a word spoken audibly from one spoken silently in the mind?

3. The ability to speak necessitates the action of the tongue. The tongue is also the organ of taste. How do we use the term "tongue" in our everyday language?

- to be tongue-tied, double-tongued . . .
- to have a tongue as sharp as a razor, to give a tongue-lashing . . .
- tongue in cheek, to speak with a forked tongue . . .

Consider how these meanings apply to your own self-image and then continue the list yourself.

4. Water is symbolic of imagination. The power of imagination, the ability to arrange and rearrange images of an abstract and a concrete nature, is an extraordinary skill.

Thinking of how they may apply to the imagination, consider these commonly used sayings about water:

- water under the bridge, don't make such big waves, cross the great water, you can lead a horse to water but you can't make it drink . . .

Add your own.

As the Lotus is sacred, the increase in the number of petals indicates an increase of expression, not only in words but, even more, in imagination. How, then, is this greater ability of expression used? The aspirant should look at every action, thought or word from the point of view of sattva (purity), rajas (passion) and tamas (inertia) in order to further cultivate speech. The best course is to remain cool, calm and receptive with emotions controlled (not suppressed), since in the heat of emotions expression can be dangerous. Strong emotions and indulgence are often linked with taste (eating habits). The urgent need for control is indicated by the Makara, with its greedy open mouth.

Thoughts on Taste

The Svādhiṣṭhāna or Second Cakra controls the sense of taste. Although there can be no clear distinction, because all human characteristics are interwoven, in the course of self-development there is a gradual refinement and escalation of the senses from the tamasic to the rajasic to the sattvic level. The senses can be compared to the keyboard of a piano. High and low keys are played in skillful harmony. This is the objective.

Taste and discrimination

In regard to food and drink, it is the tongue that we taste with, yet in daily language it becomes apparent that taste is also related to other areas besides the liking for certain foods and delicacies. The cultivation of taste in food leads to the ability to really taste a carrot or a pea by itself, without the addition of spices.

There is the cultivating of taste in dress and decoration, and in the arts. The word "taste" is also used to indicate discrimination in manners, speech and behavior. The display of good taste seems to give an individual a certain charm that opens the doors of friendship and is an advantage in various work situations. The appreciation of art is, in part, the cultivation of good taste, to which a sense of beauty also belongs.

The awareness of a particular sense becomes more acute by isolating it and by recognizing the interplay of forces that would not be understood unless attention were directed in this way. When greater awareness of the function of taste is achieved, its constant stimulation by a chain of reactions will be understood, particularly "feeding" the imagination and "feeding" the mind.

There is a saying, "We are what we eat." Let us pause to think about this. Does our choice of food point to certain characteristics of indulgence? What does it indicate about our mental and emotional make-up? Taste for something is created and recreated by memory. The actual need (for food, sex) may not exist, but memory of some pleasant experience creates the desire to re-experience. Other motivations might reinforce this, such as rewarding oneself.

Sattvic, Rajasic, Tamasic

Until the sense of taste is refined to the sattvic level we cannot experience the purity, or sattvic quality, of food. The prāṇa in food is sattvic if there is no influence from taste stimuli. Fasting gives you an opportunity to understand how the stimulations to the sense of taste affect its purity, making it rajasic or tamasic. During a fast, observe the effects of the imagination and investigate any problems that arise. Dreams should be watched during fasting. Do they contain food, and which ones? Dreams may indicate that certain foods are not good for us.

Taste has to be seen in a broader sense by understanding the connection between taste and imagination. Indulgence by any one of the senses is like swimming in murky water of unfathomable depth, with no shores in sight, no hope of reaching firm ground. Once the taste of imagination has been experienced, the temptations are difficult to resist.

Many important decisions in life have been made (marriage, business) based on unrealistic expectations – imagination kindled by desire.

Does this process of investigation exclude spontaneity? Not at all, as long as we discriminate between indulgence and spontaneity. No sense should be killed or dulled, but rather refined to the utmost degree.

Taste: Exercises

I taste. The act of tasting. What is tasted?

The exercises on taste begin with food. For the average person, the sense of taste has been dulled and so spices are used to increase taste, create more stimulation to the tongue, and thereby promote appetite. In these exercises, nothing is used that could mask the taste. They are done blindfolded so there will be no interference from another powerful sense – sight.

1. Place a piece of food such as finely grated carrot or a single pea on the tongue and experience the sensations. They are quite different from, for example, those of a few grains of sugar, a little bit of milk or chocolate. Notice the urge to bite or chew, and to swallow. It is not easy to resist in the beginning and points to greediness. The exercise should be done on a full stomach; then later, using the same ingredients, on an empty stomach.

2. Food and beverages (including water) allow endless possibilities for investigating the sense of taste and make the aspirant aware of areas that have been given little or no attention. When sufficient exercises have been done blindfolded, they should also be done with the eyes open to recognize how much stimulation comes from sight.

Interaction with the sense of smell should not be ignored. Every small detail is important in the exercise and should be carefully observed and noted.

- How does the food or drink smell?
- Is smell important?
- Or is taste?

The taste of food creates a great stimulation to the emotions and vice versa. The law of thought association brings past images into the mind. Food can mean:

- socializing, under the disguise of sharing
- obtaining recognition and acceptance for exquisite cooking and special recipes
- reaction to self-pity by eating
- rewarding oneself

3. Think about:
   - Is a person born with a certain sense of taste or is this sense developed?
   - Is taste a source of continuous desires?
   - What part does gratification or emotional satisfaction play?
   - What is the grip that taste has?
   - What compulsions, leading to indulgence, are connected with taste?
   - After the initial experience of taste, does greed take control?

The Goddess Rākinī shows protruding teeth, which means being in the grip of greediness in regard to taste. Once an attempt is made to answer these questions on a personal basis, many more questions will come up leading to insights about one's sense of taste. The finer things such as wine, caviar or other delicacies should not be overlooked. This poses a very interesting question – the refinement of taste of the tongue in comparison to taste on a higher level, disassociated from the tongue.

The following lists may help to stimulate your thinking and understanding of the sense of taste:

- indulgence, likes – delight
- aversion, dislikes – abhorrence
- indifference – neutral
- hot food and drink
- cold food and drink
- spicy food and drink
- alcohol

4. Make a list of likes and dislikes. How strong are they? Bringing them into balance makes them less extreme. From strong uncontrolled likes and dislikes arise such characteristics as: aversion, hatred, conceit, envy, jealousy, possessiveness, arrogance, passion, lust, infatuation, dullness and laziness. Observation of any of these characteristics does not mean condemnation, but rather identification of them and the slow change toward the opposite of each in order to achieve a balance. Any tendency to be judgmental would just add another undesirable quality.

5. A daily diary can be seen as a mirror in which events are recorded and which allows development in the practice of awareness to be observed. This is very encouraging and should be looked on as a reward for effort.

Cultivation can begin by developing "taste" for the more beneficial attitudes and actions in life:

- having good taste in appearance, clothing, furniture
- having good taste in arts
- handling a delicate situation in good taste

Taste as related and unrelated to the taste buds:

- being left with bitterness
- the affair that soured
- speech as sweet as honey

- a sweet person
- the taste of Divine nectar and ambrosia

6. Make a list and then try to explain the reasons for your responses:
   - What is tasteful to you?
   - What is distasteful to you?

7. When these exercises in taste have been done, some should be repeated with the guiding thoughts:
   - "I taste. What is the act of tasting? What is tasted?"

8. Now answer these questions about water and then add any others you can think of:
   - How different can water taste?
   - What is the power of water?
   - What is in a drop?

Think of:
- standing in the rain and letting the raindrops fall in your mouth.
- tasting the snow or a piece of ice.
- tasting the tears of joy or sorrow.
- Can I drink the ocean (of Divine wisdom)?
- Have I a thirst for life? or for the spirit of life?

9. Pay attention to tension in the jaws.
   - Indicating what?
   - Getting one's teeth into something.
   - Being in the grip of criticism? of oneself? of others?
   - Being in the grip of sex and emotions?
   - Spitting it out (in disgust) bitterness or negative experience.
   - Giving somebody a licking.

Swallowing insults and still smiling is a characteristic expressed by the laughing Buddha with the enormous belly. This tells us of the necessity of going beyond praise and blame.

After all these areas are explored, a taste for spiritual food has to be developed. Can this be cultivated? How? Unless taste in a general way is under control, it will not be easy to develop a taste for the Most High.

Thoughts on Imagination and Desires

The sense connected with the Svādhiṣṭhāna Cakra is taste. The double Lotus with the Crescent Moon in between indicates water, which is symbolic of imagination, a functioning of the mind. The ever-so-fleeting image brings a possible pleasant or unpleasant taste. The most important exercise is to watch the mind with all its various aspects.

Desire, imagination and emotions

Desire is an aspect of the mind that needs careful investigation. How do desires come about? Where do they come from? They are rooted in the Svādhiṣṭhāna Cakra, which controls imagination. Many impulses pass through the mind unnoticed. When the imagination gets strong impulses, they are picked up by the mind and grow by the power of imagination into desires. Some are very persistent. Like clay in the potter's hands, while desires are still pliable they can be molded into any shape or form. But once the final shape is accepted (in the form of opinions, beliefs or concepts) and fired in the kiln of the emotions, they harden and take on a certain permanence.

The scheming to fulfill those desires, and form those concepts and beliefs, is a process with many repercussions. Self-righteousness emerges; viewpoints and beliefs are fanatically defended. How does this happen? It happens by the emphasis on their importance. They provide a certain security. But we fail to realize that this is all due to the imagination and emotions working overtime for the wrong reasons. Here is the birthplace of many problems. The insistence on holding this rigid attitude keeps us asleep. Without awareness we lay our own traps.

Understanding power of desire

If this process is recognized, it becomes clear that desires have to be very carefully examined by the aspirant. Once the desires (emanating from the emotions) have been given power, it may take a long time, even years, for the manifestations to be recognized. An old desire may suddenly bear fruit at a time when the desire itself is already forgotten. We are often like children hankering after a new toy which, when we get it, has little meaning. We have already moved on to wanting something else. We need to realize this process of our development. In this respect, daily reflection and a spiritual diary are very helpful tools, enabling us to take stock of the changes and the progress made.

It may be helpful to recall what desires have been schemed for in the past. By a clear decision the energy can be redirected from the old desires, now unwanted, before they manifest, so that the energy is available for new and better ones that are more in keeping with present insights. There is a universal source of all energy, to which those unwanted desires can be "returned," as it were. In the process of that awareness, other things come up from the past, vague memories of hurts, grudges, resentments that have been left unattended. Old emotions, like old unwanted desires, can similarly be dissolved in the new insights.

It may come as a surprise to discover that even the unfulfilled desires of childhood exert energy and play on the adult. Those deep-seated desires must now be recognized as obsolete and be dismissed. They constitute excess baggage and they hinder the spiritual pursuit of the aspirant. What to dispose of and what to keep? Careful discrimination must be applied.

Renunciation

The idea of renouncing may have to be considered because of some unreasonable or illogical attachments. The concept of renunciation is often thought of as very unpleasant or even difficult, yet it presents the renunciate with a freedom which, once tasted, demands more. To be free means neither to possess nor to be possessed. The renunciate is thus placed in the middle of the teeter-totter, in a position of balance, free from the emotional swings that come with being at the ends. There will always be some desires in an aspirant's life, but it is wise not to form any attachments to them. Many a desire can also benefit others. That must be taken into consideration when forming new desires. Pain and frustration can be avoided by thinking things through: evaluating, anticipating and exercising foresight in the execution of one's desires.

Cultivated and uncultivated imagination

While the mind is the battleground of the personality aspects, it is also a playground where daydreaming can create infinite possibilities. Uncultivated imagination can lead to fear, to hallucinations, to a variety of such unhealthy mental attitudes. But directed imagination leads to creative expression such as inventions and art.

Fear has to be examined in a very clear-eyed way to see if imagination is its creator. This indulgence of the imagination in the wrong way breeds insecurity. When these emotions are not dealt with, the ego looks for a scapegoat, and one may go through life forever blaming others and defending oneself. At some time, responsibility must be accepted or one will never achieve that much longed-for sense of inner security.

Assessment, effort, work, time and energy are necessary to recognize the part played by imagination in our lives and to direct it in a positive, creative way.

Imagination: Reflections

In the previous section, there is a reference to the need to cultivate imagination because it is the source of fears. It will be practical now for the aspirant to make a list of all the fears that are experienced. Deep-seated fears are often caused by past mistakes, wrong action, intentional or unintentional, and the attendant fear of discovery. Sometimes they can be due to an overstimulated imagination, although the majority of fears are caused by an uncultivated imagination. It is up to the aspirant to make the decision to direct imagination in a positive, beneficial way.

Investigate your imagination

Here are a few questions you can ask yourself:

- Do you get dizzy looking down from a great height?
- Are you afraid of being in a confined space?
- Are you afraid of crossing a room in front of people?
- Have you any fear of being rejected?
- Have you any fear of being discovered?
- What about fear of inadequacy? in what areas?

You can extend the list but it is sufficient just to recognize your fears and use your energy to "rebuild" yourself. Most fears, when you look at them, are the result of neglecting to cultivate your imagination. Vivid imagination and powerful emotions can be terrifying and follow you into dreams as nightmares. It is not wise to become involved with too much negativity; time and energy should be applied positively.

Practice the Divine Light Invocation daily and reflect on the meaning. It is a powerful exercise giving many benefits.

Uncultivated imagination may result in thinking of yourself as:

- emperor, queen, box office idol . . .
- What roles do you play in your daydreams?

Could uncultivated imagination produce fearful images such as:

- avenger, aggressor, hunter, hunted?

Think about the qualities that cultivated imagination will produce:

- consideration, understanding, honesty, openness, loyalty . . .

Speech can be the result of strong emotions that are fed by imagination. As imagination is cultivated and refined, the aspirant's speech will reflect this.

Desires: Reflections

Make a list of desires in order of their importance and priority.

Imagination and desires

Since desires lead to scheming for their fulfillment, decisions should be made with careful discrimination. The Goddess showing protruding teeth symbolically warns us that the emotions can have their grip even on our reasoning. The power of emotions has to be realized. Their impact must be fully understood so that one can withdraw energy from them. Otherwise the energy goes into the fulfillment and manifestation of the desire. Desires created when one was still in a very immature state have to be dissolved because they become obstacles that hinder one's further development.

Visualization

Visualization is invoking an image or directing imagination. Undirected imagination is only daydreaming and has no results. Directed imagination must now be used to examine images of people and events still held from the past. Do these images influence you now?

Past desires

Think back over your life and list the things you have wished for in the past. List them in order of priority.

How relevant are they to you today? Do they still exert power over you? Here are a few to start:
I wanted to:

- become a great pianist
- be a success in business
- wield power over others

Or maybe you wanted to:

- be a perfect wife, mother
- be a perfect husband, father

What is perfection in a wife, husband or children? What is anyone's view of perfection?

When you have listed desires from the past and noted the influence they have exerted on your life, it is not difficult to see the effect of emotions and imagination, and to understand the need to cultivate and direct both.

With these lists in mind, choose an image that embodies a quality you wish to develop. Bring the image of your choice into focus, concentrating on the symbolic meaning, first to cultivate the imagination and, as a next step, to relate to your life the idea for which the symbol stands.

Imagination – Visualization: Exercises

In the exercises that follow, possible difficulties may arise because of objections to choosing an image of worship in the first place. This is a typical Western attitude. Yet the same individual cares to have pictures of a member of the family, such as his wife or child, on his desk, knowing all along that it is only a piece of paper with the image of a well-known individual on it. So why object to a picture that expresses symbolically an idea of Creation too great for the mind to focus on for prolonged periods of time?

1. Choose an image that is most pleasing to your mind. Let it be a symbol of all that is for you most Perfect, most High, most Beautiful. Remember what this image stands for: the masculine aspect, Cosmic Energy unmanifest.

2. At the spot of the Heart Lotus, see the female counterpart now representing Cosmic Energy manifest in as much beauty and splendor as you can imagine.

The male figure in its symbolic meaning is bigger, because there is so much more Cosmic Energy unmanifest than we can possibly envision.

- If you choose Buddha, see the Mother of Mercy sitting in His Heart.
- If you choose Kṛṣṇa, see Rādhā sitting in His Heart.
- If you choose Śiva, see Pārvatī sitting in His Heart.
- If you choose Jesus, see Mother Mary sitting in His Heart.

3. Now invoke a prayerful attitude and let the emotions express themselves in gratitude. To come in contact with the sacred teachings should make anyone grateful. In this way the emotions should be included in all spiritual practice, as they thereby become cultivated.

It has already been pointed out how powerful the human mind is and how quickly it can expand in its concentration. Repeat the above exercise, now adding the Invocation of the Divine Light so that all that has been imagined is "seen" as a mass of white light. The visualization of the Light will in due time saturate all forms that have been imagined. This process gives the mind enough substance in the beginning to keep it occupied over a long period of time. Through the Invocation of the White Light, the aspirant is slowly helped to recognize the Energy that manifests in so many forms.

Exercise: filling your body with Light

1. Sit in a meditation posture, cross-legged, or with your ankles crossed. Rest your hands, palms up, on your lap. (As an alternate posture, you may stand.)

2. Focus your eyes on the space between your eyebrows.

3. Try to think of yourself without the body or face; in other words, avoid the familiar reflection seen in the mirror.

4. Visualize your body as empty or hollow like a glass bottle.

5. See a small stream of White Light (the size of a thread) flowing down the center of this glass form, filling the feet, legs, trunk, arms, neck and head.

6. Soon you cannot distinguish detailed limbs. This form that you call your body is now a mass of Light.

7. Hold this image (a mass of Light in the shape of your body) as long as possible. Repeat often until it becomes familiar.

Before continuing, check all notes that have been written down after practice. Any feelings other than peaceful or harmonious ones are a signal to stop all exercises immediately. The aspirant can only resume exercises when there is an increased feeling of well-being physically and emotionally. Anything out of the ordinary indicates that personal guidance is definitely needed.

Do not skip any exercise. Learn to be persistent. There is more to learn in each one than meets the eye at first glance. Patience is hardly anyone's natural virtue and hence has to be cultivated.

Ego and pride

It becomes quite obvious that great care and time have to be spent on the "laying of the foundation" as given in the First Lotus. It is very important to be able to follow instructions. When there are difficulties, the obstacles should be searched for in the ego, which is asserting its intellectual power and expressing an unfounded pride. The antidote to pride is surrender and humility.

Thoughts on Self-Image and Personality Aspects

Where do thoughts come from?

The aspect of preservation (Viṣṇu) being together with the Garuḍa bird tells the aspirant that thoughts have wings. Where do you want to fly? Powerful thoughts can carry you to beauty, inspiration and blessing, or to destruction of yourself and others. That is your choice. Where does the power for these thoughts come from? We can see the manifestation, but what is the source?

Self-image
Imagination

A negative or poor self-image is very common. The reasons for it do not really matter since this knowledge, while it may remove the sting, does not alter the perception one has of oneself. The way to change self-image is by a systematic process that will help in cultivating the imagination. Through this process it will become apparent how great the power of imagination is. Poor self-image can be eradicated by sincere practice of the Divine Light Invocation, which has been explained in the Mūlādhāra Cakra.

Divine Light Invocation

When investigating the power of "image-creation," it is necessary to clearly understand various processes that take place without the aspirant becoming aware of them. Do not allow anyone to reduce you to an image on which you then act. Your awareness must also be clear enough to prevent you from doing this to anyone else. Such a reduction is a great insult to the dignity of a human being. But there is also the dangerous possibility of indulging in a sort of narcissism, where nobody counts but the inflated ego that nourishes a hidden self-pity by such reduction of others.

Making thought associations by images, our habitual reactions because of past experiences, also affects the self-image. This can be a bad habit, so mechanical that it escapes attention.

The images that come up in daydreaming must be

examined as they are often the source of fear and insecurity, which play a great part in self-image.

Personality aspects: the covering dust of the Self

Everyone has many different personalities, which move like actors into the foreground in various situations. The multitude of personality aspects is, in yogic symbolism, the covering dust of the glorious Self. In Western psychology, it is often referred to as "role playing." The idea is basically the same. The difference lies in the choice of symbolic expression. Many illustrations show ritual dancers wearing masks and sometimes exchanging masks. These performances often serve as a kind of entertainment or festival for various seasons and, at the same time, are meant to teach the audience some serious and important truths. Spiritual dances have the same purpose, even though the ideas may be on a higher level. They have a subtle influence on the minds and emotions of the audience, and may awaken the individual to refinement of the senses.

All your personalities and their various aspects need to be recognized. The best way is to make a list and decide on their validity. Some should be discarded. They are like tail ends hanging on from former times and only encourage vanity, pride or false modesty. Others have developed as a means of self-preservation or survival.

Ask yourself what survival means. Write this down too, because the question will come up again. It will be helpful to compare notes and see your progress.

The list of all those personality aspects will help you to recognize their power and influence on yourself and others. The face of the Śakti-Rākinī stands for self-image. You need training to think of yourself without the familiar face that is reflected in water or a modern mirror. You cannot imagine yourself without the face. The protruding teeth of the Śakti-Rākinī indicate that being in the grip of rampant emotions is very destructive. When they are connected with the self-image, it can be devastating. The ego then seeks to compensate and the situation worsens. Dishonesty, pretense and other negative aspects are expressed to the extent to which the power of the emotions is allowed to manifest.

Awareness, responsibility, and control

As the aspirant becomes aware of the facts and begins to take responsibility and control, changes for the better take place.

Self-hypnosis

The repetition of concepts of ourselves can often have an influence bordering on self-hypnosis. It will be hard to escape that trap. But it can be done. Remember, the Divine Light Invocation practiced regularly is a powerful tool in improving self-image.

Self-Image: Reflections

What is your self-image now? The need for change has to be recognized, then something can be done about it.

The image you put out to others is the basis of all responses and treatment that you get back. Even long after you have made changes, responses by others may have become so habitual that the difficulties created by the old image are hard to overcome. It takes goodwill on the part of others to accept and respond to the changes in you. These new responses will encourage you to keep working on overcoming poor images of the self.

To help clarify the image you hold of yourself, here are a few questions to be answered:

- How do I see myself?
- Is my self-image valid?
- Am I changing my self-image as I am changing?
- Can I take a new look at myself?
- Are changing goals changing my self-image?
- Can I see myself in the perspective of my new goals?
- Are the energy and discipline expended in pursuing the new goal improving my self-image?
- Am I exercising self-will (daily reflection)?

– What images of daydreams could prove useful if consistently applied?

This list must also be expanded to provide the aspirant with the basis for making the necessary changes.

Personality Aspects: Reflections

Making personality changes by sheer willpower or suggestion is impossible. The strain would be too great to be sustained for any length of time. But the goal of expanded consciousness provides a replenishing energy. By practicing identification with the Energy (Self) and by having faith in the practice, change is inevitable. (Even on a much lower level, where we are still seeking pleasure, changes take place according to the strength of the desire to achieve happiness.) Finally, the learned experience becomes second nature.

To begin, it is suggested that the aspirant make a list of personality aspects. These should not be limited to the usual ones of:

– father, wife, doctor, businessman, nurse.

Your list should also include such characteristics as:

– manipulator, game player, philanthropist, gossip, intellectual.

These are just a few random ideas. Make your own list. Clarify yourself to yourself. Avoid all judgment. Remember that there is no personality aspect that is specifically male or female; both have all sorts of characteristics.

Remember also that the Self does not own any of these personalities. Each one has its own ego, making your life more miserable than happy. These manifestations have no permanence. They appear and reappear depending on the emotional stimulus involved, to which the imagination makes its immediate contribution.

A little illustration will help to clarify this further. If you needed your appendix taken out, and the surgeon identified with your pain, his hand would falter and become destructive instead of helpful. By being completely detached, the necessary help can be given and the action (surgery) well-performed. The sympathy that is sought is expressed in the action itself. In the same way, the aspirant must avoid identification with the personality aspects in order to perform the necessary action.

The Divine Light Invocation, in due time, helps the aspirant to realize the Divine Self.

Watching the Mind

Any path of yoga has the same goal, liberation from all limitations. You have to decide to begin yourself and you have to do the job by yourself. It cannot be done by anybody else. An important part of this work is watching the mind to learn how it functions.

Concentration means to keep one object in the mind without any other intruding thought. The length of time that you can do this is an excellent way to find out more about your mind and its ability to concentrate. This practice is done side by side with the practice of the mālā from the preceding cakra, reciting a mantra a certain number of times without any interfering thought. Various images are used to enlarge one's power of concentration. Once you have learned to sit motionless for long periods of time, you can watch your mind and begin to understand the process of thinking. What kind of images appear? The mind is very quick and so an effort has to be made to slow it down. Are the images that appear in your mind concrete or abstract? Neither is right nor wrong, but these findings allow you to decide on the kind of image that is best suited to you for concentration. It will soon become obvious to the aspirant how many acrobatics the mind will perform in order to relate one thing to another. The mind will link the object of concentration to many other things that are associated with it. It will be difficult to bring the mind back to think only about the object. It is important to become aware of the tendency of the mind ever to weave new fabrics. The cultivated imagination can create a genius, but without control it produces the fragmentation that keeps the mind from relating to the object at hand.

Steps to Meditation: Exercises

1. Select a number of different objects. Concentrate on each one for 3 minutes. It will take practice to achieve unbroken concentration for this length of time. The objects must vary in kind. For example, a piece of wood, glass or bowl of water, a picture of a known person and of an unknown person, a likable and an ugly one, a picture of a bird, an insect, a fierce animal, a sweet little kitten or puppy.

2. Sit still for 10 minutes watching the mind, then note all that is observed:
   - the emerging images
   - the thought associations
   - distinguishing between concrete and abstract information
   - the influence of either concrete or abstract images

Then increase the time by 5 minutes – expand to a half hour and finally to an hour. (This can be done in two ways – first, at the start, every 10 minutes until an hour is complete, watch and take notes. However, the exercise must finally lead into watching the mind for an unbroken half or full hour, with taking notes to follow.) All notes from watching the mind should be compared. If certain aspects repeat, indicating a possible problem, this should be dealt with by continuous questioning.

These exercises will, in time, show how the mind works on all sorts of stimuli presented to it and how the mind is being stimulated apparently from nowhere. Watch what happens if, by old habit, you let the stimuli manifest or, by the new discipline of the mind, you "weed" them out as soon as they appear as thoughts. It is like a million seeds so small they are barely visible, all "sprouting" at once. This process occurs so fast that the earnest aspirant can barely distinguish them. But when control has been achieved, those thoughts die quickly and energy can be diverted toward only the desirable ones. This practice takes care of the innate restlessness that prevents focusing on a single thought or object. The mind can now become a container, open and receptive.

Memory and discrimination

Keeping notes makes it possible to practice recall and to check the accuracy of what you recall. The result of this exercise is a strengthening of memory and, more important, the acquiring of a keen sense of discrimination.

Preparation for meditation

Having learned to concentrate, to recall, and to empty the mind, meditation can be attempted because the mind is now like a vessel, able to receive thoughts of a Divine nature. In the beginning there may be insights of great significance, but as soon as intuition begins to unfold the perceptions are of a different quality, which can be designated as Divine. These perceptions flow into the mind and are often preceded by waves of brilliant hues of blue color. The meditating aspirant is enveloped in an all-encompassing feeling of peace and harmony. This by itself will become an important stimulus to keep up a regular practice. Soon it will be more than a stimulus; a deep longing will be created within the heart. Instead of color, a sense of peace may come.

A Divine image is more effective for concentration than an insignificant one. The particular image chosen can be seen in the mind's eye first in an elaborate form, but must pass into its purest form. For example, if Lord

Kṛṣṇa is chosen as such an image, all decorations must slowly disappear, the garlands, flowers and peacock feathers, as these are only symbolic of qualities.

To sum up, when desires are diminished and the scheming for their fulfillment ceases, meditation is possible without much effort. The yogis call this acquiring a PURE MIND.

Reflection on Water

Water can be used as a symbol for the mind, which can flow uncontrolled and destructive, or be directed and beneficial. The kamaṇḍalu, which is a container, implies the control of water and thus the control of the mind. Therefore, it is advised to watch the mind, looking at the thoughts and images that appear, then reflecting on both the results of the exercises and the day's events. Reasoning must be used to follow one thought to completion and to take action on whatever one has become aware of. There is no room for indulgence in emotions. This requires maturity.

What is the meaning of water? What part does it play in my life?

Water cleans and washes.
Water quenches thirst and fire.
Water is used for cooking – for diluting.
Water has various tastes according to its source and flow.
Water can give pleasure and joy, and excitement (boating).
Water is refreshing on a hot day, offers a cool swim.
Water is important to life – to growth and survival.
Water carries – debris, boats and ships.
Water can take many shapes and forms, filling spaces.
Water is soft and gentle in small quantities.

Water's large waves can destroy valleys and towns.
Water unchecked is dangerous.
Water's flow can be directed.
Water is unpredictable.
Water responds to the slightest breath.
Water wears down the hardest stone by steady drops.
Water can emerge from below.
Water can come from above as rain, hail or snow.
Water reflects the sky.
Water receives, unresisting, my projections.

What other reflections on water would you have? What thought associations come to your mind, now that you have watched your mind and seen its play, its creativity?

- Is your mind like the water?
- Does a slight stimulation create ripples of endless thoughts?
- Are the waters of your mind murky?
- Is a lot of debris floating around?
- Can you direct your mind, or is it like unchecked waters, just gushing forth?

The steady dropping of water wears down the hardest rock.

- Can you apply this to yourself in regard to spiritual practice?
- Would you want to?

Still water reflects the sky.

- Can you keep your mind still to reflect Divine thoughts?

The mind is useful in many respects, but not in all. Sometimes it assumes a rulership without proper authority. Who gives this authority? As water can emerge from below, so many suppressed thoughts emerge from below within yourself. Let all that debris come to the surface so that you know what is there. Remove what you don't want. Keep and deal with what you do want.

- Can you stay above water?

By now it must have become obvious to the aspirant that there will be no "definite" directions, only pointers to stimulate thinking into new avenues. All depends on you. Remember to keep a daily diary. It will become your treasure chest.

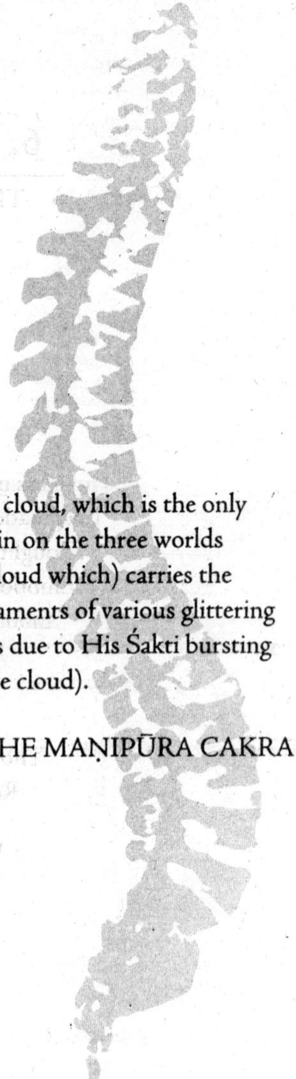

In the Maṇipūra of yours I serve Him as a dark cloud, which is the only refuge (of the world) raining down the rain on the three worlds scorched by the sun that is Hara. (This cloud which) carries the rainbow, Indra's bow, bedecked with ornaments of various glittering jewels, and which has flashes of lightnings due to His Śakti bursting forth from the enveloping darkness (of the cloud).

MANTRA FOR THE MAṆIPŪRA CAKRA

6. MAṆIPŪRA

THE THIRD CAKRA

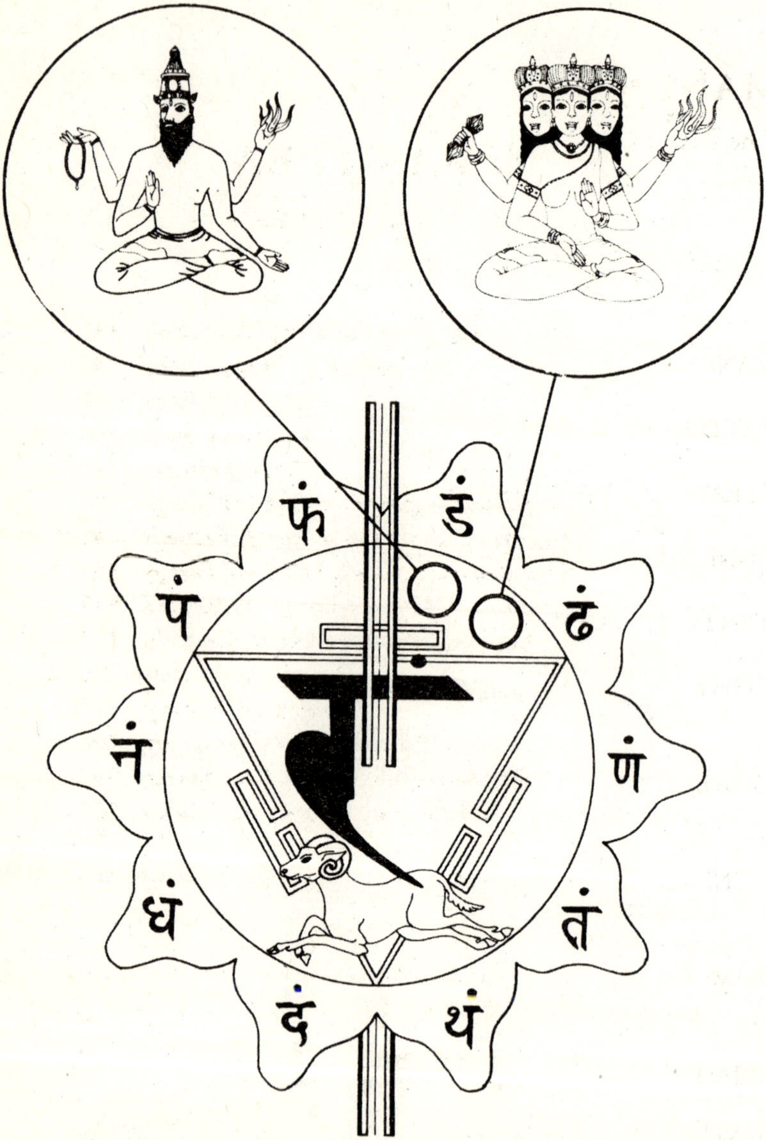
फं
डं
पं
ढं
रं
नं
णं
धं
तं
दं
थं

MAṆIPŪRA

The Third Cakra and Its Symbols

MAṆIPŪRA: The Third Cakra or Lotus

TATTVA: Differentiating faculty

62 RAYS: Relate to fire

AGNI: Sight (emotions), the Maṇipūra Cakra controls this sense

TEN LOTUS PETALS: The Lotus is sacred

COLOR OF THE PETALS: The color of heavy rain clouds, clouds prevent seeing clearly

THE LETTERS ON THE PETALS: Ḍaṃ, Ḍhaṃ, Ṇaṃ, Taṃ, Thaṃ, Daṃ, Dhaṃ, Naṃ, Paṃ, Phaṃ

AGNI MAṆḌALA: Fire wheel – a red triangle, pointing down, with swastika marks on the three sides

RAM: The animal in this cakra is a ram representing the persistence of strong emotions, which block clear sight

BĪJA: Raṃ, the Seed Sound

PIṄGALĀ: The Nāḍī on the right side of the body

ĪḌĀ: The Nāḍī on the left side of the body

SUṢUMNĀ: The central channel of the spine

CITRIṆĪ: Three in one (sattva, rajas, tamas), body, mind and speech

GOD AND HIS OBJECTS:

Viṣṇu: The male aspect of Energy unmanifest, preserver of life (Rudra)

The intelligence on this level is symbolized by Viṣṇu (Rudra), the aspect of powerful emotions.

We have to preserve the body through which we can raise the Kuṇḍalinī. When all exercises in meditation are completed, the aspirant acquires the power to create worlds. This means the worlds of one's mind, because one now has power over imagination and emotions.

Rudrākṣamālā: Rosary

Powerful emotions need to be expressed. This can best be done for one's benefit by turning them to the worship of one's Iṣṭadevatā.

Śakti: Fire Weapon

Fire weapon, so called because of the fire of emotions which will manifest and are inherent in the Śakti Power.

Gesture: Vara(da), granting boons; Abhayamudrā, dispelling fears

GODDESS AND HER OBJECTS:

Lākinī (Lakṣmī): The female aspect of Energy manifest

The intelligence on this level is symbolized by the Goddess Lākinī. Three faces, three eyes to each face; the face is the seat of all five senses. The third eye is the increased power of inner sight that is available – clairvoyance.

Vajra: Thunderbolt

The thunderbolt is a symbol of power. It is a very powerful expression of nature that can strike and set afire that which it strikes. So the aspirant has to clearly decide if he or she wants to be set on fire with enthusiasm for success, name and fame, or wants to be consumed in the fire of seeking the Most High. Again, it does not seem possible to serve two masters or pursue two goals. In this cakra, the fire of passions is strong and powerful, as can be seen in the next object.

Śakti: Fire Weapon, having an innate power of destruction

Gesture: Vara(da), granting boons; Abhayamudrā, dispelling fears

The Goddess of Speech – Śakti

Awareness and levels of consciousnsess

The power of speech that has been given in the previous cakras can now, in the Maṇipūra, focus on compulsive talking, compulsive criticism and the compulsive gratification of what are termed "needs." It must be realized that all human beings go through five stages of development: mineral-human, vegetable-human, animal-human, human-human, god-human. While it is right for us to fulfill needs in the first three groups, human-human, now in search of the path by a decision of his or her own, must look at these needs and cut them down to the very essentials. Giving in to needs that should be discarded could exact a high price.

Language

Language is born of the unconscious. The drive to express oneself comes from the unconscious. Behind many a word lies a whole range of ideas allowing numerous interpretations. For example, the words "time" and "space" spring from very different ideas when used by a housewife, an architect, a scientist, a social worker or a psychiatrist. Each profession has its particular language for specific communication with those of like mind.

Energy wasted in useless chatter is easily recognized when we are sick. We are then aware that energy is quickly depleted. There is a reluctance to conform to the social conventions that decree that one must always make talk, however small or worthless. What is the difference in the useless drain of energy in talk or in sex? If greater awareness of its preciousness does not show a purpose for the energy, then it is spilled down the drain. Observing the mind has to be carried out as an exercise to find out how it functions and to obtain greater awareness.

Changes in ourselves are frequently unnoticed. They come to the foreground, however, when attention is given to the use of words and language. In each cakra the

Goddess (the Śakti) of Speech increases. Higher levels of consciousness are approached as awareness expands. Exaggerations, superlatives, coarse language have to be left behind as one evolves; after some time, these simply drop away. The voice becomes a magnet that attracts others; the magnetism of personality comes into effect.

The scriptures speak of the Devī of Speech. The reason for giving speech a female character is that the letters of the alphabet give birth to language, to words, the sound body. They are sound symbols.

Just as complicated mathematical formulas are unintelligible to the untrained mind, so are higher aspects of the meanings of words like mantra. A magnetic/electric field is created by the chanting of mantras. The benefits are evident to those who practice Mantra Yoga. Sound has an effect on the human body in general and, in very specific ways as well, on certain limbs and organs.

Sound

First there is the sound or word, second the sense, and last the manifestation (vāk). This is mantra, Nāda Brahman. The summary of all these ideas is expressed in the deity (vibrations). A mantra is, therefore, not limited to the letters themselves but is also in their audible pronunciation (vibration).

Vibration

Speech: Exercises

In this cakra, the Maṇipūra, we will investigate the power of the spoken word and realize that in certain respects the power of language is not different from the power of thought.

1. To begin this investigation, think of the following:
   - What is speech?
   - How do I speak? Clearly? Mumbling?
   - Do I want to be heard?
   - Am I afraid to be heard?
   - Is there clarity of thought?

2. After having asked these questions and added many more of your own, the brief answers that you may supply in the first moment of response have to be further clarified.

- Do I see the light of the day?
- If I do, what is it that is seen?

Daylight, sunlight, moonlight – all have the word "light" attached to them.

3. Many expressions that are commonly used in everyday language show the reflection of sight in speech:

- in my eyes (in my estimation)
- to cast an eye (to look over, evaluate)
- the eye is the mirror of the soul (honest reflection of thoughts)
- an eye for an eye (equal revenge)
- have an eye for (to desire, to assess)
- keep an eye on (watch)
- keep your eyes open (stay alert)

Sight is also reflected in such expressions as:

- foresighted decisions
- shortsighted decisions
- eyewitness (someone who was present)
- an eyesore (untidy place)

Add your own expressions to this list.

4. Another step toward the cultivation of speech is the emphasis on mantra. The power of sound, the power of vibration, can only be achieved if the aspirant is very careful not to allow the mantra practice to deteriorate into mechanicalness. In the same way that somebody will say, "I love you," using a great deal of emotion to convey deep feeling, so in mantra the voice (speech) and emotions must work together.

The emotions expressed can be hope, longing, determination or desire to achieve the power of the mantra, to experience the power of sound working in others as well as oneself. Prolonged mantra chanting, which means a couple of hours a day for some months, will bring the effect of directing and pinpointing the vibrations in the body.

Power of the Mantra

The aspirant must also renounce a very common need these days, the demand for results. This may be necessary in the beginning to make the aspirant feel secure that he or she is on the right track. In the same way, while it is all right to be aware that at a certain stage in one's life one "needs to be needed," the aspirant must guard against a dependency on that emotion. The importance of the practice of mantra can be summed up by saying that the eventual goal of mantra consciousness is obtained when the power of the mantra manifests during sleep, when you awake not with a dream but with a mantra.

Listening to one's voice

1. Chant a mantra of your choice, paying attention to the breath. This links emotions with sound and is a good way to hear the emotion in your voice. This is an outlet for the restlessness caused by the emotions.

2. Hold an imaginary conversation, allowing the play of emotions to take place.
   - Repeat, controlling the emotions.
   - Record the conversation, then play back and listen to the emotions in the voice.

Listening to one's speech

Hearing yourself speak can bring attention to several things:
   - Is the voice soft because of fear of saying the wrong thing?
   - Is it soft because of a poor self-image?
   - Is the voice strong and powerful?

– Is there determination to be heard, to override others?
– Or is the voice strong and clear because the mind is clear, the emotions are clear?

These again are only a few focal points to pay attention to. Each aspirant will have to discover the various differences and possibilities in these random lists, think of the meaning of the expressions that are used, and add and clarify any other personal ones. Again you are reminded that this is a small selection and your lists could be very much longer.

Thoughts on Sight

The tattva of this cakra is the controlling (differentiating) intelligence of sight (agni). When dealing with sight, we have to recognize the different manifestations of this sense in sattvic, rajasic and tamasic expressions. It is necessary to clarify our thoughts on sight.

What would your life be if you had no sight? Have you taken sight for granted? Is there a difference between "I look" and "I see"? What is sight? Do the eyes record as efficiently as a photographic camera? Watch the process of seeing, then analyze it. When you "look," do you "see"? When does awareness come in? Can sight be cultivated?

In fact, all five senses have to be exercised to bring them to their highest potential. If seeing is a mental process as well as physical, then the question of "How do I see?" carries more importance. If the eyes register the visual impression and the mind interprets it, is "clear sight" really possible? When the mind interprets, what is the basis of the interpretation? What prevents clear sight?

Mind the interpreter

The answer might point to the emotions. Mind the interpreter is perhaps not as reliable as it is often considered (particularly when logic is claimed as its attribute) because the emotions insert their own filters, different-colored filters for different emotions.

This is evident in the number of different ways an accident can be seen by several witnesses. In each case the personal emotional filters, formed from past experience, likes and dislikes, or even the thoughts that were in the mind immediately prior to the event, influence the perception of what has been observed. Clear sight is sattvic, uncolored perception.

Investigate sight

Sight has to be investigated in the same way as the previous senses to understand what it means and how it functions, not so much from the anatomical point of view as to be aware of what is happening when one sees something. For example, food is selected by the eyes for its appearance, its freshness. Immediately one sees appetizing food, the mouth begins to water. The saying that the eyes are bigger than the stomach is well-known. It might be very helpful to know which of the senses is most stimulated toward eating and what part sight plays in this.

A quick glance at surroundings can give information about conditions. They are speedily assessed by the mind as to whether they are favorable or unfavorable. If an object is in the way, seeing it makes us either remove it or walk around it, unless the sight has been diverted, in which case, we will probably trip over it.

Concentration, meditation, contemplation

If the exercises are done as they are laid out in the following pages, the aspirant will find that the control that is achieved is a power in itself, and that a more intense level of concentration, meditation and contemplation will be reached. The power of concentration is obvious in the lives of yogis and yoginis, but it is present also in people who are successful in daily life. With respect to Kuṇḍalinī Yoga, the books tell of yogis who have siddhis (special powers) capable of accomplishing phenomenal feats, bordering on the miraculous.

This may be difficult to believe for the Westerner. However, proof will lie not in the witnessing of someone else's extraordinary acts, but rather in one's own achievements. Power of concentration does increase and when, after a few years of practice, a greater level of intense concentration is achieved, it must be realized that one has still not reached the highest limit. The power can continue to increase to a miraculous degree.

Seeing facts as they are helps to build confidence and make a person stronger. If we can see what is, instead of what we want to see, there is much less self-inflicted pain. It may seem cruel to be urged to give up our illusions, but to insist on seeing what is not there must someday lead to a rude awakening. The result is pain and this pain is self-created.

The sattvic, rajasic and tamasic qualities apply to sight as well as to emotions. Both need to be cultivated. The physical eye that can appreciate high-quality craftsmanship will develop creative inner sight that will manifest in due time. Raw and powerful emotions have to be cultivated into refined feelings through this in(ner) sight. Sensitivity to our own emotions, to our own ego, has to be cultivated until we respond with fine feelings, with understanding (I see what you mean), until eventually the cultivated feelings reach the level of compassion – compassion for others. All self-development must be used in helping others if a higher level of consciousness and the goal of Liberation are to be achieved.

After examining sight, insight and the mind's eye, investigation of the sense of sight can be taken one step further, to the third eye, which is indicated as having its location in the space between the eyebrows. No physical eye is involved. We are dealing with the center of sight that is in the brain, in which the power of sight is located.

The power that has created the eye can see.

Intuition

This would also apply to all other senses. Intuition is the highly refined expression of a sense, in this case of sight, which takes on almost the quality of the third eye. Like the blood that moves through the whole body, the Energy moves through all the senses to a greater or lesser degree.

Sight: Exercises

I see. The act of seeing. What is seen?

How do I see myself and others?

1. You might start this investigation with: "Do I see myself? How do I see myself?" When these questions are asked for the first time, the answers should be written down. At another time when that same question is posed again, the answer will be significantly different because of the previous "insight."

Identification

2. Continue this investigation with such questions as: "How do others see me – my husband, wife, son, daughter, co-worker? Do I identify with others? How do I see them? Do I see myself in others? What should I identify with? How can I see myself? When do I screen things out? What is it that I don't want to see? Why?"

Intentional blindness

3. It is necessary to see where we keep ourselves intentionally blind and to clarify what screens are put up in front of things we do not want to see. Every emotion erects its own screen, preventing clear sight.

Try to identify the screens, the emotions, expressed by:

- I saw red and didn't know what I was doing.
- I can't see this person or this object going out of my life.

To see something that is not there means we cannot see clearly what is there.

4. Check your habitual way of looking at things. Find out where you are not recording what you have seen – with the inner eye as well as the physical eye.

In all these investigations, there must be the overriding thought, "Knowing myself will make me free." Here in the Maṇipūra or Third Cakra, the interplay of the forces of sight and emotions is particularly powerful.

5. Look at an inanimate object such as a piece of wood, glass of water, piece of cloth or sheet of paper, for 3 minutes and note the intruding thoughts that prevent single-pointedness of sight in regard to the object. Now, for comparison, look at a photograph of a loved or revered person, or the image of a deity, or the picture of a child, a bird, a flower. Afterward, notes can be compared and the ability to concentrate established. The exercise could be timed for greater accuracy.

6. Sit comfortably facing another person and look into each other's eyes for a certain period of time, without moving or talking, trying not to blink. Observe the activity of the mind and the emotions and later record these observations.

7. Create a painting or sculpture in your mind's eye, or use an image from the first exercise. Again observe what happens and check how long you are able to hold your concentration and which of the objects holds your concentration longest.

Sitting quietly and observing the mind is like seeing with the mind's eye, seeing what appears on one's mental screen. Notes should be taken periodically and the material later looked over and dealt with where necessary. There is much to learn about one's mind and about thought association, which in time becomes extremely helpful and revealing. Problem areas that appear over and over have to be dealt with, otherwise they will become a disturbance and an almost insurmountable obstacle to meditation. The time spent doing this exercise can begin with 10 minutes and then be doubled, tripled, and so on.

8. Look at an ordinary stone for not less than 3 minutes.

Then shift to a semi-precious or precious stone, whatever is available, and recognize its symbolic meaning for you.

9. Look at the colors in your room. Fix your eyes for a few minutes on one color at a time. Clarify what the colors mean to you.

10. In your mind's eye see a flame. Does it consume anything? Or is something emerging from the flame? Now visualize your Heart Center. Imagine a blue flame on an altar there. Take the flame and place it on the heads of friends or loved ones. Write down what comes to mind during this visualization.

11. Chant Auṃ mentally. Then visualize the word in block letters as clearly as possible.

12. Place a colored dot on a plain background. The dot should be one-half to three-quarters of an inch in diameter. Look at the dot without blinking until the eyes water. Practice must be kept up to lengthen the time.

Now, looking at the dot, breathe in, hold the breath, tense the hands, let the breath out and relax. Again write down all observations.

Make a comparison of concentration on the dot and on looking into a person's eyes (exercise #6 above).

13. Sit in a comfortable position and think of the navel. Focus your eyes on the spot between the eyebrows. Form a clear picture of a silver disk (the moon) on top of your navel. When the picture is clear, bring in feeling and watch the coolness move in concentric circles, mingling pleasantly with your body heat. If the mind becomes active beyond the concentration on the silver disk and the cool feeling, add some bold letters such as LOVE, PEACE, GOD or LIGHT.

14. Sit with the spine straight, neck and shoulders relaxed, your breathing steady. Make yourself comfortable. Think

of the Buddha or an image of your choice. Focus all your attention on this image. Now see the figure sitting on top of your head. Think of your spine continuing into the spine of the figure. Choose the most meaningful image of perfection for you and see it as a human form sitting cross-legged on top of your head. Record all that happens.

15. Gaze in a mirror at your face, portrait size, including neck and shoulders. What do you see? A face of resentment or pain? Is it a face one can trust? Does it look deceitful or does the inner Light show through? What kind of face do you see? Look at your face for 2 or 3 minutes, then close your eyes and visualize it. Make brief notes. Double the time for the next period of looking and continue closing the eyes, visualizing, making notes, until you are able to hold the image with closed eyes. When you can successfully see in your mind's eye the image of yourself that was reflected in the mirror, project your image into the sky.

16. Continue the practice of the Divine Light Invocation, now putting more emphasis on sight (visualization) and on feeling.

There is no depth of understanding of the sense of sight unless these exercises are done, and these are only a beginning. With every exercise, always remember, "I see, the act of seeing, and what is seen?" Follow this process to understand the sense of sight and its effect.

Thoughts on Imagination, Mind and Energy

At each turn in the practice, the aspirant is reminded of the fact that the Energy is originally formless and shapeless, and the contribution made by the imagination to its manifestation is the responsibility of the user. The

Energy, having moved from the Mūlādhāra Cakra to the Svādhiṣṭhāna, is here now in the Maṇipūra Cakra where the imagination and strong emotions, in interaction with the sense of sight, have welded it into desires. The images welling up are like clay, with a form yet soft, able to change shape. But once they are put into the kiln of the emotions they are hardened by self-will and, if left there, can in the course of time become as hard as rock, difficult to destroy when the aspirant becomes aware that this must be done.

Passions are not limited to sex. One can be passionate about forms and shapes, and also about ideas and concepts.

Concepts that have been formed on this level can be compared to the clay images, put into the emotional kiln and burned with passion. We love our concepts and they occupy a large place in our lives. Such concepts acquire, in due time, an almost hypnotic power. Sometimes it seems impossible to act contrary to them even when reason indicates that we should. Also, our emotions cause intentional blindness. From earlier times of development there seem to be some appendages, old habits that constantly cause difficulties, such as procrastination, self-pity and the desire to compensate.

By the time the aspirant comes to practice Kuṇḍalinī Yoga, many habits have been established: habitual thinking, habitual feeling, habitual defenses to things we do not want to hear, actions and reactions, compulsions, and the teeter-totter of the pairs of opposites. A very important pair of opposites is the power of positive thinking and the power of negative thinking. Negative thinking exerts such a strong power because of the pushing up of the emotions, which are controlled by the ego. The power of positive thinking needs to get its push from repeated (cultivated) visualizations of ideal responses to situations in the mind's eye. This point will become clearer through watching the mind.

Gradually we will become aware that the mind interprets everything we experience in reference to ourselves.

The awareness has come through the refinement and cultivation of the senses, which are the doors and windows to the world. Such refinement will bring us into more sensitive touch with those around us, because no one is an island. The single cell of the body functions in conjunction with all the other cells and its very existence depends on the cooperation of all other cells. Similarly, each individual could be compared to a cell in this great cosmic body that we name in various ways. Self-importance makes for a separation that will only lead to isolation.

Because of imagination, the images in dreams need to be observed. To know them, their influence and even control, is very important when exploring the already known powers of the mind. It is important to know what the mind manufactures when the consciousness is dimmed in sleep. It takes a great deal of courage to accept the messages, which often tell the dreamer an unpleasant truth that ought to be known. A combination of humility, prayer and courage will help the dreams to become very clear, very much to the point.

There are many schools of dream interpretation, but it is wise, particularly in the case of the beginner, not to mix schools of thought.

Imagination, Mind and Energy: Reflections

How do you create your world? Are you happy with it? If not, can you destroy it and create it anew?

Habitual looking at things and people, groups or individuals, belongs to the pattern of mechanicalness that indicates blindness. At this point, it will be helpful to reflect on the habitual pattern of mechanicalness in regard to sight, illusions, and perhaps even cherished beliefs.

See your beliefs.

- Where do they come from?
- What is the foundation?

- How much is wishful thinking and how much true knowing?
- What happens when you assume an opposite position from your beliefs?
- Does this become disturbing?

If you can follow through with this process of looking at facts clearly, there will be no flaring emotions if someone else opposes your beliefs, because you have already done it yourself. That investigative process may have moved you from one end of the teeter-totter closer to the center. Functioning closer to the center and the benefits of such functioning will now bring new insights.

In reflecting on mechanicalness and habits, it may be helpful to go through the day in your mind and think of all the things you do habitually.

Do you always:

- Eat certain foods at certain times of the day or on certain days of the week?
- Limit some activities to definite times?
- Allow too little time for activities, resulting in rush?
- Perform routine tasks with little awareness of doing them?

Mechanical behavior

In these reflections, think of your actions and reactions.

- Do you become defensive when criticized?
- Do some mannerisms make you feel hostile?
- Are you intimidated by certain people?
- Does a person's appearance cause you to react favorably or unfavorably?
- Do you have an emotional response to witnessing certain situations?

Both of these lists of questions can be expanded greatly and will be helpful in understanding yourself and increasing awareness, in awakening from that "sleep-walker" state.

The work of laying a foundation is mainly done in the first three cakras and it is, therefore, very important because any imagined shortcoming is just that – imagined. It is not a fact. The intense examination of the use of the senses up to this point – smell, taste and sight – with emotion and imagination shows the immensity of the work that has been done by a yogi who has achieved even a small degree of realization. Each step may seem to be cruel and the aspirant will attempt to resist fact and to hold on to imaginary conditions or circumstances, or to desires and hopes. Any dreams in daily life are only illusions and the awakening from those dreams is sometimes much more cruel than the demands of the yogic path. To see facts as they are helps to build confidence and makes us stronger. If we can see what is, instead of what we want to see, there is much less self-created pain.

Sight, Emotion, Imagination, Desires

Straight-walk thinking implies straight-walk living, and means meeting situations head-on instead of imagining that things are different and covering them up by foggy thinking, or just doing nothing and hoping that the problems, worries and decisions will go away.

Sight (inner sight) is strongly linked with concentration. The ability of intense concentration is the key to success in all walks of life and also in the cultivation and the development to greater depths of all physical, mental and emotional tools that are available to everyone.

Concentration can be roughly described as seeing in the mind's eye at will, for a specific length of time, a chosen object. The aspirant must find out how long the span of concentration is and learn which objects hold the attention for the longest time and which for a shorter period.

The understanding of whether the aspirant visualizes an image of an abstract or a concrete nature is important when the choice is made for concentration. (For example, can you think of yourself without holding on to your physical appearance? Can you see yourself as a mass of

Keeping a record

Light? A body of Light without density?) The daily diary reporting the happenings, the exercises and the emerging thoughts about them, as well as dreams and their interpretation, becomes a kind of gold mine in your own backyard and makes clear which way your mind works. Careful study will show how, step by step, you get in touch with your innermost being, which becomes the guiding force to further development. It also becomes a source of energy which you can draw on for the necessary enthusiasm and drive needed to carry on this formidable task of continued self-development.

Put the spotlight of attention on:

- Where are my dark clouds?
- How do these dark clouds develop?
- Can I detect them when they emerge?
- Which are the areas where I act under compulsion of the emotions?
- Do I value "emotional investments" more highly than reason?
- What would be a good key sentence if I want to make changes? (Example: first think, then act.) Key sentences are reminders in a nutshell.

How would this compare with using another person as a sounding board or brainstorming?

Can I detach myself sufficiently to be clear in my own mind which of the processes (sounding board, brainstorming or key sentence reminder) will be most effective for me in a specific situation?

A few more focal points would be:

- Delay tactics of the mind-emotions.
- Traps laid out by the mind-emotions.
- Habits of criticism and judgment-emotions.

Delay tactics and traps:

- to do the job tomorrow.
- to deposit in the past, or postpone until the future, matters that should be dealt with in the present.
- to remain intentionally blind to avoid taking action, making decisions.
- to pretend unawareness.

Where do I use delay tactics?

- job, study, work, cleaning up, tidying . . .

Ways to practice awareness:

- paying attention
- recording observations, dreams, diary
- physical exercises (Haṭha Yoga)
- mental/emotional exercises (yoga): watching the mind, concentrating on one object, reflecting on daily events, reflecting on the meanings of words and ideas

Please remember that reflecting for your own clarification must not lead to the habit of looking for loopholes. A wide area of choices for development must be recognized and evaluated, but the greater responsibility that goes with the new awareness can be more easily accepted through clearer thinking, by whatever process you choose. It is impossible to cover the countless possibilities of which the mind and emotions of each individual are capable. Again it is suggested to expand the process of clarification as you progress.

Thoughts on Emotions, Mind and Energy

Emotions

For a long time in the aspirant's life, it seems that emotions are always upsetting the balance, and so observation is clouded by vanity, pride or false modesty. A critical attitude toward ourselves and others and the resulting emotions are responsible for the drive of competition. In the life of an aspirant there can be no competition. The aspirant is like a flower in the field. It grows and it does not measure itself against other flowers of the same kind or of other kinds.

Competition

Need for reflection

Reflection means mirroring the events of the day and trying to assess our performance on all levels. Without reflection we would not know when pain is unavoidable or when it is self-created. By our own attitude, we can take situations as helpful or hurtful. Often we are simply inconvenienced, not hurt. If there is an accident, such as cutting our finger, when we are physically hurt, the accident may be due to lack of observation and, therefore, also self-created. Pain has to be recognized as a great teacher. There might be painful experiences from past lives which, because they were not dealt with at the time, show up again in the present life.

The average person may never encounter a process of developing latent potentials, but, as in law created by humans, in Divine Law ignorance is no excuse. For the ignorant person, life often appears to be merciless, making that person feel like a leaf in the wind, blown here and there, helpless. The possibility of self-mastery on the physical and on the mental-emotional levels seems to be hidden from such persons. The Eastern teacher defines a secret as that which is not known. The average human being assumes that what is not known does not exist.

The Maṇipūra Cakra, located in the region of the navel, is the seat of the emotions. The powerful influence of that center on the body needs to be studied and understood. The aspirant is probably aware of the hypnotic effect of his or her own negative emotions. By applying positive thinking in concrete images, this power can be used constructively. Emotions can be of different kinds, like fire and water. When one "sees red," the emotions are so powerful that they prevent clear sight. Later, upon reflection, one can observe what has happened and by a

Positive use of emotions

process of reasoning, balance can be re-established.

As a means of increasing control over such disturbing emotions, do an exercise of 3 minutes' concentration on water. A drop of water is like a drop of emotions: small, it can be wiped off easily. A bucket of water, if it spills, is much more work to clean up. Think of a lake as symbolizing emotions – what is the depth? Murkiness of the water prevents clear sight to the bottom. Water takes on a shape and form of its own if not controlled and regulated.

Emotional blindness

Let us suppose that the eyes wander to the sky. There are some clouds screening out the sunlight. "Can I see things only in reference to myself? Then what about the clouds of my mind? What are they made of? . . . emotions? If emotions can interfere with clear sight, then I must 'look' at the emotions to keep myself from 'blindness.'" When blindness is physical, other senses in the blind person take over and become more acute. But when blindness is emotional, it means we do not want to see. How many times do you say, "I don't want to know"? In order to see more clearly, it helps to say to yourself, "Let me look at some of my emotions – like jealousy, attachment, self-pity, and the old habits of procrastination and self-justification, to name only a few."

Emotions, Mind and Energy: Reflections

The image of God in the mind serves these purposes:

- to focus attention for a longer period of concentration
- to refine or even develop through acts of worship certain emotions such as gratitude, empathy and loyalty
- to break the monotony of spiritual practice so that it goes beyond one's "time limit" (the limit of one's inclination). This means that there is at the beginning a length of time of concentration and enthusiasm, but when this

is exhausted the aspirant needs to be inspired either to make a new start or to be encouraged to continue to reach for higher and higher goals in concentration and refinement of emotions.

The next step in cultivation of emotions is replacing in the mind the concrete image of the deity with the Light. This is much more difficult and demands greater awareness, discrimination and a deep sense of gratitude.

For every emotion you experience, there is an opposite one. Think now of as many emotions as you can and find their opposites. Try to think of ways in which you can change negative emotions into positive, using the following examples as guides:

Gloom – cheerfulness:

- Create cheerfulness by singing a happy tune.
- Go for a walk, or do so mentally.
- Imagine a beautiful garden; look at the flowers.

Anger, harshness – love, mercy:

- Think how one person full of love and mercy can have an impact on the lives of many others.

Criticism – acceptance:

- All are precious in the eyes of Śakti. Form similar sentences yourself to act as reminders.

Dependencies are numerous. List them. Then realize that the process of thinking is dependent on the brain. "I" (as a personality) depend on the ability to think. Without thinking, "I" do not exist, there is no awareness. "I" (as a personality) depend on discrimination to recognize illusions.

Emotions, Mind and Energy: Exercises

Silver disk

1. Repeat the exercise using the silver disk, which was described in number thirteen of the previous section on sight exercises, this time putting the emphasis on feeling.

Returning to center

2. Start by standing with the hands palms up just above the navel. Smoothly lift the hands up to the heart center as if lifting the emotions up to the heart. Then extend the arms out full length, forming a circle as you bring the hands back down to the area above the navel. Walk around the room in a circle, making this circular movement with the arms. As you do so, say aloud and listen to your voice reinforcing, "I am functioning from my center." The reinforcement of hearing this repeated aloud is very effective. Doing this exercise 10 times, even once a day, will bring a good reminder on other occasions when you may be off-center, that it is possible to return to the center at any time it is so decided.

3. See in the mind's eye some esthetically unpleasant, or even violent scene that may have been witnessed on television, or one involving a strong emotion such as revenge or resentment toward some individual. Imagine what you would do if you had the courage to do it. Observe the rising emotions. Repeat several times and observe any other emotions such as satisfaction at having done it, even though only in the imagination. Observe the destructiveness of the emotions of which you are capable and that they are not justified. Consider that such emotions could be directed against yourself and think of how you would feel.

Observing and balancing emotions

From this exercise you will be able to recognize the source within yourself of forces that manifest harmfully.

Then, for proper balance and understanding, it will

be necessary to create and imagine an ideal situation – elevating, happy and joyful. Of course, in the same way that there was a receiver of the negative, now there will be a receiver of the positive. So choose your ideal companion or circumstance and observe the emotions involved in this situation.

The objective of the exercise, now that both parts have been done and the emotions have been observed, is to balance these opposites and to tone down the harmful and destructive, as well as the benevolent emotions. To achieve this balance, the emphasis on the daily diary has to be intensified. The reflection has to result in accepting the facts as they are, with as little emotional coloring as possible.

The exercises given here can be replaced with actual people who are known in your life, actual situations from the past or those anticipated in the future.

The aspirant has to take full responsibility for the cultivation of the emotions. Even your own Higher Self is only going to cooperate if there is evidence of effort and will and desire to achieve a higher state beyond the ordinary.

It is necessary to develop a feeling of gratitude, so that it becomes natural and emerges on its own account. It would be wise to make a list of all in life that you have reason to be grateful for.

Also list the actions done to other people that you feel they should be grateful for, in order to examine your own need to receive gratitude from others. The renouncement of the fulfillment of your needs has to be properly understood. It is not about repressing needs, it is rather controlling the fulfillment of those needs. Clarification can reduce the compelling pressures from needs. It is important not to fall into the trap of our times, which advocates the fulfillment of needs. If we felt this to be essential, we would have to allow our children to have everything they wanted. What counts for the baby on the human level also counts for the spiritual baby. Discrimination and self-control must be exercised. Discipline has to be accepted.

Clarifying needs

Thoughts on Dreams

In dreams we are able to contact the Higher Self, the guru within. The understanding of our own dreams, and the discipline that comes with it, has exceedingly useful results which the aspirant will discover from the practice: independence from the criticism of others and from habitual self-assessment and the awareness of a new dimension that becomes more and more available.

As an aid in recalling dreams, keep by your bedside paper, pencil and a light of some kind. Just before going to sleep, repeat to yourself, "I will remember my dream and write it down." If this is said with conviction and repeated at least twice, you will find that you do remember your dreams. Write down whatever you do remember, even if it is not complete, as even fragments can carry a message. Dreams should be written down immediately after awakening. If no dream is recalled, the first thought should be written down. A brief interpretation, even if incomplete or partial, should be noted in a separate paragraph. Another commentary that is useful to add is the events that took place, or the mental preoccupation that was present, before the dream occurred.

The daily diary can in this way be used in conjunction with the record of your dreams. The two go together like one hand washing the other.

Pay attention to how the mind functions during the sleep state, how it changes perception of time and space and the way it can shift very quickly. It is useful to ponder the meaning of time and space and the shifting of events because, in our mind, we do the same thing in daily life. In our thoughts we move from one thing to another without awareness of doing so.

You will find it useful to incorporate the symbols that appear in your dreams into a dictionary of your own. It is wise not to consult dream symbol dictionaries, but to discover how that part of the mind expresses ideas over and over again in symbols that are very personal to the dreamer. With practice it becomes obvious that dreams, too, take on various levels and become more clear, more easily understood and more direct.

Thoughts on Worship

The transmuting of emotional forces into spiritual energy is accomplished through the practice of worship. Worship in temples and churches has been a means of escalating raw emotions and their powerful manifestation into genuine feelings of high quality. Modern life has lessened the activity of worship of supreme beings, but the inborn need for worship is suppressed only in part by intellectual pride, and it emerges in many disguises – in worship of power and money. Many people worship football heroes, boxers, or movie stars; even intellectuals hold in great reverence persons with power, social status or high academic achievement.

When worship in any religion becomes routine and the ideals are lost, the fire of enthusiasm dies and corruption follows. In a church or center, all activities such as worship may, in the course of time, become regimented for the sake of discipline and harmony. Such stabilizing of rituals and worship to maintain a high level of performance inevitably leads to an atmosphere in which the personal experience can no longer take place.

Once again the aspirant is advised to use discrimination and awareness to avoid falling into the numerous traps that worship of the wrong power can set. In the beginning, worship is a wonderful way to cultivate emotions and transmute them into a high level of refined feelings that will become a spring of spiritual energy. Ego pride that hinders such a necessary step as humble devotion, eliminating this important rung of the spiritual ladder, can result in disaster – the disaster of worshipping false gods.

In worship, one can take a picture or image of a deity that is the total of one's understanding of the Supreme Intelligence, such as Śiva or Pārvatī, and use it as a reminder. Most of us are not so bad, but we do tend to forget, and the serious or earnest aspirant who wants to make headway should make use of such images to keep memory alive.

There is an alternative to the worship through the eyes in conjunction with the emotions, and this is worship through speech and hearing in conjunction with the emotions – chanting. Anger and agony, laughter and pleading, sorrow and peace, gratitude and humility, can all be expressed beautifully through the voice. If gratitude and admiration for the Cosmic Intelligence as it manifests are intermingled, understanding on a higher level is nearing. That cultivation will result in such a state that never again will you have a sense of pleasure when someone else falls or fails and there will never again be unhappiness and jealousy when others succeed.

The innate Divine majesty in everyone is remembered through the practice of worship. Each aspirant is entitled to create or develop worship in a most personal way.

Additional Thoughts on Sex

In view of what has been discussed so far, it becomes necessary to have another look at sex. See the compulsion with which it manifests, passionately, with burning fire, in contrast to the spontaneity of feelings that have been refined from strong emotions.

If emotions cause compulsive action, trouble will follow. In contrast to compulsive emotion stands spontaneity. The difference between the two has to be clearly understood because of the possibility of misinterpretation. Spontaneity is empowered to surface suddenly from cultivated feelings of goodness, even selflessness.

Now that you have clarified many of your ideas and thoughts about sex, here are a few more for your consideration:

- Sexual impulses generating by themselves or through another.
- What is creative sexual expression?

Avoid using many words, but truly give your ideas on the following:

- Sex as a seduction game by men, resulting in what?
- Sex as a seduction game by women, resulting in what?
- The sex game of the conqueror, the hunter, the seducer?
- What is sex without affection?
- What is affection without sex?
- Does sex remove the scars of rejection?
  Are sex and spirituality different?
- Are sex and spirituality expressions of the same energy?
- By yielding to sexual spontaneity, is the door kept open to higher consciousness?

Thoughts on Kuṇḍalinī, God, Energy

Mind and consciousness

If God or an image of Him/Her is the creation of the mind, then mind should also be investigated. What is mind? And it may be practical to find out if there is a difference in meaning between mind and consciousness, or if these two terms are used interchangeably. Whatever the concept of an individual, let us agree on a starting point: consciousness is Energy.

Energy – the Great Mother

How can Energy be known? Its presence is recognized in its manifestations. The old yogis stated that Energy and its manifestations are inseparable. Some texts refer to that Energy as Light, some use the mother as symbol – she gives birth to the child. Energy gives birth to various creations. She is the Great Mother. As the Mother of all, She is called Śakti. This is a simple way to explain what cannot be said in the words that are used in daily communication. This is poetic expression and poetry is the language of inspiration.

The yogic path is the pursuit of liberation from all limitations. We have to begin where we are. It has to be recognized that our human drive and inner restlessness are there, but by courageously changing the viewpoint from old established positions, something different can happen. New avenues of thought can come into focus. At first these may not be too clear and therefore they cannot be accurately defined, yet that very unclear, foggy notion puts us onto the search for higher values in life. Maybe there is a purpose in all that happens, be it pleasant or unpleasant. In any event, it is worth finding out.

Could it be that the Energy is one underlying force pervading all things manifest? Maybe all the effort to separate things for classifying, organizing and recording is, if necessary at all, only a self-gratification, a need for self-importance.

At this point, take a deep breath and decide to begin the search. Take only one step at a time to explore the new territory safely. It is like emigrating to a new country. One collects facts, as many as possible, plans wisely, avoids undue haste. The old habit of separating, organizing and recording is very useful in this new territory, but now it is done for the purpose of clarification of all concepts and ideas.

Kuṇḍalinī: a precise path

In this pursuit, arrogance and blindness, coupled with insensitivity to finer forces within and without, can be changed. The path of Kuṇḍalinī is precise in its minute development; it is a good and safe guide. If, at this point, we cannot say what Kuṇḍalinī is, we can anticipate results from following certain instructions. By recording thoughts, dreams, daily events and, most important, the outcome of those instructions, all of which mirror where we are, we can anticipate the next step, nourished and encouraged to pursue the path.

In this way, the aspirant comes to personal conclusions and learns to accept that these, too, are constantly changing as the process goes on. It is wise never to think that the final answer has come. This would mean limiting what is Unlimited. Kuṇḍalinī Yoga includes all aspects and characteristics of the human being. There is Divinity in all of us; the difference lies only in the degree of that awareness. To achieve greater awareness is what Kuṇḍalinī is all about.

What about the unhappiness, confusion and tragedy in the world? We must understand that all human drama, joyful or tragic, is but a means to the expansion of consciousness – to realize the imperishable Divine Self.

If we have learned to read and write, we have power over those who have not. Any position of power can lead to abuse. If we have money, we have power over the poor. If we have awareness, we have power over the sleepwalker. All powers are a temptation. If there is a latent weakness in the personal makeup, power will lead to corruption, whatever the power is.

We know about the balance of power in world affairs – if the balance is tipped, wars of aggression result. In our own lives, the balance of our positive and negative characteristics and ambitions is important, and the constant interplay of forces between the senses and the levels of consciousness must be controlled if the power is to be used wisely, in our own development and in the service of others.

The warnings about the practice of Kuṇḍalinī Yoga, particularly without the help of an experienced teacher, are well-founded. Carelessness will exact its price. When one cleans a gun and does not remove the bullet, somebody may be killed. Disregarding traffic signals may cause two cars to crash. Not listening to instructions, so that one can follow them precisely, will lead to problems on any spiritual path. There is no need to be fearful about the path of Kuṇḍalinī when it is practiced with the help of an experienced teacher, or if scrupulous attention is paid to following each step in this book.

The Absolute will remain in the far distance as long as we struggle with concepts about the different aspects of Kuṇḍalinī or God. It is like seeing a huge mountain in the distance; the snow-capped peak instills an awesome feeling and a desire to get there. Yet, as we begin to climb, sight of the peak is quickly obscured. The emotional reaction that we might be lost can turn into fear. We must have faith that the path will lead to the top. Even the experienced mountaineer will occasionally encounter a feeling of fear. Courage does not drop into our lap. Courage is gathered by overcoming fear. Faith is not gained unless we are willing to accept the darkness.

If we can know Kuṇḍalinī only by experience, then what kind of experiences are they? As has already been pointed out, these experiences are individual and words are inadequate to describe them. But they can inspire the listeners to experience their own.

An important practice such as the Divine Light Invocation, which is given among the instructions, will bring about a unique experience. Careful observation will show that first the "grooves" of the old mental record have to be changed so that the nervous system can get used to a different rate of vibration, in the same way that one has to learn to sing in a high key. The voice does not jump there, but has to be trained and become flexible to expand its present limitation to reach the high notes.

The question, What is Kuṇḍalinī, what is this Cosmic Force?, does have an answer. But the answer goes on expanding according to the level of understanding from which the question is posed. The answer comes also in that particular language that is unique to the questioner, in the same way that for one person God is a Supreme Being, for another God is the Energy in the atom.

Reflection on the Body as a Garden

In the garden of the body there are many paths.
Choose one.
Eyes sweep over this beautiful garden.
See with the eye of LIGHT.
An urge to touch.
Touch with sensitivity.
A deep breath brings fragrance to the nostrils.
A deep breath feels like expansion – unending.
What is this fragrance?
Who perceives it?
I? Who is I?
That little leaf bobbing up and down
on the waves of the mind's lake.
What direction?
Don't care – let go.
Surrender.
A floating leaf doesn't resist – it doesn't leap either.
It allows itself to be carried.
A river of thoughts – where will they go?
To a big ocean?
One thought like a drop falling,
falling into the ocean to be lost.
What is reality? What is mind?
An overwhelming feeling of gushing concepts
barely escaping the fire
of the emotional kiln.
Do you light the fire in the kiln of your emotions?
Can you blow it out when you want to?
Can you soften it?
Can you stay cool in the blazing fire
of emotions of another?
Do you get ignited?
Try to put the fire out – by the water of your eyes.
Close your eyes.

See how the red veil changes.
Pink is love without passion.
Love, the center of being –
Love, the center of Light radiating –
touching others,
touching others and expanding.
Heart filled with love, lungs filled with air,
breath is gentle, breath is life.
Power of life – breathing the breath of life.
Inhale inspiration.
Exhale despair.
Swing with the rhythm of breath and life.
Let the air flow back of its own accord.
Stop and wait, hold the breath – but for how long?
Nothing lasting, constant movement.
Sailing thought on the mental lake.
Music of the waves.
Smell their fragrance,
feel their vibrations.
Feel the breath in the sound of the voice.
See the fragrance of the flower
moving through the air,
dancing in the sun's bright Light
subdued by the clouds,
warmth touching gently, softly.
Swirling Light, swirling air – vibrations,
inside – outside.
All Energy vibrating in unison.
Love without passion.
Love without fire.
Luminous Light that reflects in dew drops
on the thousand-petaled Lotus.

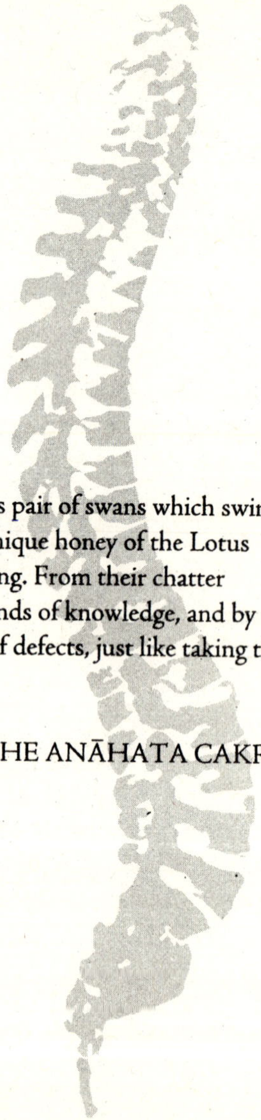

I venerate (revere, render devotional service) this pair of swans which swim in the mind of the great, feeding on the unique honey of the Lotus (heart) that is the opening of understanding. From their chatter comes the development of the eighteen kinds of knowledge, and by using them one acquires all qualities out of defects, just like taking the milk from water.

MANTRA FOR THE ANĀHATA CAKRA

7. ANĀHATA

THE FOURTH CAKRA

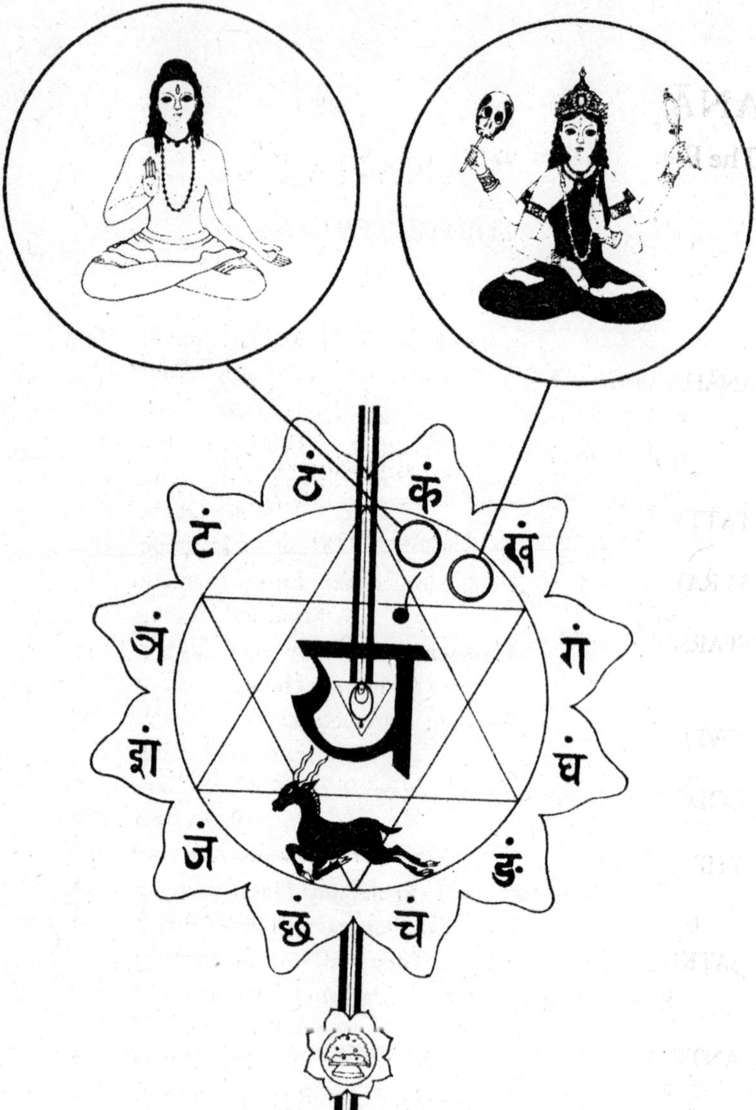
ठं
कं
टं
खं
ञं
गं
झं
घं
जं
ङं
छं
चं
यं

ANĀHATA

The Fourth Cakra and Its Symbols

ANĀHATA: The Fourth Cakra or Heart Lotus (Celestial Wishing Tree)

Sound of Śabdabrahman (sound of bell) is heard without the issue of striking two things together.

TATTVA: Differentiating faculty

54 RAYS: Relate to air (vayu)

SPARŚA: Touch (feelings), abode of Mercy (spiritual experiences), the Anāhata Cakra controls this sense

TWELVE LOTUS PETALS: The Lotus is sacred

COLOR OF THE PETALS: Vermilion

THE LETTERS ON THE PETALS: Kaṃ, Khaṃ, Gaṃ, Ghaṃ, Ṅaṃ, Caṃ, Chaṃ, Jaṃ, Jhaṃ, Ñaṃ, Ṭaṃ, Thaṃ

ṢAṬKOṆA: Two Triangles, one pointing up, one pointing down, the one pointing up symbolizes the aspirant's rise to the Greater Power

ANTELOPE: Black, the antelope is similar to the deer – a very shy, fast and graceful-moving animal

Its symbolic expression here is connected with spiritual experiences that go before the self can grasp them and know them, moving quickly away from the eye of the ego.

BĪJA: Yaṃ, the Seed Sound

PIṄGALĀ: The Nāḍī on the right side of the body

ĪḌĀ: The Nāḍī on the left side of the body

SUṢUMNĀ: The central channel in the spine

CITRIṆĪ: Three in one (sattva, rajas, tamas), body, mind and speech

GOD AND HIS OBJECTS:

Īśa: The male aspect of Energy unmanifest (Haṃsa, swan, also the Sun)

The intelligence on this level is symbolized by Īśa, the Lord of Speech, on a black antelope. The Iṣṭadevatā is worshipped in the heart.

Gesture: Vara(da), granting boons; Abhayamudrā, dispelling fears in the three worlds (past, present and future)

GODDESS AND HER OBJECTS:

Kākinī: The female aspect of Energy manifest

The intelligence on this level is symbolized by the Goddess Kākinī, also on a black antelope.

Pāśa: Noose, being caught in expectation of spiritual experiences

Skull: pure mind

Gesture: Vara(da), granting boons; Abhayamudrā, dispelling fears

Black Antelope: symbolizes fleetness; spiritual experiences are fleeting

ĀNANDAKAṆḌA LOTUS: Below the Heart Cakra is the plane of mental worship, there the Kalpataru (celestial wishing tree) grants all one asks, leading to mokṣa

The Goddess of Speech – Śakti

The cakras, as levels of consciousness, represent dynamic processes in people.

The Anāhata Cakra controls air as well as touch. It is important to observe how speech comes about. A person who is out of breath can speak only with great difficulty. Obviously, speech without air is impossible, but the use of air, or the kind of breathing, affects speech in loudness or softness, melodiousness or abruptness. When we speak, we set up currents in the air and we are responsible for these currents. The evolution of tamas, rajas and sattva has to be given an important part in our awareness.

The Devī holds in Her hand a noose. This warns that we can be caught not only by our emotions in speech, but by speech itself. We can love to hear ourselves talk and be caught in this infatuation. The aspirant must be committed to truth in speech and thought.

The process of clarifying the meaning of terms must be continued and, in this cakra, you will have to define such words as "consciousness," "psychic" and "spiritual." This definition does not necessarily limit them, because the meaning is open to many levels of understanding.

The refinement of the senses finds its expression in speech through poetry and sometimes in prophetic poetry, because then the sound is not of the tongue but of the heart (Śabda). It is like a well from which water is gently brought up from deep within. One becomes aware of the source only in those rare moments of surrender, stillness and intuition at its deepest level.

Here one may easily reach the Spirit, coming through the poetry, of a travel companion on that royal highway of spiritual life. Here the aspirant is only one step away from the communication of Selves (souls), which is beyond all words.

At this point, when the senses are refined, coarse

speech is a painful experience, almost unbearable. The Devī of Speech (Śakti) is word power. Mantra is its highest expression. The sound of the voice and the vibration of it pervade the area in which the mantra is spoken. After some time, the mantra purifies the mind and the immediate orbit, which enlarges as the time of practice continues. Finally, the power of the mantra becomes a self-generating energy. At this point it is said that the Devī, the Divine Mother, is manifest. Waves of joy and peace flood over the aspirant and a great surge of energy is experienced, expressed in most delicate, gentle feelings of devotion and surrender. The Heart is the meeting ground and some of Her Divine gifts are received here. If they are treasured and kept secret, She will be most generous. But the moment the ego puts itself on the throne that belongs to Her, the "Divine love affair" is ended. To prevent this from happening, humility has to express itself naturally, devotion to Her has to be given first place, in complete surrender. This surrender is easily attained by stilling the mind to receive Her Divine "messages," your intuitive perceptions.

The Heart Lotus is your personal temple, as indeed your whole body is. Let your mind create the atmosphere, let your feelings express that mood. Be alone when you worship in your own heart. This cakra is also called the Abode of Mercy. Mercy in feelings only is of no benefit to anyone unless this mercy is also expressed in words or actions. Mercy is forgiveness, understanding coming from the heart. As we give it, so we will receive it. There is perfect balance in the law of karma.

The Wishing Tree, the Kalpataru, is located in the Ānandakaṇḍa, which lies below the Heart Lotus. We can pick the fruit from the Wishing Tree, words of sweetness and truth. This miniature Lotus is regarded as being the inner courtyard to the Anāhata Cakra. It is the way of approach to the Most Holy, in an attitude of gratitude, awe and wonder. It is symbolic of the process of discovering the Divine within, and the mysteries and awesome powers of the mind. The inner courtyard then represents the experience of the manifestation of psychic energy, while the Anāhata Cakra houses the tabernacle of the Most Holy from which the spiritual energies manifest. To this the whole chapter is devoted.

Thoughts on Touch

The Fourth Cakra is called the Heart Lotus. Air and touch are the particular expressions of this cakra. The air indicates lightness; it cannot be grasped and held onto. Breathing is vital to human life. A touch as light as breath is only possible when all self-gratification has been renounced. Grasping is different from touching.

To touch a silken cloth is to feel its softness, but to touch a piece of rock is to feel its roughness. We can think of touching the human skin, feeling the softness, warmth and the pulsating life; or we can think of allowing someone to touch us and responding to what that touch conveys. A touching gesture can be more helpful than words in comforting someone, yet the right words can also touch one inside.

Touch and feeling: tamasic, rajasic and sattvic

"Touching" and "feeling" are interchanged in everyday language. Should they be? Touch and feelings can be seen as emotions that are being cultivated from tamasic to rajasic to sattvic. Uncultivated or tamasic touch will be rough, without awareness for the sensitivity of what is touched, be it a person or an object. Touch is often emotionally stimulated and serves as a barometer to find out if "the touch of my hand is well-received," which conveys to me that I am accepted. So it serves my own emotional needs rather than being of a giving nature. This motivation to touch would be called tamasic. Rajasic touch would be partly the fulfillment of my needs, but there would also be a willingness and a readiness to meet the needs of the other person. The underlying factor would be my desire to accept and my need to be accepted. The most desirable touch is the sattvic approach that will give without asking anything in return, a spontaneous from the heart action.

Touch: Exercises

I touch. The act of touching. What is touched?

Once the aspirant begins to practice Kuṇḍalinī Yoga, small details have to be given great attention. Here in the Heart Lotus we must investigate the sense of touch as has been done with other senses in the previous three cakras.

It is now time to check out emotional impulses to see how they have changed into refined feelings and how much still has to be done. As the process of awareness goes on, emotions change too, but sometimes more slowly. To become aware of something disturbing that one has been unaware of can trigger feelings of hurt. By the use of discrimination, as part of awareness, you can quickly discard old experiences and the desire to take revenge for them now. There is no point in getting angry now about something that occurred years back. Awareness should be a tool for a more balanced way of living. Revenge is never good, but this type is very unfair.

Investigate what touch means to you

In a dispute between parents, children should be left out and not used as objects of revenge. If a mother blesses her child by a gentle and loving touch of her hand and touches the child with her eyes, the father can turn that blessing into a curse in subtle ways. Or vice versa, the mother can turn the blessings of the father into a curse.

– When you say that something touches your heart, what do you mean by this?
– What does it mean to be touched by a smile or a look of understanding?
– Think of being touched by the sunshine. In what ways?
– Prāṇa touches every part of your body and moves around within it. What does this mean to you?

- Is a healing touch necessarily limited to the laying on of hands? Can it be comfort in emotional desperation?
- Is there ever a time when touching people is an imposition?
- Do you consider touching an imposition when you are tired, nervous or wish to "keep your distance" and retain privacy?
- Does fear of touching or being touched mean a fear of not measuring up?
- Does your sense of touch have a powerful influence on your moods?
- Do you like or dislike being touched and stroked by others?
- Do you use the sense of touch for differentiation and organization?
- The hands are the part of the body most used for touching. Hands build and hands destroy. Can this be related to touch and feelings?

The following exercises will be of assistance in learning more about the sense of touch and the details of this perception, which are usually given little or no attention. The exercises are divided into theoretical and actual parts.

Theoretical:

1. What is your present perception of touch?

2. What can you touch and what can you not touch?

3. How do you relate touch to feelings and to emotions?

4. Do you really experience touch, or do you only remember? How big a part do memory and thought association play in the actual experience of touch?

5. Investigate the sense of touch in relation to the other senses. What is the influence of the other senses?

Actual:

1. The first exercise for the actual sense of touch is to hold or touch objects such as a piece of wood; metal objects, one that is smooth and one that is sharp such as a knife; a smooth stone and one that is rough; hot water and cold water; a leaf; the hair, skin, feet, face and eyelids of another person. Observe all your thoughts and reactions and carefully take note of them.

Touching an object for 3 minutes

2. Take a piece of perfectly clean, white cloth. Rub your hands on the cloth, saying aloud, "Dirt be removed. Dirt be removed," over and over again. The cloth will, of course, become dirty. The remembrance that it was perfectly white at one time will lead gradually to insights.

Clean white cloth

3. Sit comfortably facing your partner and touch just the fingertips of your hands together. Observe all impressions, thoughts and reactions and write them down afterward. This exercise can also be done with each partner holding the hands close to, but not touching, the other's hands. Observe the difference.

Touching another person's fingertips

4. If you have the opportunity to make observations of people while they are chanting a mantra over a period of three hours, you will be able to feel the vibrations in different parts of their body. Place your hands lightly on the head, the neck, the shoulders, the back, at the end of an hour of chanting. Do this again at the end of two hours and again after three hours. Note how the vibrations vary in intensity and in different parts of the body.

Effects of chanting mantra

5. Choose a stone and hold it in your hand when you go to sleep. Try to keep it in your hand until you awake in the morning. Observe your feelings or thoughts in connection with holding the stone and note any dreams that come from this experience. Recall dreams you have had in which the sense of touch was involved.

Dreams and the sense of touch

Value of personal experience

The insights obtained from these exercises will be more valuable than information given by someone who, through a misguided idea of helping (sentimentality), shares an experience, thereby depriving the aspirant of self-discovery. The very much needed personal experience becomes a well of strength and energy to pursue the path.

Powers of the Mind

Now that the foundation has been laid in the first three cakras, some development will take its own course and bring about new experiences. Development takes place all the time, usually without the awareness and understanding of the individual. It is circumstances that force this process, which is long and slow in the ordinary course of life. The yogi and yoginī aim at conscious co-operation, which is like cleaning out the cupboards of the mind, taking down from the shelves old accumulated concepts that have collected dust over the years without yielding any benefits. This process makes "space" for extraordinary experiences that may be psychic or spiritual.

When the Divine Light Invocation exercise is practiced with the utmost attention it will bring indescribable results. For instance, the aspirant may experience the body as a mass of Light, or the sudden expansion of the head or the whole body. When this happens for the first time, some discomfort or even anxiety may follow, since this is something of which he or she has previously had only theoretical information but no personal experience. Psychic happenings are intriguing and we can easily be caught in them. How do they come about?

Everyone functions primarily through one of the five senses and it thereby becomes dominant, by choice or by circumstances. Therefore, it is through this sense, which has become trained and heightened in perception, that a psychic manifestation comes about. However, the experiences themselves are not a source of the continuous flow of energy needed to pursue further personal development. A psychic experience is seldom a strong enough inspiration to bring about continuing self-development, greater awareness and expanded consciousness. The terms "clairvoyance" and "clairaudience" mean clear sight and clear hearing, not necessarily character development.

Psychic & spiritual experiences: knowing the difference

Here in the Fourth Cakra, both psychic and spiritual experiences can take place, which makes an understanding of the difference between the two a necessity. The spiritual experience is unforgettable. It cannot be repeated at will and becomes the source of energy to further our development in becoming truly masters of our Self, a sustaining energy that seems to keep flowing. This is not the case with any type of manifestation of psychic energy, of which there have been repeated experiments. Psychic experiences have no particular aftereffects, except a stimulation as from anything enjoyable that one can repeat.

Explicit recall (memory) is a practice that takes time and effort, yet it is a necessity to develop this, not only to recall dreams as precisely as possible, including all details and feelings while dreaming, but also to recall events. Recall and observation go hand in hand. The yogic student should concentrate on recalling important events, particularly in regard to personal development, feelings, hunches and insights, in order to have an increase of those experiences that are valuable for understanding the mind in its various activities. To illustrate this point, if a muscle is exercised, its strength increases. If insights are acted upon, more insights (often of increasing importance) will come. Hunches and insights are evidence of increased sensitivity and when pursued will lead to a high degree of perception, by which other mental processes can also be understood and expanded.

Memory is increased when the aspirant is interested in the subject. Memory does not diminish with age, but age leads to differentiation of what is important to remember and what is not.

Recall and observation are very important because of

thought association, which is recall of the past. Together with observation in the present, we can get a clear understanding of our reactions. A certain person's facial expression, color of hair or eyes, type of clothes or mannerisms, may bring back the memory of someone else and perhaps a situation connected with an entirely different person. Sometimes these thought associations are very clear and sometimes they are barely recognizable, only making their presence known by a mood that may leave the individual puzzled.

An illustration of a small incident that everyone experiences will help with the understanding of certain powers of the mind. Two persons in the same room may voice the same thing at the same time, because they had the same thought. However, most people are unfortunately only temporarily amused and do not consider the very extensive influence of the interplay of the mental forces of and by those around us. An example of this is when one finds that a friend or neighbor comes repeatedly to mind. It should not then be a surprise to be contacted by that individual. If observation has been practiced, many such things will already have emerged. These qualities of mind are present in everyone. We can become aware of these abilities, increase them, and finally exercise them in a conscious way.

The yogic practices leading to awareness and control of the mind, keeping the mind single-pointed, receptive and on the Most High, lead to such mental powers as clairaudience and clairvoyance. Telepathic communication between guru and disciple is not at all unusual. Only when we do not pay any attention to what happens do we think that some people are gifted with phenomenal powers in these areas, which from a yogic point of view are quite common. We do not see anything phenomenal in such contact between a mother and child or a husband and wife.

What makes the manifestation of these mental powers so unusual is that the merry-go-round of the conversations in the mind has been stopped. The energy that keeps the merry go-round going is easily traced back to self-justification, self-glorification and self-gratification. This kind of wrong preoccupation with self is a great stumbling block. The still, small voice is drowned out by the merry-go-round of the mind. Flashes of awareness, flashes of insight and moments of inspiration are brief because the space is already filled to capacity.

Let us ask questions and listen to the answers from within:

- Do the cells of the body have a consciousness of their own?
- What triggers in the mind memory of a pain or a need?
- Is the mind the manager, assuming authority by suggestion, by determination, by self-hypnosis?
- What makes up the many details and events of our lives?
- Who else would be responsible for the interplay of these forces?

In technological inventions, humans have recreated their own abilities with greater accuracy and a wider range of functioning than they have discovered in themselves. It is doubtful that we could invent anything that is not in some way already existing in ourselves. We could only invent the camera because of the example of our own eyes. Television could not have been developed if the mind had not shown it was possible. The greatest obstacle to self-discovery is lack of mental discipline. The concentration exercises aimed at single-pointedness of mind should have a superior position in the daily schedule.

The need for surrender

The ability to surrender opinions and preconceived ideas means being able to relax the mind. To achieve a state of mind that is truly relaxed, we have to begin on the physical level. Body and mind will relax simultaneously in steps when supported by breathing exercises, which create the necessary conditions for complete relaxation. This state of relaxation and receptivity of the mind is a necessary prerequisite for obtaining the awareness of spiritual inspiration that will provide the spring to nourish continued development.

Mind: Doubt

Doubts, like clouds, sail on the mental horizon occasionally. They can be dark and heavy or small and wispy. Sometimes they disappear, but often return unnoticed because of an influx of new experiences. The mind, often not able to deal with experiences of psychic or spiritual content, is tempted to premature assessment, which contributes to doubt. It is wise to suspend all judgment and wait things out.

A record should now be kept, giving as many details as possible of any unusual experiences. Spiritual practice is a positive way to clear doubts. Then limitations created by doubt will be only temporary, not binding, if we do not insist on drawing conclusions from incomplete observations.

Doubt can be healthy or destructive, depending on the attitude of the aspirant. If doubt is destructive it can result in a depressive mood; it can open the back door to allow escape from the previously assumed responsibility and commitment. Impatience and restlessness create doubt, but the aspirant is warned that both also prevent certain spiritual powers from developing. Remember that impatience is an expression of arrogance of some sort which, if allowed to linger, will undermine faith, hope and will, and only strengthen the moods of depression. Arrogance is of the ego and is therefore destructive.

Healthy doubt stimulates questioning, which allows expansion of awareness and a widening of horizons on which the sun of spiritual life will continue to rise.

Every now and then, the wind of imagination creates

waves on the surface of the waters of the mind and the boat is rocked by doubt. But persistence in following the set course will give strength to weather the storm. Each victory then becomes a new source of strength from which we can draw when another storm arises. But we also learn to keep more and more control on emotions and imagination, and thus the waves lose their power in due time. Faith thereby becomes a self-generating energy that is at our disposal when needed. Faith practiced becomes strengthened.

Mind: Observation

Knowledge and self-reliance

There is power in knowledge, our personal knowing, which is inner wisdom. The process of attaining that wisdom is a long one on the path of Kuṇḍalinī Yoga. Concentration on ideals, keeping the mind fixed on these qualities, together with daily reflection and straight-walk thinking, will lead to that wisdom. It is necessary to be able to break away from the herd, free ourselves of the conditioning of upbringing, and stand alone on our two feet, responsible only to the inner authority. The practice of straight-walk thinking, getting straight to the point, while reflecting on the events of the day, then using the spiritual diary to record these observations, helps in the process of becoming self-reliant.

Humankind's unexplainable desire to believe in the occult, religion or mysticism may stem from an inner knowing that there is a Power greater, creating the tantalizing question – Where did I really come from? – Who am I?

Refined perception

During sleep, sensations are perceived on a different level of consciousness. They seem to emanate from a plane of finer forces. All spiritual practice aims at sensitizing our gross senses so that we can become aware of these finer forces. We must not be in a hurry to allow the gross mind to translate the perception into something understandable just for the sake of mental security.

One way to increase that perception is to use the imagination and bring Light into the Heart Lotus, which is situated in the spine just above the physical heart. If you have a guru, it will now be possible to reach a level of intuitive perceptions when, by first invoking and then projecting the inner Light, the personality of the guru disappears and the listener perceives only what comes through the Light.

As a result of the sensitizing and refinement of the senses and the practice of control of the energies thus revealed, an energy field around the body can be produced that is strong enough to prevent the passerby from seeing the physical presence. In other words, "A" can produce an energy field strong enough to become invisible to "B." It is like jamming a radio station with an interfering overlay of sound. The body of "A" does not actually disappear, but the state of mind of "B" is being affected like a person in shock who cannot clearly see or think. The senses are temporarily out of order.

The creation, use and control of the energy in the energy field and its increase become understood during periods of practice.

Mind is a miniature universe.
Universe is the expansion of the mind.

Investigating mind

Control of mind means control of thoughts.

- Can you change the pattern of your thoughts?
- Do you have thoughts that are self-destructive?
- If so, can you subdue them?
- By what means?

Thoughts are reproductive, like seeds.

- What kind of thoughts do you want to plant in your mind?

Become aware when you and another person have the same thoughts. Try to find out how this came about and observe if these influences can be brought about at will. Watch how you do it.

Mind has a drawing power.
- Where does your mind draw you?
- Does it draw you to something desirable and uplifting?
- Does it take you beyond the physical-emotional level?
- Does it take you to the Self, over the mind?

Memory exercises

To practice recall of different states of mind:
- When do I have these states of mind?
- At what time?
- What are the cycles of my mind?
- Have I had any hunches?
- What is the difference between hunches and intuitive perception?

Think about promises:
- What are the promises I have made to other people?
- Have I fulfilled them?
- What are the promises I have made to myself?

Watch any aspects of today, the past or the future in your dreams. Write down what you recall of dreams you had three months or six months ago and compare them with your original notes.
Now watch yourself falling asleep.
- Can you take an active part in this?
- Can you redirect your dreams or stop an unpleasant dream?
- Watch how you do this.

Now consider your moods:

- Watch your moods three times a day and record.
- Assess your mood – 10 the lowest, 100 the highest.
- See what your cycles are.
- Compare surrendering to a mood with resisting one.
- Observe moods, thoughts and habits.
- Recognize the difference between habitual and spontaneous responses connected with the mood.
- Recall how this happens.
- Spontaneous responses have to be watched like the habitual ones, three times a day.

Catch the stimulations of the moment.

- Separate ordinary events from inspirations (of a Divine nature).

Mind has to be controlled in order to free it from its own inherent doubts. They create the need for security. Oversimplification and reluctance to reach beyond the ordinary have put reason and logic on the throne from generation to generation. This emphasis has become a self-perpetuating indulgence to meet the demands for security. It has kept people comfortable and so it has prevented the expansion of old limits and thereby the discovery of new territory and new possibilities.

Divine Mother Śakti: Energy Manifest

"I am a gross body, a subtle body, a causal body – I am myself Turīya Caitanya – I am in all. I am all aspects of Māyā – I am with attributes – Māyā; I am without attributes – beyond Māyā."

– S. Shankaranarayanan, *The Glory of Divine Mother*

Energy manifest

Femininity and masculinity exist wherever there is creation. The Śāstras (scriptural texts) call the male the Deva and the female the Devī, in accordance with the male and female principle in all fathers and mothers in the world. Energy per se is symbolized in the male aspect. Energy manifest is symbolized in the female aspect.

Śakti is the Great Mother. In glory She surpasses a father at all times. Mother Śakti holds the child, the seeker, the aspirant in Her womb, which is the world. She nourishes the child with Divine nectar, which brings the child back to Mother, after the enjoyment of the play of Māyā.

All practice in Kuṇḍalinī Yoga must be understood as an approach to the Devī. Śakti is the origin of all. Śakti is the source. Whatever one worships and admires, it is Śakti. She is the form, the ideal, the Power – the Goddess of the spoken word. It is for this reason that Śakti is also life, breath – existence itself. Śakti is one power becoming many. All that is manifest has an innate power that is from the same source. There is one sun having many rays. All rays emanate from the same source.

In order to understand Śakti Power it is necessary that one recognize power in its most simple manifestations. Electricity is a familiar energy. It is easy to focus the mind on its physical forms, such as a light, a heater or a running motor. When the mind has to focus on the electrical power itself, without the familiar gadgets, the difficulties become quickly apparent. Even an abstract symbol is not the power itself.

The light and the heater can be seen as concrete symbols of electricity. The mind needs a particular training to understand beyond the symbols. The difficulties become apparent when we practice thinking of ourselves without the body or face. Yet we are familiar with ourselves and often even quite emphatic about what we know of ourselves.

We can use these illustrations and carry them a step further. To understand terms like "God," the "Absolute" and "Cosmic Energy," special training and new experiences are necessary. How can we otherwise overcome the old familiar process of creating and recreating the Absolute or God in our own image and even adding human characteristics to it, however perfect these may be?

Energy manifesting

In Eastern thought, God is understood as Energy manifesting in many aspects. The mind and its many possible manifestations are an expression of that one Power, Energy.

The process of thinking is an energy process. How much energy is used to produce a thought? Where do we take it from? When thought is put into action, combined with emotion, we use the terms "energy expenditure," "emotional investment" and so on, because we can "measure" our "energy output" by our feelings of tiredness or exhaustion. In order to understand the Śakti Power, it is necessary to list all the different faculties of the mind. What about telepathy and hypnosis? How do they come about? Can this be done at will?

What is the Śakti Power that is at work in the mind? Before the term "phenomenon" can be used, the heightened power of perception should be considered. This is what the practicing yogi develops in regard to the senses. To truly heighten perception, one condition is necessary – the clearing of one's conscience. Otherwise, much energy is bound up and that hypersensitive state cannot be attained.

The human body would be another good illustration of the many manifestations of one source. There is one body with its many manifestations and very different expressions: eyes see, tongue tastes, feet walk, blood flows. Within these gross manifestations there are minute details of each limb, organ, cell, yet in spite of the "individual expression" of each, the power emanates or is drawn from one source that we call life force.

Sandcastles do not last; they become sand again. But only the form is destroyed – the essence (sand) remains to be formed again.

It must be understood that these are all oversimplified illustrations and that each aspirant has to do his or her own "straight-walk" thinking. In all areas, each aspirant has to draw conclusions that are personally meaningful.

For a long time, the need of substituting a concrete symbol for an abstract idea has to be accepted. This kind of mental acrobatics is very helpful and will lead naturally to a point where it is no longer necessary.

Anything that is manifested takes on a life of its own. Therefore, the individual is responsible for every thought, word and action that he or she produces, and this increases at each level of consciousness.

The four Powers of Divine Mother Śakti:

1. Maheśvarī: preciousness, comprehending wisdom, majesty, greatness.
2. Mahākālī: strength, will, irresistible passion.
3. Mahālakṣmī: harmony, secrecy, compelling attraction, seriousness.
4. Mahāsarasvatī: perfection, intimate knowledge.

Śakti's power is the manifestation of the microcosmos as well as the macrocosmos.

Power of Divine Mother Śakti

To use the power of Divine Mother Śakti for our own purposes is to enslave it to the ego. Greed has no limitations. This is an important area that needs to be given attention in daily reflection. ("God, Divine Mother, provide everything for me from a parking place to a fat increase in salary.") Such thinking backfires badly at a later time when this attitude is already forgotten.

Śakti is all the Power there is to be experienced. She is called the Devī of Speech, the whisper that is in every illusion. She is also the thunder of the cosmic voice. The two extreme gifts that one can obtain from Divine Mother are Her Māyā (continuous illusion) and Liberation from the bondage of all illusion. Each human experience is at some point on the sweep between these extremes of Māyā and Liberation. The movement of every human life shows the intermingling of countless possibilities. Only by a decisive act of will can we stop running all over the place. Remember, by the manifestation of Her power is this whole universe set in motion – revolving, moving constantly.

On the path to Liberation from illusion, the relationship of the aspirant to Divine Mother must be built on the firm foundation of good character, self-discipline and a faith that ever deepens. Eventually, when this faith is no longer blind, the aspirant knows within the heart the presence of Divine Mother, and an intimate play of forces follows, which no verbalization can truly express. The description "Living in Divine Mother's grace" fits perfectly.

As long as the aspirant keeps the contact with Her, She will take care of Her Divine child with a love and a tenderness unknown before. Life takes on a new meaning.

The kind of life one decides to live is up to the individual. After obtaining Her grace, an aspirant may not want to grow more into Her Light, but may desire to resume the previous activities but with another dimension. Yet, an aspirant having once tasted Her Divine nectar may become an inspiration to others and continue to expand in the desire for a higher state of consciousness. Another may perfectly surrender to Her and desire nothing more than to be led by Her, wherever She takes Her Divine child (servant).

The end of pain and illusion

If She is wanted for Herself, all illusion comes to an end, and so does pain. It sounds easy and yet it seems to be, and really is, a constant battle against the stream of life. Life is not to be rejected, but to be transformed.

The last illusion is Śakti Herself.

Mind and Healing

Compassion: the basis for healing

The power of healing attracts many aspirants. When the aspirant has gained control over the emotions and cultivated them into finer feelings, compassion will be allowed, in due time, to find true expression. When one desires to help because help is needed, rather than for rewards of any kind or for sentimental reasons, this desire has the right basis. It is far more likely that a healing will take place when motivated by noble feelings such as compassion. However, many more aspects come into both success and failure in healing.

An interplay of forces

If the aspirant has become aware of the power of the Divine Light Invocation, the interplay of forces is recognized. This contributes a great deal to understanding the functioning of the processes that are needed to gain conscious control of various energies. Opinions, concepts and beliefs are all loosened up through the practice of the Divine Light Invocation, gradually becoming ethereal as the firmness dissolves into Light. This is more than increased flexibility. Do not miss the subtlety that is expressed by the word "light." Meanings of words will become more and more elusive. This is inevitable when more subtle regions are reached.

Thoughts on healing

When we desire healing for ourselves or others, a few questions come up about the energies involved:

- Does healing have anything to do with the mind? or with the heart? What is it that heals?
- Is another person needed to assist healing?
- Does one have healing power within oneself?

By asking numerous questions and trying to find the answers, we grow in understanding.

When healing is being considered, the healer must find out how the illness came about. If there has been a continuous violation of some physical principles which has led to the breakdown of health, spiritual healing might be successful only once, if at all. In this case, the person should be properly instructed in taking care of the body and observing the laws under which it will stay healthy. If these are neglected, trust in spiritual healing will be weakened both in the healer and in the one who is ill. It is rare that illness is sudden. It is more likely that preoccupation of the mind with other concerns has been too intense, so that early signs of breakdowns in the body have gone unnoticed. Pain is a great teacher, and illness is often the only way to become truly grateful for health and to see the healthy body as a precious instrument that should be well taken care of.

The attitude of the sick person might be a reason why spiritual healing could not take place. It could fail if there were no will to live, no purpose to life which would give the impetus, or if the purpose had not been grasped, or if the person believed that he or she was too great a sinner to deserve to be healed. Add to this all the psychological advantages of love and attention that go with being ill, and it becomes obvious that there could be little or nothing to promote healing.

So the mental and emotional preparation of ill people is very important. This means that there has to be real concern, not sentiment, to help them to help themselves and to understand some aspects of their predicament. There has to be the cooperation of the desire to be well and the will to live a purposeful life. The healer has to inspire and reinforce these positive thoughts. Emotions, which have been discussed at great length in the Maṇipūra Cakra, play a very important part in the healer and the ill person. There have to be cultivated emotions, feelings of deep gratitude on the part of the person being healed for regained health and on the part of the healer for the privilege of being a channel. Gratitude, being one of the finest of human feelings, plays an important part in the practice and the results.

Is healing a power of the mind? Or is healing by Divine grace?

Healing

Looking at the various powers of the mind, it becomes obvious that there is no simple and direct answer. Illness is a combination or, to use a now familiar term, an interplay of forces. The genuine concern of the healer can be a subtle suggestion, or, if there is a powerful personality involved, it can be a powerful suggestion, which will lift the self-image and infuse new hope into a purposeless life. This regenerates the healing forces that are in every individual. Confidence, trust, hope and will to live, and the view of a goal or purpose are some of the basic principles involved. As a plant needs certain conditions to grow, so the human "plant," when its basic requirements are met, will grow into a normal healthy human being.

It is now necessary to see that there is another factor in healing that we will call spiritual. The process of life itself, be it a plant, an animal or a human being, is still an unanswered mystery. A healer is a person who has an awareness and perception of those forces that promote healing or correct what is detrimental to health. This awareness makes it possible for the healer to let this energy flow through and direct it to the person who is in need of additional energy that will correct the weakness in the body.

The Divine Light Invocation has the proper combination of all that is necessary to bring about a healing, either spontaneously or by repetition. In the practice of the Divine Light Invocation there has to be a true feeling of compassion and total involvement on the part of the healer, which communicates itself to the sick person. Sometimes psychological problems have to be removed first, and there has to be a healing in the mind before a healing can take place in the body. It is essential that the healer refrain from determining how the healing should take place in order for the Divine Light to flow and set in motion what is necessary for a particular individual. Geographical distance need not be a barrier to healing. The ill person may be 3000 miles away, but our old space/time concept should not prevent us from attempting to help.

At the moment when the needy person is deeply relaxed and in a state of surrender (perhaps because of weakness) he or she becomes receptive and thereby allows the energy to flow and do its work. The healer must observe and understand the state of surrender and deep relaxation. If such a state cannot be achieved while awake, it will naturally take place when the individual falls asleep. In the following two hours when there is a dropping from the conscious level to the unconscious, the body is extremely receptive to repeated suggestions of healing directed toward its own resources. This in itself may lead to healing in some cases.

The efforts described may have to be repeated over a period of from one to three months. It must be realized that in some circumstances healing may not be best for the whole person. The Divine Light cannot be told what to do, but immeasurable benefits will be derived whatever the visible results.

The power of faith and hope should not be underestimated. They are also Energy, which can be increased with concern and involvement through the Divine Light Invocation.

Thoughts on Humility and Gratitude

Humility and gratitude go hand in hand. The feeling of gratitude is an interaction between the mind and the body. Both will benefit from it. Awareness increases so that we become grateful for everything we are given. We have to learn, literally learn, to be grateful for what we receive day by day, simply to balance the criticism that, day by day, we voice because of powerful emotions. When the question of initiation came up for a certain young man, my Guru said that he would not consider it because this young fellow was not grateful for what he had already got, therefore he should have no more.

In Buddhist tradition, the aspirant gives 100,000 prostrations to develop humility – a virtue that is thus expressed appropriately through the body. Some people will say, "But I feel I have gratitude and humility, so what is wrong?" You may think and feel you have gratitude, but if you never express it, does it have any meaning?

When you have helped a friend over and over again, but no gratitude has ever been expressed, you may wonder what you are doing and if you are wasting your time and energy. But perhaps you are unable to recognize your friend's love and gratitude because they are not expressed according to your expectations – because your friend's spontaneous expression of those feelings is not an echo of your own. Then we enter into playing games. A good sense of discrimination is necessary to see through all the tricks our mind and emotions play.

What else can we do to cultivate gratitude and humility? The East Indians use the worship of the guru, which appeals only to some people. But this act of worship has very good psychology behind it. People have an inborn desire to admire and worship. They look for an example after which they can mold themselves. False gods such as success, food, sex, possessions, unproven beliefs and personal convictions are often worshipped until there is an awakening to their emptiness.

Another way to develop gratitude is to truly look at yourself, to see the marvel of this human body and the intricacy of the sensitive organs. Be grateful to have the full use of your senses through which you perceive all that is around you, the world and the beauties of nature. Appreciate the strong body and the state of good health you enjoy.

What has been said so far only scratches the surface. It is meant to stimulate your mind into the kind of thinking from which you will benefit. The mind is always so active scheming to fulfill selfish desires that those shy and modest thoughts of gratitude and humility get pushed into the background. We allow the mind to be stimulated by all sorts of things that often prove to be useless, even detrimental, to our mental and emotional well-being. Thoughtlessly we establish bad habits and allow those to remain, then cry when we experience the pain of our own carelessness. We even interpret this as an unfair destiny, entirely missing the point that we have laid our own traps and we have to take responsibility for those acts. In the course of life, there are many little "miracles" but our hearts are so hardened that we don't pay any attention. Instead we take things for granted. Yet we never allow anyone to take us for granted. When this happens, we protest loudly.

The lengthy prayers to all gurus and all Buddhas fulfill this function – the cultivation of the finer feelings and the acknowledgement to those who have paved the way and share their hard-won experiences with us, helping us to gain insights and to travel the narrow road with faith and endurance, in humility and gratitude.

Additional Thoughts on Sex

Quality and commitment

The process of cultivation and developing quality in regard to sex, which has already been pointed out in the First Cakra, now has to reach a level of refinement where neither partner becomes demanding and where the commitment to each other is clear. With the grosser emotions refined into true feelings, sex must become an expression of love and an ability to surrender to each other. In other words, all that has been practiced can now be synthesized.

Light blending into Light

A married couple meditating together is coming together on a different level, even if the image of meditation is not the same. The Divine Light Invocation can be supportive because, with continued practice of it, the gross image of the body and identification with it are diffused. It may become the underlying thought that in the surrendering of the sex act, Light blends into Light. This would indicate that, with all possessiveness and self-gratification gone, there is a real giving and a receptivity to each other.

The mistake that is very easily made by an aspirant is seeing the powerful life force only in extremes – from simple survival of the species to the mystical marriage (of yoga and religions). An attitude like this entirely misses a wide range of differences in experience. If the enjoyment of sex were compared to the enjoyment of food, it would be like the creativity that goes into the preparation of a meal. This brings enjoyment for the eyes, for the nose, for the touch when it is eaten by hand, as well as for the taste. If it is cooked with a deep feeling of love and concern for the health of those who will partake of it, and if it is presented in an attractive way, the table decked with candles and flowers, it becomes a festive occasion. The enjoyment goes far beyond simply filling the body needs.

In the sexual area, we can see that the important activity that also brings another human life into being has to be given the same care and attention as the preparation and enjoyment of food.

We must look at sex, besides being a procreative force, in its psychic connotations. Since no human activity can be isolated, in a sexual relationship each partner is affected on all levels, from the purely physical to the psychic. On the mental level, the interplay of forces between two minds has already been pointed out.

In Western culture, there is an unnatural overemphasis on sex. Orgasm is not the ultimate goal of human beings. The woman's point of view is naturally different from the man's because of the fact that she is the bearer of children and has the greater burden and responsibility.

So the woman's viewpoint on sex in a yogic life has to be re-evaluated. Additional offspring can be a great hindrance at a certain point in her yogic life, particularly if she has done her so-called "duty" to society. She may find it extremely difficult, if not impossible, to serve two masters and will therefore have to resign herself to limit her spiritual activity, for a certain time, to increased self-development. This, however, will then provide the foundation for later spiritual life, provided that she has made herself emotionally independent of the male. That emotional independence is, in any case, a desirable basis for any male-female relationship.

There is an additional problem that the householder yogin or yoginī has to face in the West because of the social setup of the single-family unit. In many other human societies, the whole family, several generations, lives together and the children are accepted by everyone. So, if one parent were to take a few hours a day for several weeks or months to do a particular work or spiritual practice, the children would not suffer. Even so, men and women of the East postpone more intense spiritual practice until the middle or later years of their lives when the young members of their family no longer need them.

It cannot be stressed enough that for the yogi or yoginī sex is not a sin, as it is often seen in the West.

Cooperation with evolution

The Divine union is an ongoing evolution and, as such, in some lifetime the decision has to be made to cooperate with this process. This does not mean a hindrance or discouragement in the development of intellectual or mental powers. On the contrary, the whole system of yoga is one of cooperation with the evolution of the human being in all phases of life.

Kuṇḍalinī Yoga offers an equal opportunity to any man or woman who is willing to pursue that path.

Thoughts on Brahmacaryā (Celibacy)

The many functions of sex have been discussed in the cakras and in each the horizons and levels of meaning have been expanded. The symbolism of the cakras shows the change of meaning, and it has already been pointed out that brahmacaryā (celibacy) is not a moral issue with the practicing yogi or yoginī, but a matter of choice. A quick review would be in order. First, energy is expressed through sex for the purpose of procreation. Then the energy is expressed in art or invention or in healing. Without energy, neither our thought processes nor any of our senses would function. We have seen that even mechanicalness uses energy. But let us not give in to the natural temptation of classification. Energy cannot be put into a pigeonhole.

Through the process of clarification, the aspirant will have observed the attachment to all our sense perceptions, to which we give such weight that they dominate our lives. Attachment to anything is binding, preventing us from seeking something else outside of the habitual thoughts and actions. Sex is not excluded from this. Attachment to sex and its pleasures, and the enormous energy that goes into defending the attachment to those pleasures, would be worth a scientific investigation.

The path of brahmacaryā is only for the very few who will set aside a period of three or four years to thoroughly investigate the truth in the old teachings to see if there is any point in pursuing this new path, this new outlook on life. Most people are only willing to allot that amount of time to accomplish something more tangible and ego-pleasing, more emotionally satisfying.

The objection that celibacy, in those religions where it is practiced, has not brought any outstanding results but often the contrary, points again to mechanicalness. It is like the repetition of a mantra, whose power will indeed manifest if it is recited with the right attitude, concentration and understanding of the purpose to be achieved. Similarly, celibacy must be practiced with the right motivation to give sufficient support for the times of temptation that are bound to come. What makes brahmacaryā meaningful is not the moral implication, but the aspirant's active participation in the process of spiritual evolution.

The necessary division of the duties and responsibilities of a householder do not allow the practice of brahmacaryā unless the offspring have reached a certain age and there is a mutual agreement between the partners.

This is a complicated situation and for this reason gurus have discouraged the combining of family life with yogic life when the goal is the pursuit of a higher state of consciousness. It is difficult enough to attain a true state of brahmacaryā, not only on the physical-emotional level, but also on the mental level.

The cultivation of imagination and desires has been thoroughly dealt with in the first three cakras. In order to practice brahmacaryā successfully, this groundwork has to be done and the goal has to be set.

Psychic powers, which can perhaps be little goals along the way, are also not attained without the necessary exercises to bring about certain physical-emotional-mental conditions. If a magician needs years of practice to perfect his act, then the sharpening and refinement of sense perception that allow the unusual manifestations called psychic must be given at least an equal amount of time. The moment psychic energy is experienced, not just intellectualized, the whole world appears on quite a different level. Anybody who has given the time and effort required for three or four years of intense practice knows this to be true. Only those who are blind would deny the existence of the sun.

Brahmacaryā is not easy, and without the help of a teacher experience has shown that this decision seldom lasts more than two years, because of the lack of other supportive exercises which are necessary to keep control of the expression of the various senses and their gratification.

It must be recognized that at a certain stage of spiritual life an authority is needed, not to cater to dependency, but simply because the guru knows what the disciple does not know, but wants to learn. The guru becomes an authority by that fact.

Spiritual practice and authority will very slowly lead to self-reliance and freedom from the pressures of the senses. Without proper discrimination and knowledge, freedom cannot be handled. Release from any kind of attachment will therefore only be possible in the proportion to which the individual has learned to cope with freedom. Learning in all areas, I would like to remind you, is a process. The process of learning in Kuṇḍalinī Yoga is interwoven with awareness, observation, reflection, discrimination, and the practical application of all these things.

Thoughts on Worship

Worship for the aspirant can be symbolized by growing white flowers as a reminder of the purity one wishes to attain. Blue flowers may be grown if the color blue means spirituality to the individual, if in moments of quiet, blue lights have been experienced. The meaning of the color should be very definite for the individual. Grow flowers of a color that is for you symbolic of purity and the Most High. If you desire to unfold like a lotus, grow these plants, and when you care for them, think that you are looking after your own development.

Worship in daily life

Bring this attitude into all areas of your daily life. Beware of mechanicalness and routine. When making beds, think of straightening out the wrinkles in your mind, smoothing out your thoughts. When you light a candle, think of all the meanings associated with the Light. Think that people you have formerly considered primitive, such as fire worshippers, were in reality worshipping the Greater Light. This brings appreciation for other forms of worship.

The aspirant is warned not to allow worship to become dependency in the garb of tradition and authority. Worship must also have its evolutionary processes. That needs a thorough investigation. The almost inborn tendency to worship is obvious in the worship of power. This can be seen in the lives of all revolutionaries, who are first called murderers destroying an old power structure, but then when they are successful and attain power in their own way, they have the admiration of those same people who criticized them.

Symbol and ritual

We no longer worship many gods and goddesses, with the numerous rituals and ceremonies of the old religions, and we smile about the accuracy with which such rituals and ceremonies are performed. We think it is pagan, or at least outdated, but we seldom stop to consider that symbols are still used. Only their expression has changed and now we worship personalities or offices.

Worship as performed with intricate rituals and ceremonies has to be understood on the same variety of levels that we can still see today in some of the Christian faiths. The simple person, for example, feels much closer to St. Anthony than to Jesus or God. The more developed is able to accept St. Anthony, but is closer to Jesus. The next stage would be seeing the saints and Jesus as stepping-stones to God as Supreme Being. Finally, it takes a person with quite a different mind to accept a Cosmic Intelligence no longer put into a shape and form that have been created by the human mind.

Once we have advanced to this point, we recognize that all these other ways of worship lead away from the realization of the Self. Let us then use worship to cultivate the senses, to escalate the mind, and to achieve greater perception to discover the Divine within. The fire or sun worshipper is doing the same thing, being on the evolutionary path toward the Divine Light without color.

This is not to deny the value of developing human virtues, but for too long we have been conditioned to avoid carefully the discovery of the Divine within. Only a few have had enough rebellious spirit to break their dependency on the authority of established religion and make that discovery.

Guru-disciple relationship

The aspirant, then, is warned against taking a guru who will strengthen the bonds of dependency for too long. The true guru's purpose is to set the devotee free. The guru can only be seen as a symbol for the cultivation of the senses and, therefore, be worshipped or adored for only a certain length of time. Swami Sivananda sent away after twenty years a disciple who did not want to be independent.

The Heart Lotus is the place of the crossroads where the aspirant has to make a decision that everything in life must now be subservient to the pursuit of the goal, and where the actual worship of a guru will dissolve in the tabernacle of one's own heart into the guru within. Such an experience takes place when the disciple has accepted responsibility.

Certain levels of achievement may take lifetimes, but a disciple who has doubts will see that bonds dissolve in the Light, almost by themselves, at the right time. Again let us take an illustration from ordinary life. The baby learns to walk, clinging tightly to the mother's finger. When it has gained enough self-confidence from the practice of walking and the process of learning, there comes a moment when the baby of its own accord will let go of the mother's finger. What a great triumph the baby experiences and how it cherishes the joy of this demonstration and the delight of those around it!

The true guru is in the same position with the disciple (devotee) who, having had the encouragement of the guru all along the way, will know when the moment of independence has come. At this point timetables no longer need to be checked by the guru, nor all questions answered. The disciple finds that answers are within. The increasing awareness of the disciple makes it clear where it is necessary to take action. Before this time, the ego, every now and then, may interfere and make the disciple wish to be free of the guru's authority. Any such premature wish is of the ego. Daily reflection, in conjunction with the Divine Light Invocation, will develop the light of understanding in the disciple clearly enough to know when that time has come. But let us not be foolish and let go the attachment and the dependency to the guru before all other attachments are taken care of. That sacred relationship will dissolve into Divine Light. It does not need any conscious separation.

Worship is not done for the benefit of a God or a guru, but simply for the spiritual aspirant to recognize his or her level of development. Worship makes a great contribution, particularly when it is allowed to grow out of the individual temperament and cultivation of all senses. Traditional worship and ceremonies that have become meaningless to an aspirant are certainly not encouraged, but by individual inclinations, each aspirant should develop worship personally.

Either in your garden or in your house you can have a special place with white flowers or white candles for a spiritual idea such as Śiva or the Absolute, and have colorful flowers with colorful candles, symbolic for Śakti, the Divine Mother. Searching for the right plant or even seed, caring for and nurturing the flowers, all this activity will help cultivate feelings and the mind. Reflecting on these symbols, intentionally lifting them to higher levels, is a beautiful process of worship.

Synthesis of Exercises for the Anāhata Cakra

The aspirant has been given many details and carefully outlined steps for exercises in connection with each cakra. Here, for the first time, is a synthesis for the Anāhata Cakra. That step must also be done by the aspirant for all other cakras, then finally for the whole path of Kuṇḍalinī from the First to the Sixth, the Ājñā Cakra. All the symbols that have been helpful in giving directions are now changing levels of meaning.

In the Fourth Cakra, the aspirant is at the crossroads. A large portion of the work has been done and the changes in the aspirant may have resulted in attracting different people, people of like mind who offer support. At this point it will be necessary to review ideals to discover if some require refining and escalating from what was originally established. Others may need more intensive application. This can be accomplished with the help of a review of the daily diary, which has become a valuable chart of your progress and development. This process of evaluation will provide the base for laying out the next step on your path. Special care must now be taken in applying your new awareness to daily life. You will notice changes that have taken place in your self-image and thus recognize your ability to develop in the directions you have decided upon. This recognition can provide the enthusiasm needed for your continued development.

What is a friend?

A question that may be appropriate at this particular stage of development is, "What is a true friend?" What would be the characteristics of a person whom a seeker can call "my best friend"? As a starting point, one can ask what were the characteristics of your best friend up to this point.

- Somebody to do things with, see a movie, listen to a concert?
- Someone with whom little favors were exchanged?
- Someone to talk about the job or business with?
- Someone in whom comfort or sympathy could be found?

At this crossroads it may now appear that those characteristics of friendship are no longer sufficient and perhaps the friend of the past is in fact no more than a very good acquaintance. So, the list of characteristics of one's best friend would look quite different now.

Acceptance, discussion and support of:

- ideas that specifically come up in spiritual life.
- times of uncertainty and doubt.
- temporary instability.
- continuous questioning and searching.

These things require a friend with depth of character, understanding and someone who will, in the moment of doubt, not drag you away from the goal, but rather give support to your commitment and help you to bring out the best in yourself.

After you have found your guru, it may take a long time before your spiritual teacher is recognized as your best friend because of many moments of painful awareness. This awareness, even though painful, means that the process of attaining mental and emotional maturity is still going on. However, in the early stages of development, one reacts with resentment and it is only much later that a sense of gratitude emerges from within naturally.

It takes sensitivity and awareness to bring out the best in someone else, to be a best friend. The choice of friends and the extent to which we criticize others are reflections of self-image. Improved self-image and a beneficial kind of self-perception come from the pursuit of mental worship of our Iṣṭadevatā in the heart.

Divine Light Invocation and self-image

The Divine Light Invocation makes the greatest contribution to the change of self-image because of identification with the Divine Light. The Divine Light Invocation, which has been practiced in preceding cakras, now becomes the preparatory step for the Meditation on the Light at the end of the following chapter.

Mantra is an ever living embodiment of Power and Truth. It is another important tool in changing self-image and whether the voice is strong or feeble is not important, but the underlying "emotion-desire-longing" which, when given expression in chanting or reciting mantra, becomes a magnet attracting the Higher Force. This Higher Force will someday spark a "flame" deep within and develop into a self-generating force.

By using these tools with attention and concentration, you can affect the images of the mind.

- The mind is ever creating – what?
- That which is created – what happens to it?
- The mind creates beautiful images (manifesting them or not).
- The mind creates ugly images (manifesting them or not).

Value of character building

Now that you have examined the characteristics of a best friend and your own self-image, it is time to investigate if you have the qualities yourself to become someone else's best friend. Character building in ourselves is what attracts or makes us worthy of another person who is also building character. From the review of the ideals and the diary, it should now be clear what you need to cultivate. Personality changes take place according to the strength of the desire to achieve the goal. Here you should once more go over the exercises in the Maṇipūra Cakra on negative qualities and their positive opposites, bringing in your newly developed awareness. Listing such qualities and feelings makes clear the subtlety of the obstacles one encounters.

Emotions

When emotions arise, catch them, look at them, take all power out, withdraw identification from them. This practice takes time, but it may be better than to struggle with them. It is harmful, even destructive, to suppress emotions or to deny their existence. Transform them into refined feelings. If the emotions have erupted before awareness could catch them, replay the situation and take the position of an onlooker. This will help you to become detached. Emotions are attached to certain personality aspects – the Self is always only the Witness.

Desires

Desires arise from memory of experiences of the past. They are also projections into the future. Selfish desires are outgrowths from competition and comparisons. Whatever the root of these desires, take the battle-ax of the Devī and cut them off before it is too late. Discrimination serves very well as a battle-ax because not all desires are detrimental to our growth. A desire to grow in character and spirituality is necessary for growth to take place.

Discrimination

Evaluation

Desires have to be carefully evaluated. What can we do about old desires manifesting when we have progressed beyond that point? Pray. Ask that the desires that accompanied a lesser state of development will not be fulfilled. With a greater awareness of needs, there is a greater attempt to simplify life in order to remove all possible distractions from the chosen path.

Renunciation

Renunciation of desires can be achieved without pain and frustration if the contents or the fulfillment of them are well reasoned out. Leaving them to the emotions means that the attachment is still there, that we really want this or that, but are denying ourselves. It is important to make a list of desires, to look at each, and to evaluate with discrimination.

Mind, body, speech

Negative thoughts, if left unattended, bereft of energy, will die by themselves, like a plant without nourishment. However, the control of thoughts has to be preceded by control of body and speech.

Here are a few methods to help with the control and cultivation of speech:

- Choose subjects carefully.
- Avoid stimulating talk about sex.
- Avoid stimulating talk about money.
- Avoid stimulating talk about various pleasures.

Realize that you lay your own traps by indulging in careless conversation. It is this carelessness that is the beginning of temptation.

Investigate beliefs

Another investigation to be made at this time concerns the core of beliefs of which one may or may not have been aware. Part of the process of clarification that is now necessary is to discover beliefs and where they came from. Beware of mindless conformity. The path of yoga means personal responsibility. Clarification of such words as "sympathy," "kindness" and "compassion" leads to acceptance of others and then to an inner union in yourself.

Pay attention to what people really think and whether they say what they think, or if they make you guess. Do you get a message that is different from the words? Do you say what you think, or do you imply and insinuate? How does this go with straight-walk thinking?

Words and their meanings

You must fully comprehend the important words you use. Make a list of them, clarify their meanings, and note the way you use them. Do not use books written by others. The aspirant must take responsibility for what is meant. The list below is by no means complete. A minimum of three minutes should be given to each single word, first thinking about and then writing down the meaning:

- perspective, thought, concentration, memory, observation, imagination, learning, humor, discrimination, waking state, sleeping state, trance, telepathy, clairvoyance, clairaudience, hypnosis

Clarification and refinement

Sometime later in the course of development this exercise should be repeated and notes compared to ascertain that your horizon has widened. By repetition of this exercise, understanding grows in depth and becomes refined. All perceptions go through a process of refinement. Each aspirant should extend this list of words to include those that are frequently used, in order to gain the maximum benefit.

Continue this process of clarification with questions such as:

- How is pain experienced?
- What is my concept of energy? in general, in the body, specifically in the brain (because it records all sensations, like pain).
- Do I consider light as a byproduct of energy, or vice versa?
- What is my concept of consciousness? How does it function in the brain?

Touch as expressed in speech

Phrases like the following are common in everyday speech. Think what they mean to you and then add to the list yourself:

- touch and go
- a finishing touch
- a touching scene, person, tone of voice
- a soft touch

- touch with the eyes
- touch my heart
- as soft as butter
- as hard as nails
- see how it feels

Such idioms are very revealing in their use.

Preparing for intuitive wisdom

In the Anāhata Cakra, the aspirant becomes aware that attitude is extremely important. The preparation for perfection in yoga is control of the mind. The right attitude and motives result in the clear conscience that is necessary to receive intuitive wisdom. The heightened perception of the five senses on which this depends is only possible through proper relaxation. In all spiritual practice surrender has to be stressed, as in the death pose of Haṭha Yoga. Special attention is given to prāṇāyāma in this cakra. Mind can be controlled by breath. One has to learn to accept unjust criticism and must forego self-justification. The meaning of symbols has to be understood on a much more subtle level than in the preceding cakras and the previously given exercises have to be continued with greater sensitivity.

On a more advanced level, there will be a greater ability to surrender. As the mind is carried on the waves of the breath, so the swan, Haṃsa, is carried on the waves of the water to know the Ātman (Self).

Prāṇāyāma

Prāṇāyāma as traditionally presented refers to:

1. Prāṇa: life force, often interpreted as breath. Prāṇa is consciousness, the most subtle life essence that pervades all manifested forms. Prāṇa is the sum total of all existing energy in the universe, that primal Energy manifest, unmanifest, or in a nuclear state.

2. Yama: the Lord of Death (Naciketas, as told in the Kathopanisad, obtained enlightenment through Yama's instructions). In the eight limbs of yoga (Aṣṭānga), Yama is also described as ethical discipline.

3. Āyāma means extension, stretching or restraint.

Prāṇāyāma is the yogic practice of breath control, which enables the yogi or yogini to attune to the cosmic rhythm. Prāṇāyāma is a process through which we can isolate our inner Self from the influences and influx of mechanical thoughts. Through the practice of prāṇāyāma the yogi gains control over the central nervous system and, most important, over the mind itself. Prāṇāyāma involves control by a triple process: the inhalation (pūraka), suspension (kumbhaka) and exhalation (recaka) of breath. There are two phases of kumbhaka: antara-kumbhaka, the interval between full inhalation and exhalation, and bāhya-kumbhaka, the interval between full exhalation and inhalation. Kumbhaka is also used to denote all three aspects of the prāṇāyāmic process.

Prāṇāyāma must be practiced in conjunction with character building. The selfishness and passions of the lower self, symbolized by the trunks of the elephant in the Mūlādhāra Cakra, have to be brought under control. With a purified character, prāṇāyāma is one of the practices given by the guru to awaken the dormant Kuṇḍalinī energy or Śakti. The nāḍīs or nerve channels through which the Kuṇḍalinī energy flows may be cleansed by the practice of certain prāṇāyāmas. Prāṇāyāma must be learned from an experienced teacher.

The yogis teach that we have only so many breaths in each lifetime. An emotional or rajasic temperament will "burn one up" and thus shorten one's life span. Practice of prāṇāyāma leads to emotional control and limitation of selfish desires, so the mind is prepared for the higher stages of yogic practice.

Practice of prāṇāyāma increases the alpha waves in the brain. If done correctly it leads to control over the emotions, calmness of mind, curing of nervous disorders and the refinement of sense perceptions. Awareness of the internal noises of the body and other finer, subtler sense perceptions develop through the practice of prāṇāyāma. All impurities of selfish desire are removed and a sense of peace and harmony is experienced, which naturally leads the mind to meditation. The mind becomes the abode of extrasensory perception. Intuitive knowledge increases as scheming is eliminated.

For the practice of prāṇāyāma, relaxation is essential. This is a very important point. Preliminary exercises for the body as a whole, and the neck and shoulders in particular, should be done prior to prāṇāyāma practice. (The lungs should be filled three-quarters full without tension and with complete relaxation in the body.) In the beginning, do only the practice of 4-16-8 prāṇāyāma with finger counting, no more than six rounds daily for the first six months. (See Finger Exercises in the next section.) Do not attempt too much at one time. The ideal time for prāṇāyāma practice is after Haṭha Yoga āsanas and end relaxation. If desired, a glass of milk or cup of tea may be taken beforehand, though it is best to do prāṇāyāma on an empty stomach. Always breathe through the nose during prāṇāyāma. Take time to relax after each prāṇāyāma. Savāsana (the corpse pose) is ideal for relaxation. Prāṇāyāma should not be done by people with high blood pressure.

Any sitting pose in which the spine is straight, chin slightly in and the body relaxed may be used for prāṇāyāma. To relax the neck and body, relaxation exercises are given below.

Mantra repetition during prāṇāyāma favorably influences the subconscious, giving spiritual suggestion to the mind. The medulla oblongata (the uppermost part of spinal cord next to the brain) may be used as a center for concentration only during prāṇāyāma.

Benefits of Prāṇāyāma:

- Karma can be burned up.

- Illusion is destroyed (latent fire in the mind). Calmness and one-pointedness of mind attained.
- Vagus nerves brought under control.
- Proper elimination of carbon dioxide; proper absorption of oxygen.
- Control over the restless mind.
- Sense of peace and harmony.
- Increased awareness and ability to observe.
- Relaxing effect on the heart and nervous system.

Prāṇāyāma: Preparatory Exercises

Relaxation of the whole body:

1. Neck
   - stick head out
   - pull head back
   - gently drop head to right shoulder
   - gently drop head to left shoulder
   - gently drop head forward
   - gently drop head backward
   - gently roll head in a full circle clockwise, 10 times.
   - gently roll head in a full circle counter-clockwise, 10 times.

2. Abdomen
   - Stand with feet shoulder-width apart.
   - Place hands on hip joints.
   - Slightly bend the knees.
   - Bend forward from hip joints with straight spine.
   - Pull abdominal muscles in.

– Relax abdominal muscles.
– Take a deep breath and stretch at the same time, lifting arms up.
– Exhale, relax arms.

Repeat 10 times.

Prāṇāyāma: Finger Exercises

Finger counting is done in prāṇāyāma so the mind can concentrate on something else, such as a mantra or short prayer.

Below is given the finger counting for 4-16-8 Prāṇāyāma, in which one inhales for the count of 4, holds the breath for the count of 16, and exhales for the count of 8.

1. For count of 4: Start on left hand with the little finger and continue to left forefinger.

2. For count of 8: Start on right hand with the little finger and continue to right forefinger (count of 4). Then continue from left forefinger to left little finger (another count of 4), making a total of 8.

3. For count of 16: Begin on right hand with little finger and continue to left little finger for a total of 8, as in number 2. Repeat this for a count of 16.

4. Inhalation has to take place for the full length of 4 counts. Holding for the length of 16 counts. Exhalation for the length of 8 counts.

After the finger counting has become familiar, mentally recite a mantra or short prayer with each count.

Bhastrikā-Prāṇāyāma: Bellows Breath

Stand with the feet shoulder-width apart. Place the hands on the hips. Bend the knees slightly and bend forward at the hip joints, keeping the spine and head in a straight line. Using the abdominal muscles, breathe in and out, following a rhythm of tensing and relaxing the abdomen. Do 20 inhalations and exhalations. Keep a steady, even rate; the speed of inhalation and exhalation may be increased with practice. Do not continue if there is any dizziness or tension. Breathe through the nose throughout. There is no need to fill the lungs completely. After the 20 rounds take a deep, slow breath, stretch up and raise the arms above the head. Exhale and slowly lower the arms. Relax in the corpse posture.

Repeat this prāṇāyāma only once a day for the first three months, then increase slowly by capacity. This prāṇāyāma may also be done in a sitting position, with the spine and head kept in a straight line.

Alternate Nostril Prāṇāyāma

Sit in a relaxed position with the spine straight and head erect. In this prāṇāyāma each nostril is alternately opened and closed using the fingers of the right hand.

Place the hands palms upward on the knees. With the left hand touch the thumb and index finger at their tips. Keep the other fingers outstretched. Straighten the left arm and rest the wrist on the left knee. The touching of the finger tips in this manner forms a hand position known as Jñānamudrā, the symbol or seal of Knowledge. This mudrā symbolizes the union of the individual consciousness (index finger) with the Divine or Cosmic Consciousness.

Bend the right arm at the elbow and bring the hand

toward the chest. The right hand is to be used to open and close the nostrils. Bend the index and middle fingers to rest in the center of the palm.

The ring and little fingers are used to close the left nostril and the thumb to close the right nostril, by placing the fingers and thumb against each nostril respectively.

1. Alternate nostril prāṇāyāma:
Close the right nostril with the right thumb. Exhale through the left nostril, then slowly inhale through the left nostril. Close the left nostril and exhale through the right nostril. Now repeat the process in reverse. Slowly inhale through the right nostril. Close the right nostril and exhale through the left nostril. There is no kumbhaka (retention of breath) in this prāṇāyāma. Twelve inhalations and twelve exhalations complete one full round.

2. Alternate nostril 4-16-8:
Close the right nostril with the right thumb and exhale through the left nostril, then inhale through the left nostril to the count of 4. Close the left nostril with the ring and little fingers. Hold the breath to the count of 16. Open the right nostril and exhale to the count of 8. Now inhale through the right nostril and repeat the process in reverse.

3. Alternate nostril 4-16-8 with A-U-Ṃ:
Close the right nostril, exhale, then inhale through the left nostril, and meditate on A (sound as ah) to the count of 4. Hold the breath to the count of 16 and meditate on the sound U (as oo). Exhale through the right nostril to the count of 8 and meditate on Ṃ (as mm sound). Now inhale through the right nostril and repeat the process in reverse. Begin with four or five times daily. Increase to 20 or 30.

Kuṇḍalinī Prāṇāyāma

Prepare as for previous prāṇāyāmas. Concentrate on the Mūlādhāra Cakra. With hands placed as for alternate nostril prāṇāyāma, close the right nostril with the right thumb, exhale and inhale through the left nostril to the count of three Oṃs. Imagine drawing in praṇā with the breath inhaled. Close the left nostril. Retain the breath for 12 Oṃs. Send current down the spinal column into the Mūlādhāra Cakra. Imagine the current striking against the Lotus in the Mūlādhāra Cakra. Exhale slowly through the right nostril to the count of three Oṃs. Now inhale through the right nostril, repeating the process in reverse. Practice three full rounds twice daily.

Prāṇic Healing

Prāṇa can be stored in the medulla oblongata, then released at will toward the patient in need of healing. Laying on of hands can be done simultaneously. Or a gentle massage can be used while prāṇic energy flows into the patient's body. Keep a positive attitude, free from any criticism, with deep concentration on the healing Light. Let the Light flow through – through – never from you. Give of the overflow of Light, see yourself as a channel for the healing Light. If the mind becomes active, divert this activity by talking to the body parts or cells in need of healing.

The Mantra So'haṃ Haṃsa

The rhythm of life is breath – inhalation, exhalation; expansion, contraction. The mind has its own polarity also. Practice of this mantra as described will establish a rhythm in harmony with the rhythm of all the life force around you. A great inner stillness is the result of this practice. Awareness of the body ceases entirely. This exercise is very useful as a preparation for the more complex practices that are given later in the book. This mantra can also be used preceding the performance of the Divine Light Invocation.

Results in all practices seem to be very far away, perhaps even impossible to attain. Do not let this affect you. Remember that only half of the moon is visible at times and yet the light of the moon is always there. It is only that it is obscured from view.

When you begin to do this exercise, use your fingers to count. In time, the rhythm will become a natural flow. The meaning of So'haṃ is "I am He" and Sâhaṃ is "I am She."

Exhale – mentally repeat So or Sâ.

Inhale – mentally repeat Haṃ.

Repeat this for a few minutes and then reverse, mentally saying Haṃ on exhalation and So or Sâ on inhalation.

Thoughts on Reverence for Life

Saying grace before eating is a very common habit with many people, but it is equally common that the conversation is resumed right after, which indicates that there was not much reverence for life expressed in that prayer. In order to overcome this kind of unawareness, a day should be chosen when more time can be devoted to a meal. The ingredients should be simple and few. For example, the choice could be spinach, egg, carrots, bread and perhaps fish, if you are not vegetarian. Have the meal all prepared and on the table, covering the food.

Clarify to yourself or, if the meal is taken in the company of others, take charge and guide the thoughts of those present.

– I am hungry.
– I want to eat.
– My body needs nourishment.
– For what?
– To stay alive?
– To indulge?
– For self-gratification?
– Or to give some selfless service to others?

Then close your eyes and visualize the source of your food and how it is obtained.

I go to the garden where the carrots are grown and dig my hands into the earth to wrench out the living, growing roots from the ground. Then I walk to the field where the wind moves the grain in waves and the sun plays and gilds it. How does this beautiful life form become bread? When I cut the grain and take big bunches home to crush into flour, is it a painful process? I stop to gather the spinach. How much attention do I bring to the task? As I slice the green stems or pull out the plant by the roots, do I recognize the life force that is again being sacrificed to sustain me? Entering the hen house, the birds squawk and scurry off as I take their eggs from their nests and carry them to the kitchen to be boiled in hot water. Although this is sufficient for my needs, how the sense buds vibrate at the thought of a tasty fish, so I walk to the water and throw in a line to catch the fish. When I'm successful, I hold its thrashing body and remove the sharp hook from its mouth before killing it. I catch a few more. Now I am ready to go back to the house to finish preparing the meal.

I chop and steam the carrots and spinach, bake the bread, boil the egg, scale and fry the fish. Perhaps I think of myself as a good cook and hope to receive compliments for my care and preparation. Perhaps someone will even say, "You really cooked with love." Did I?

Open your eyes, and uncover the food. Can you give thanks with true feeling? As you eat, bring awareness to the gifts of life that are sustaining you. If you use your body as an instrument for your search for the Most High, all life that has been killed in the process of nourishing you will benefit from the vibration of holy thoughts.

Reflection on Māyā (Illusion)

My body is like the mountain.
My eyes are like the lake.
My mind is like the sky.

Plants feed on the mountains.
My body feeds on the plants.

My eyes are like the lake.
Water reflects the clouds, the clouds of my creation.
My creation is but the shadow on the water that reflects all images.

My mind is like the sky.
My creations are like the clouds that float across the sky.
Old images surface on the lake of my mind and bounce on its waves.
Vision widens to embrace the Void.

In your Viśuddhi I serve Śiva, the progenitor of the sky, transparent like a pure crystal, and also the Devī who is like Śiva and attached to Him. It is through their beauty and graceful movements, shimmering like the rays of the moon, the world shines, its internal darkness having been dispelled, like the Cakora.

MANTRA FOR THE VIŚUDDHA CAKRA

8. VIŚUDDHA

THE FIFTH CAKRA

VIŚUDDHA

The Fifth Cakra and Its Symbols

VIŚUDDHA: The Fifth Cakra or Lotus

TATTVA: Differentiating faculty

72 RAYS: Relate to ether (ākāśa)

HEARING: The Viśuddha Cakra controls this sense

SIXTEEN LOTUS PETALS: The Lotus is sacred

COLOR OF THE PETALS: Smoky purple

THE LETTERS ON THE PETALS: A, Ā, I, Ī, U, Ū, Ṛ, Ṛ, L, Ḷ, E, Ai, O, Au, Aṃ, Aḥ

ĀKĀŚAMAṆḌALA: Circle, the ethereal region and gateway of Liberation

BĪJA: Haṃ, the Seed Sound (Mantra of Ambara, the bīja of ether)

PIṄGALĀ: The Nāḍī on the right side of the body

ĪḌĀ: The Nāḍī on the left side of the body

SUṢUMNĀ: The central channel of the spine

CITRIṆĪ: Three in one (sattva, rajas, tamas), body, mind and speech

AIRĀVATA: Elephant, as white as snow

The elephant symbolizes will subdued because of surrender. The triangle with the point down indicates that the Divine Energy, now properly used and understood, is available to a greater extent. When control of mind and emotions, and surrender is achieved, the cakra promises constant, gentle, steady peace of mind. One sees the past, present and future. One becomes courageous, forgiving, free from greed, malice and pride.

GOD AND HIS OBJECTS:

Sadāśiva: The male aspect of Energy unmanifest

The intelligence on this level is symbolized by Sadāśiva. Sadāśiva is the three-eyed Deva in the lap of Ambara on a white elephant. The third eye is the eye of wisdom. He has five faces and ten arms, is clothed in a tiger skin, and has a garland of snakes.

The five faces represent the presence of the qualities of omniscience, omnipresence and omnipotence, and also the sublimation of the five senses, each face having an eye of wisdom. The ten arms imply efficiency and the power used with wisdom, which is symbolized by the snakes.

Pāśa: Noose, warns of being caught in the pride of knowledge

Aṅkuśa: Goad, shows that goading or pushing is still needed

Gesture: Abhayamudrā, dispelling fears

Nāgendra: Snake king, symbolic for temptation or wisdom

Śūla: Trident, symbol of the trinity (physical, ethereal and causal body)

Dahana: Fire, the fire of ambition – in what areas?

Ghaṇṭā: Bell, symbol for listening

Vajra: Diamond scepter, awareness of power

Kṛpaṇa: Sword, the sword of discrimination

Ṭaṅka: Battle-ax, used to cut away old personality aspects

GODDESS AND HER OBJECTS:

Gaurī (Eternal): The female aspect of Energy manifest

> The intelligence on this level is symbolized by Gaurī Eternal. She is half of Lord Śiva's body. Gaurī is the Mother of the Universe and also the other half of Lord Śiva.

Pāśa: Noose, warns of not being caught in sound

Aṅkuśa: Goad, one is being goaded on to the last efforts

Arrow: direction must be clear

Bow: tension (alertness) is necessary

The Goddess of Speech – Śakti

Speech, now refined, shows in the Fifth or Viśuddha Cakra the limitations of words. Perceptions can come by thought, but these are not the highest experience. "Perception beyond words" has to be clarified. Does "beyond words" mean mental speech, or beyond mental speech? If we say "beyond mind," we must ask, "If it is beyond mind, then how can it be known?"

The Devī (Śakti) is the source of what is perceived beyond words, beyond mind. This is usually expressed by saying "a knowing of the heart," another dimension. Such perceptions are beyond verbalization, without color or form, without concepts, all-encompassing like the sky. As an example, the rays of the sun travel in all directions. They do not form part of the sun, but are the sun. If consciousness is Energy (Śakti), and Energy is indestructible, then an unusual manifestation of consciousness can be perceived as coming through the guru or the Devī. When the aspirant has refined the sense of hearing to that point, this will undoubtedly be verified by personal experience.

Speech beyond words is also saying something by a gesture, by a touch, or by an expression of the eyes. Speaking from the heart, while audible through the use of words, is expressing inaudibly at the same time. The Divine Word (holy name, mantra), through the process of practice, will become inaudible on its own account and thus Divine speech is engendered. The power of the spoken word is derived from a forceful desire and therefore that power is not different from the power of thought.

First we have the word (sound), then the vibration of the sense that receives the sound, and third the manifestation of what has been received. The summary of all these ideas is expressed in the Devī of Speech (vibrations). Sound and its resonance are inseparable and can result in powerful emotional responses. Perceiving the Devī is on the subtle level of the power of sound and its resonance, which is missed by the average person.

Beware of using words for laying a trap for others or for yourself. This can be done by asking leading questions, "putting words into the mouth" of another person. Look at your life's situation to discover where and when you have done so and which traps have already been laid. Great effort is necessary to discover these traps.

Speech that is praised is like a sweet drink or a strong spirit, bolstering the ego or the emotions. However, when the voice is the magnet that attracts others, and a chord resounds in the heart of the listener, this is a sign that the aspirant is in contact with the Devī of Speech, with Sarasvatī.

The Devī of Speech can be approached through reflection and the following salutation:

O Devī! O Sarasvatī!
Reside Thou ever in my speech.
Reside Thou ever on my tongue tip,
O Divine Mother, giver of faultless poetry.

From the Devī of Speech we learn that when the oil of worldly desires is burned up, She Herself, the Mother and Creatrix of all, is realized. She also tells us that unfavorable karma is burned up when Her spiritual child, the aspirant, turns the gaze fully on Her. This clears the way for the aspirant to have the strength, persistence, wisdom and circumstances necessary to achieve the goal of the full realization of the creative energy (Kuṇḍalinī). The difficulties in using everyday language to express the underlying principles make them seem almost secret. All wisdom is secret to the ignorant and that makes it difficult to interpret such knowledge in daily language.

When we recognize that the term Devī, Divine Mother or Śakti, means power or intelligence at its highest, then we can speak of "Cosmic Intelligence" and see the Energy on an impersonal level.

Performing certain exercises that are meant to give perfect control of sense perception and the mental background noises of the mind may result in the manifestation of psychic energy or even in spiritual experiences, as was discussed in the Anāhata Cakra. The spiritual experience is an enormous transformation and perhaps it would not be an exaggeration to say that the Cosmic Fire indeed lights up the horizon of life. While the psychic phenomenon is of the senses and the powers of the mind, the spiritual experience is of a Divine nature, beyond the mind and beyond the control of the aspirant. It cannot be repeated at will. Living in such a state would mean living in the blissful state of truly aware being.

In moments of quiet and reflection, a kind of meditative mood emerges. In this stillness of mind, lights can be experienced, beautiful hues of color – very bright blues or yellows. They may dim and flow into each other like a display of northern lights. When such experiences are new, they create a wave of enthusiasm in the aspirant and that is what they are meant to do. They are a signpost saying, "You are on the right path, on the right road." But to indulge would mean turning those experiences into a spiritual entertainment. Every good teacher discourages a student from giving those manifestations any significance beyond encouragement.

The seeing of lights shows that, for a brief moment, the mind was free from thoughts. The importance was in simply being an observer and refraining from interpreting that which was observed.

The Cosmic Fire is a Light that is beyond all those little lights that are experienced in quietness. They are the boon of the Devī for effort. While we may have some difficulties with terms like "Cosmic Fire," "Intelligence," "Light," they have to suffice as they are the best we have until we can familiarize ourselves with the language of the Gods. They should not be discarded because they are in themselves limited, but should be recognized as useful stepping-stones to approach another dimension.

In a moment of meditation or reflection, the aspirant may have a sudden insight, a state of awareness not previously experienced, in which all mistakes are recognized, all things are seen for what they are. The aspirant should try to recall a moment in life when he or she was very conscious of something of great importance. Such an experience has nothing to do as yet with Kuṇḍalinī but, at that moment, the aspirant stopped the habit of mechanical thinking, habitual responses and reactions.

The Cosmic Fire is a term that the aspirant has to bring to a personal level in order to truly understand its meaning. It is a term related to energy on a cosmic level where the aspirant has a cosmic vision and hears the cosmic sound of Auṃ. Cosmic Fire is a great Cosmic Light existing beyond all names, shapes and forms, and at one point even the concept of the Higher Self, if it has any trace of the personal form, has to be let go.

Thoughts on Hearing

The Viśuddha Cakra stands for the sense of hearing which is, from the Western point of view, the last of the five senses. In the East, mind the interpreter is considered the sixth sense. The element of the cakra, ether, means something very elusive, ethereal, and yet very powerful. The influences on a human being are subtle and yet can bring about great changes in the body and mind. The dictionary definition of ether indicates that it has three aspects: the abstract, the physical and the chemical.

Ethereal is defined as: light, airy, heavenly, of unearthly delicacy of substance, character or appearance, something of great subtlety or transparency. To hear the music of the spheres would be an ethereal experience. To hear the Goddess or Devī speak and the sound of the cosmic Auṃ is the crown of all experiences through the sense of hearing. This indeed may start delicately and subtly, but can become very powerful, lifting the listener into a different ethereal world.

Hearing is a subtle process. It is indeed ethereal because the interfering voices that prevent us from hearing are our own thoughts. Much energy is wasted listening to those thoughts, which are based on mental speculation, self-defence and self-justification, so that it becomes impossible to truly hear what another person says. Pain results from this lack of communication and that is why so much attention must be paid to removing the screens that we erect in front of our senses. When the refinement of the sense of hearing permits us to rise above the level of ordinary daily existence and observe from a more subtle level (ether), we see that the clarity and the understanding that we assumed we had vanish into thin air before we can grasp them.

Listening is an art. To hear the true message through all the veils demands a very skillful listener who can extract from the words what the speaker truly says. How much more sensitivity, then, is required to hear the still, small voice within. The acquisition of powers, which may be a hidden desire, depends on the ability to concentrate, the ability to mentally relax and receive, to be in control of the merry-go-round of the mind. Listening ability in present-day life is cut down by a variety of strident noises that are not only imposed on us by industry, work and so on, but that we choose ourselves. There is little protection outside the home, but the aspirant must become conscious that there are places where control can be exercised.

The emphasis on mechanical habits in regard to the sense of hearing is just as important as it was in dealing with the previous senses.

There are many potentials that can be developed in the human being and the ability to be a good listener is one of the most important. In certain professions it is essential to be able to listen with depth of understanding. Many skills can be developed quickly. Listening, however, is only excellent when the listener has also developed the ability of recall. The human mind is an incredible storehouse of memory, but without recall we cannot retrieve what is known. Many psychics have simply learned to draw on this storehouse, which contains our past lives as well as our present. Information about ancient civilizations could be gained if this faculty of recall were more fully utilized.

The refinement of the senses that has been emphasized in each cakra applies to the sense of hearing, perhaps even more than to the sense of sight. There are many stages, from the basic state of hearing only the rough, the harsh, the arrogant to the level where we can hear the music of the spheres.

Surrender: the key to hearing

Before it is possible to still the mind and surrender to what is heard, we can start on the physical level with the "Death Pose." The name of the Death Pose itself explains its meaning of no reaction, complete surrender to what is, ending all arguments. The only validity for listening to one's thoughts is when positive key sentences have been put into the mind to replace the old negative ones.

Ego: the opponent to hearing

It must be recognized that assertions of self-will, which subdue the message spoken by another person, have no validity outside ourselves. It is an illusion to think they will bring good results. For example, a typical reaction when speaking to a person who does not understand the language is to speak louder and louder, in the false belief that this will bring comprehension. The motive for speaking in a low key must be genuine. If it is hiding pushiness or dominance, while giving the appearance of being soft and gentle, it is a lie. In how many ways do we lie? Dominance and pushiness are uncultivated will, and even if speech is sweet and gentle it is an act of deception. Like the other senses, hearing has to be understood on the tamasic, rajasic and sattvic levels.

The ear that listens is precious and that preciousness is expressed symbolically in the descriptions of the designs and precious stones of the earrings worn by the Divine Mother. It is not within the range of this book to include all the meanings of the jewelry worn by the gods and goddesses of each cakra, but they all have important symbolic meanings.

Speech is of no relevance if there is no listener. The trident reappears here in the Viśuddha Cakra to point out the ever increasing delicacy of the interaction of the energy in the body, in the mind, and in its most exercised expression of speech. This interaction may not be recognized to its full extent for lack of awareness of how the control comes from the mind. Āsanas are a silent manner of speech and the cells in the body, each with its own consciousness, are the listeners. The body is very teachable and can become a spiritual tool.

Tools of Sadāśiva

The goad (aṅkuśa) says to the aspirant, "Keep going, move on, pursue development, discriminate." At this point, "stand still" can mean a loss of all previous input and the still, small voice, that is precisely the source of those urgings, needs to be heard by the inner ear.

The noose (pāśa), held in this cakra by Sadāśiva, warns us not to be caught again in the noose of the intellect, the emotions or wild imaginations, not to be trapped in old habits, mechanicalness, preoccupation with self, or turning a deaf ear. The daily diary will help to discover old traps and even recognize traps before they have been completely laid.

The arrow can only be shot in a straight line by direct commitment and by having a clear goal as a target, by straight-walk thinking and straight-walk action. The target has to be well-defined. Problems that still remain have to be tackled head-on. All five senses need to be brought under control by awareness and refinement. The forces of the Maṇipūra Cakra, the fire-wheel of emotions, will make a last attempt here to flare up again with all power and imagination in order to prevent the surrender of self-will. Doubts invade the mind. It is easier to talk oneself out of one's determination than into continuing the pursuit of the goal. But the fire can be lifted from the purely emotional struggle to the fire of enthusiasm where ignorance is burned in the fire of wisdom.

What, then, keeps interfering with progress and makes all those warnings necessary, as expressed by the symbols of the goad, the noose, the fire and the arrow? It is the lurking of the old personality aspects. The battle-ax must be wielded, but it has to be used skillfully. Ego tries again to raise its head in a last attempt to reassert its power. The lower nature will put up a fierce fight in some areas. The battle-ax is sharpened by discrimination and razor-keen awareness. The sword of discrimination, having two edges, indicates the seriousness of the aspirant's situation; to cut away the undesirable characteristics without hurting oneself demands great skill and strength and clear assessment of what needs to be cut and what needs to be preserved.

The bow and arrow show that tension has to be expected. If the bow is not tense the arrow will not fly. The tension has different sources. Doubts and strong desires can be really troublesome. Only by withdrawing the power from them will they diminish. Sometimes another source of tension is the influence of so-called friends who do not understand the road to spiritual success and who will, by comparison, only respect such strenuous effort by the aspirant if the goal is monetary, political or social. When the goal is a higher state of consciousness, their negative arguments seem to be logical and reasonable, and this type of friend is very difficult to deal with. The spiritual road is indeed lonely until you meet your first spiritual companion. How often we already have such companions but do not recognize them!

The more tense the bow, the further the arrow will go and the greater the impact on the target.

Hearing: Exercises

I hear. The act of hearing. What is heard?

In the Viśuddha Cakra, the emphasis is on hearing. This often neglected sense has to be carefully examined to understand all implications. The preparation in the first three cakras and in the Anāhata Cakra specifically will have proved to be fruitful. However, this has to be extended.

True listening means the ability to surrender, thereby speech, as well as mental talking, must be controlled in order to hear clearly. At this point it may become clearer why the Goddess of Speech appeared in each cakra and why speech is called our greatest performance. The almost insatiable need to hear ourselves talk feeds our self-importance almost to the exclusiveness even of those whom we profess to love. In the daily reflection, there should always be an entry in the diary of whether you have been able to surrender to another and how well you can stop listening to yourself. Our habitual way of hearing has to be changed in order to attain quality in listening. Most people who have authority complexes do not recognize that the ego is really the biggest authority, most of the time preventing the aspirant from doing what he or she wants to do. If the ego listens, what does it listen to? Possible hurts or criticism? Compliments? When it comes to praise, the ego can be a real glutton.

By investigating the process of hearing, we may become aware that many things are screened out and only those things accepted that we want to hear. Sometimes what is heard has been so twisted that what we think we hear is far from correct. The questions to ask are, "Am I listening? Is the ego listening? Who is listening?"

It becomes more complicated to control the ego if we think in short negative key sentences. The influence of these can range from strong to subtle and their effect may be hypnotizing. "I always make this mistake" . . . "I have never been able to do this" . . . "I would rather die than try that" . . . "I could never handle that" . . . These are habitual thought patterns that are verbalized in the mind, listened to, and then acted upon. It is obvious that this is destructive. Yet there is a choice to think positively, to turn to the opposite. "I have never done this before, but if I give it my attention and try,

I am sure I can do it." When acted upon, this becomes a small success that can be used as a stepping-stone to even bigger ones, which become a good foundation of inner security.

Investigation of all ideas about security on a physical, emotional and mental level can bring us to new conclusions. Habitual actions and reactions that have been investigated already must also be reviewed and shifted to higher levels. Discrimination has to be refined and self-will needs to be subdued. Speed is not efficiency. It may indicate good intention to say, "I wanted to do it fast to go on to something else," but this will not justify sloppy performance. In order to get self-will under control, we must first understand the difference between will and self-will. Self-will is an expression of the ego, and if we can understand that "In the will of the Most High I am free," the distinction is clear.

Will and self-will

The power that is given to self-will in daily life keeps individuals apart and relationships become a battlefield for dominance. Instead, we can use the will to pursue a way of life that brings out the best in ourselves and makes us a blessing to others. A good way to understand the power of self-will is to choose someone and submit to the wants or suggestions of this individual for a certain length of time. The chosen person should have no knowledge of such a decision. The choice should be made alone, silently, and in the utmost sincerity of wanting to have a clear understanding of self-will. In this surrender, we begin to perceive our ability or lack of ability to listen to others. We become aware of the power of the background noises of the mind or the talkativeness of the ego that prevents any kind of real listening.

Understanding surrender and self-will

The god and goddess of the Fifth Cakra, Sadāśiva and Gaurī, while apparently separate, like consciousness and mind, are really one. If the rational is considered the male aspect and the irrational the female, when we accept both on an equal basis we understand the union or the first spiritual marriage within ourselves, an important step in the development toward maturity. If the rational and the irrational are in the proper balance, the perceptions of each can be heard, truly heard. This can be called listening with the Third Ear.

There is often competition between the sense of hearing and one or more of the others. If you find that what is seen interferes with hearing, listen with closed eyes or focus the eyes away from the speaker. Hearing must be through the ears, not through the eyes, and must not be destroyed by what is seen. To understand what is heard it must be "digested." Listen to the pure sound, without interference of the emotions.

To help in the clarification of what the sense of hearing means to you, think about each of the following and then add to the list:

- sounds of a music box
- a running brook
- laughter and sobs
- hearing yourself think
- hearing thought associations
- creating noises in the mind
- garbling the thoughts:
    - to avoid listening
    - not to be involved
    - not to be confronted
    - not to have to do anything about it
    - not to have to make a decision
    - not to face up to certain problems

Here are some questions that may be of practical help to the aspirant in further investigation of some important areas of the Viśuddha Cakra.

- Am I listening?
- Do I get the message?
- Do I hear only words?
- Do I screen things out?

- What are the reasons for the screening?
- Do I hear my voice?
- Do I like my voice?
- What can a listener gather from my voice? . . . arrogance, warmth, kindness?
- When I listen, what is it that listens? The ego?
- Can I keep the ego suspended, finally withdraw its power altogether?
- Is my self-will behind the ego?
- Have I conditioned myself with negative key sentences that I have been telling myself for many years?
- Should I form new key sentences that will be of benefit and open the door to more perception and listening?
- Is surrender to listening to another a giving of myself?
- What is my ability to perceive new insights?
- Are these insights coming from my Higher Self, or from the heart, or an unknown source?
- Can I discriminate between self-will and surrender?
- Do I understand the fine dividing line between self-will and Divine will?
- Do I keep the sword of discrimination truly sharpened to find the balance between reason and emotion, logic and intuition, fear and courage, clumsiness and lightness, strength and softness?
- Do I have the humility to ask for help when the ego puts up a fierce battle?

A few exercises are given to start the aspirant in the observation of listening and of what is heard. Note the process of screening out what we do not want to hear, or what we claim to have heard. This will bring some surprises. When these exercises are done, we find that lack of awareness is staggering. With persistence, they will truly lead to liberation from self-centeredness.

Listening to a variety of music, carefully selected, preferably with earphones and in a reclining position, will tell you by your emotional responses to the music where you are. Sound and careful listening can trigger long-forgotten events, be they painful or joyful. Later it is advisable to proceed to listening to nature, the wind, birds in the trees, the sounds of the city in the daytime or at night. Listen to your chanting and how your voice undergoes changes from the beginning and how it shows the release of your emotions.

After doing these exercises you will find that you can really listen to the voices of your loved ones and that what they say is music to your ears.

Exercises

1. Listening to yourself:
   - Choose one person and investigate your way of speaking with that person. Try to remember a conversation. What do you observe about your speech? Do you know your own voice? What does it sound like? Do you like it?
   - Record yourself speaking. Give an assessment of yourself.
   - Choose a partner and record a 10-minute conversation. Challenge the other, try to convince. Note how you sound when emotional. Observe yourself and your partner. Do you hear what the other person says? What do you hear besides the words? List the emotions detected, such as joy, elation, strength, anxiety, pain, begging, confusion, tears. The words may not convey any of these. Do you hear it in the voice? Note.

2. Listening to body noises:
   - your stomach, your blood, your heartbeat
   - Note everything down carefully.

3. Listen to the mental conversations in your head:
   - What do you hear? Describe.
   - Can you stop these mental talks?
   - If you can, how do you do it? Describe.
   - If you cannot, would you want to learn how?

(It will be necessary to have this mental control if you wish to pursue the spiritual path of Kuṇḍalinī.)

4. With the new insights on listening, chant a mantra of your choice for 2 hours.
   - Watch the mind carefully.
   - Write observations for 15 minutes after the first hour of chanting, then after the second.
   - At the end of the 2-hour period, make more detailed notes.

5. Say your own name aloud for 2 hours.
   - For the first hour, look at yourself in the mirror while saying your name.
   - For the second hour, do not use a mirror.
   - Make notes for 15 minutes after each hour of the exercise.

6. Say aloud someone else's name for 10 minutes.
   - Choose a name that is symbolic in some way or important to you.
   - Watch yourself and all your reactions.
   - Make notes of all you observe.

7. Listen to music for 15 minutes.
   - Choose a piece of recorded music.
   - Listen to the music while sitting, lying down, lying down and listening through carphoncs.
   - Again note all observations.

8. Listen to an unpleasant sound:
   - Have someone make an unpleasant sound such as scratching on a piece of glass.
   - Repeat three or four times for just a few seconds.
   - Write down reactions at once.

9. Listen to sounds of:
   - different bells for a period of between 5 to 7 minutes each.
   - Write down reactions after each.
   - Note if listening was done with eyes open or closed and if there was a difference.

The Viśuddha Cakra controls the sense of hearing. These exercises will help the aspirant to understand the filters that prevent the hearing of pure sound and that prevent communication. Following instructions, which is necessary on the path of Kuṇḍalinī as in all walks of life, presupposes the ability to listen.

Synthesis of the Viśuddha Cakra

At this point, the aspirant who has faithfully practiced the given exercises will have proved the value of knowledge gained through practical experience. For those who find the path difficult, it has to be remembered that there is no easy route to a higher state of consciousness.

The symbols of the cakra set out clearly the lessons to be learned at the level of the Viśuddha Cakra. In the colors of this cakra we can recognize easily the coloring of what we hear in our own mind. The purple is a mixture of red and blue, red standing for life as we live it and blue for the spiritual. So the mixture is a combination of these two aspects. However, Sadāśiva is silver and gold. This shows how all symbols can be lifted to higher levels, from the very gross to the very high. The smoky color of the petals expresses symbolically that until we can really listen, clarity of thought and even clarity of understanding are not achieved.

The noose is a warning not to be caught in the old traps of mechanicalness and intellectualization. The fire of emotion shows that rebellion and opposition flare up easily. The goad urges us to plod on, doing what is necessary for the last part of the journey.

Balance: the male and female within

The fine balance of reason and emotion, logic and intuition, tension and letting go, are expressed in the symbols of Śiva and Śakti with a clarity that is beyond doubt. These pairs of opposites, now balanced, become a unit and create the sensitivity that allows the overwhelming experience of hearing the cosmic Auṃ. The Most High cannot be commanded and, if invited, will come only after we have prepared ourselves. We must surrender and wait patiently for this immense moment.

The number of the petals of the Lotus is now 16, meaning that language has increased. With the development of language, humans have become more clever but unfortunately not more wise. The aspirant will find that the intellect, through the exercises, has sharpened considerably and therefore can now cleverly talk one into or out of almost anything. Yet the aspirant is reminded that the petals belong to the Lotus, which is sacred. When all the smoke of the ego is gone and complete surrender to listening is accomplished, one can truly hear the message, be it audible or inaudible. When the clever aspects of the mind and speech are overcome, the struggle with the ensuing temptations will be less intense.

The white elephant shows by its color the spiritual intention of the aspirant's way of life, thinking and action. The elephant, reappearing from the Mūlādhāra Cakra, is considerably subdued. Only one of the trunks is held up – one more obstacle to overcome. The elephant has also shrunk in size. The obstacle has become smaller, however, not necessarily less intense. The aspirant is no longer subject to the power of driving instincts.

Sadāśiva means Ever Śiva. He is ever present to the call of any devotee. He has the third eye of wisdom and five faces, the five senses. The five faces indicate such qualities as omniscience, omnipotence and omnipresence. Ten arms symbolize efficiency in dealing with difficulties. He is the Compassionate Lord. His body is clothed in a tiger skin and garlanded with snakes, which represent evil and wisdom, both of which can assail the aspirant. The skin of a tiger is used for spiritual practice to insulate the sadhaka or aspirant from the influence of the vibrations of the Earth that keep one earthbound. The aspirant may even sleep on the tigerskin (or pure wool) to preserve energy and assist efforts to go beyond all the influences of the Earth and the many tempting fruits of life itself. The tigerskin is a symbol of the power that has to be developed to resist such influences and yet stimulate sufficient enthusiasm to pursue the difficult path.

Abhyamudra

The gesture abhaya indicates that the sincerity and humility of the aspirant will dispel all unnecessary fears.

Lord Śiva is often shown with a hooded snake, the cobra. The snake approaches in silence. So it is with wisdom, but also with temptation. The cobra is considered the king of all snakes and reminds the aspirant to be observant, to consider carefully every move and how intelligent discrimination must be used in all experiences.

The daily diary is most important because it will help to show the difference between the two functions of intuition and reasoning, to know when intuition is operating and when it is simply wishful thinking. The process continues of reviewing and adjusting ideals and making sure that the daily practice is stressing the areas that require development and refinement. The perception of the results and new insights provide the enthusiasm to continue the practice.

Thought association

When listening to a story, events or special happenings, mind the interpreter immediately uses the opportunity to allow its own past events to be triggered. This becomes particularly clear when the mind replays what it has heard when there is no more outside interference, when the aspirant is alone and can watch what happens in the mind.

In the state of sleep-dream, pictures are seen and voices may be heard. Only when there is "clear listening" will one be able to hear voices in the state of sleep-dream. Not only are such dreams very important, carrying meaningful messages, but they are also little signposts of gentleness, peace of mind, courageousness and forgiveness. When the "voice of the Self" or the still, small voice within is heard and given attention, recognition and gratitude, the aspirant can truly be said to be in touch with the Higher Self, which is now given back its rightful rulership. It is again like listening to the conch shell with surrender. One cannot tell the conch shell what sound it should produce.

It would be wise here to investigate thought associations that spring up mechanically. These can be subdued, if they are of a nuisance nature, by the practice of mantra in an audible way. The time for mantra practice could be increased. All the garbling noises in the mind are first subdued, then discouraged, and then eliminated. Instead of fighting those mental background noises of the mind or the intruding thought associations, the energy is rather put into the practical application of mantra.

Voices, pleasant or unpleasant, from the past – that means from early childhood – can surface because of a certain intensity connected with them. Also voices from a past life can re-emerge.

Yoga is a path of evolution and, while the physical body may have at one time emerged from the apes and developed to its present state of perfection, that process may have been necessary so that the body and the brain, in particular, could become a vehicle for increased consciousness. It seems that nature always provides before the need arises. A mother already has the milk before the baby is born. So we seem to have a sufficient mass of brain for the next stage of development.

Reincarnation

Birth and death simply mean that a body is created and at some future time dies, and will again be recreated.

Birth and death are "actions" born of desire to create. Desire is the cause of all "birth." Mind-born, then, simply means "idea – desire – manifestation." One purpose of rebirth is to fulfill all desires.

With regard to genius, for example, the groundwork that has been laid in other lifetimes provides the basis for full development in this life. This may appear in childhood when there can be a great love for music, for some instrument, and the evidence of unusual talent and perfect pitch. While these gifts are brought over from the past, the energy must originate in this lifetime. One may also in the present life reach only the first level of genius or potential genius. Therefore, when the desire is held alive at the time of death, the circumstances of rebirth will be such that the unfolding of what has already been gained can come from budding into full flowering.

Dreams play a part of increasing importance and the experience of significant past lives may appear first as dreams to prepare the aspirant. Those past lives are indications of what has been left undone, so that the mistakes can be corrected in this life.

The ego is responsible for all the pain we experience. But we must come to a realization that the Self is Divine and its vehicle, the human body and mind, deserves respect. Therefore, when we are constantly trying to subdue the ego, we must use careful discrimination to keep intact our human dignity. This requires great perception, as the line of balance is as fine as a hair.

Emotions and energy

The power or energy is neutral. Emotions give it the color of expression. Self-will and indulgence motivate emotions and bring pain. Unresolved problems and anxieties have to be dealt with directly and unemotionally.

Negative emotions such as hostility and resentment should not be suppressed. It is better to deal with them thoroughly, come to grips with them, and direct awareness into the area from which they spring. If they are expressed against another person, the ego is strengthened and it will be impossible to ever achieve peace of mind and come to inner harmony. The ego is the worst taskmaster.

It judges, condemns, criticizes ourselves and others. Life is black or white, good or bad. And so is the "wearer" of the ego, living between punishment and reward.

It is seldom suspected that feelings of worthlessness and helplessness often derive from not getting one's own way. "My opinion is not appreciated. I am not important enough." It should not matter if you truly "know in the heart" your own intrinsic worth. The greater the awareness of your own Divinity, the less you are subject to the demands of the ego. Then you can open yourself to learning, free to acknowledge the fact that you do not need to know everything.

The ego, in its unchecked need to assert itself, becomes possessive, thus preventing any true feeling of love. Many people can only accept or believe in love in ways that they themselves determine, thereby preventing the expression of a true feeling in themselves or in another.

The ego is teachable. It can be taught new concepts that are more beneficial. In the early stages of development, substitutes are often the only way. It is like giving up a habit such as smoking and indulging in something else instead. We can and must be constantly aware of the choice of the way in which energy is used. One way of recognizing the choice is to first become aware of and list all habitual, mechanical thinking, acting and evaluating.

Ego is like a rope made of many strands – pride, greed, illusions, self-importance, desires, passions, cravings. The sacred texts mention nine types of pride:

1. in one's physique and strength
2. in one's intellect
3. in one's morals and virtues
4. in one's psychic powers
5. in one's spirituality
6. in one's noble birth, social status
7. in one's wealth and possessions
8. in one's beauty, handsomeness
9. in one's talents, power of command

The interdependence of body and mind must also be recognized in the aspects of material (bodily), mental (abstract) and ethereal (spiritual). The aspirant will by now comprehend the use of mantra in bringing these aspects together. The practice of mantra (refined speech), the Divine Word, undergoes a process of becoming inaudible on its own account. Audible recitation improves the listening capacity and so this should be stressed rather than reciting the mantra mentally. Only when the listening capacity reaches a certain point will the mantra become self-generating.

In the previous cakra, the aspirant's attention was directed to the useless conversations in the mind. The screens we put up to filter what we want to hear need to be removed in order to listen clearly to what others have to say and to what the inner or outer guru says. By learning to listen and by practicing listening, we will know when words do not ring true, even those in our own heads.

It is fascinating to see how hearing and listening are used in daily language, which makes it clear that there is support for our need to listen.

- turn a deaf ear
- up to my ears (with work)
- I was all ears (intense listening)
- perk up your ears (pay attention)
- in one ear and out the other (not listening)
- the walls have ears (spying)
- bend your ear (talk a lot)
- music to my ears (something we want to hear)
- to sound him out (to test his reaction)
- to hear her out (to hear all she has to say)

The old saying that as we think, so we become still holds true. Every thought has its own mental image. It is possible to put into the mind the image of what we would like to be and to use autosuggestion to achieve some desired quality. In the case of eradicating a negative characteristic, we can phrase the suggestion in a positive way, emphasizing the goal to be achieved. For example, criticism is not overcome by telling ourselves, "I shall not criticize." In fact, we become more critical because the emphasis is on the word "criticize." The goal is achieved by saying, "I will be more accepting of people."

The use of the word "should" raises our deep-seated resentments of old authority figures. Therefore, it is best to use positive suggestions, such as "I am going to . . ." or "I will . . ." which indicate a firm decision.

The average person is very suggestible. A good way to become conscious of this in yourself is to watch for it first in other people. Clear thinking and discrimination help you to see the influence of the power of suggestion. Awareness is the mirror-like quality by which we can establish our true identity.

Let us consider what is meant in the Mantra of the Divine Light Invocation by, "I am created by Divine Light." When we make this statement, we have to clarify to our selves what it means, otherwise it is utter nonsense. We do not want to become parrots and just repeat the words (even though the repetition, in the course of many years, would also bear fruit). Hence we must think about it and understand it on a level that goes beyond the words. Feelings and emotions must also be involved, that is, the understanding should be on more than an intellectual level.

When I say, "I am created by Divine Light," I must know that at this moment I am not identifying myself with my physical body. I am identifying with the source of my being, with that creative energy to which some of us give the name "God."

Identification

The big problem for many people is not having a meaningful identification. With what do you identify? Is it your body? Then, are you only a body? If you are not the body, are you the mind? The mind has countless personality aspects. If you identify with the mind, you have to identify with one of the personality aspects that is in the foreground at the time. In a moment this can shift to another personality aspect. What security is there in this?

When you identify with anything other than your Higher Self, you make a very serious error which at some time you will have to rectify. The wrong identification will bring a number of negative consequences. When you identify with another person, only one small part of you is involved. It is one personality aspect which you recognize both in yourself and the other. For example, the personality in you that is jealous identifies with that aspect of jealousy in another person. It is not necessary to identify in this way in order to understand the other person. You must recognize that jealousy is a negative characteristic belonging to one personality aspect shared by you and the other person, and in no way expressive of the Higher Self. Knowing this should give you an understanding of yourself and a true sympathy with the other person. Beware of making any such identification, because in so doing you forget your truly Divine nature.

In the beginning of the path of Kuṇḍalinī Yoga, we are like spiritual babies under special grace. Now the time has come for maturity. The expression "flowing with it" does not mean not caring, but includes acceptance of responsibility.

Life becomes more steady because the aspirant has become more gentle and more modest. From the Heart Lotus, peace of mind spreads and because of self-control there is a freedom from greed, malice and pride. The aspirant has become courageous and forgiving. The feelings (refined emotions) are now truly a stepping-stone toward compassion. However, it should be remembered that the cakras have been explained as levels of consciousness and that each cakra has many levels.

If, by this stage, you decide that you really do need a guru, it must be remembered that to find out if a cake is good, it must be tasted. Philosophizing about the recipe or psychoanalyzing the cook still leaves you in the dark about the cake and its taste. To recognize your guru, you must study the teachings yourself and practice in daily life what the teachings direct.

As has been stated, surrender is necessary to be able

to truly listen. Surrender has to be practiced first in the physical, in the body, by learning to relax completely – surrender to the flow of breath coming in by itself, flowing out by itself. To flow with the breath of life is to do so with discrimination, not resignation. Then, as has been pointed out, the mind will also become still. As discrimination and sense perception become refined, intuition will flow as never before. The still, small voice within may now be heard. The passion of activity no longer destroys these Divine insights. All passionate activity is tempered by love that has a Divine quality and whatever interference from old personality aspects there might be, at this point the aspirant is more skillful in handling the battle-ax, to sharpen it and to cut away the appendages by determination and will.

Once again the lower nature will put up a furious fight. The ego, having been in charge for so long, is now seen in the proper light. It will be observed to be merciless, never allowing a response to the inner being. This is the moment to take careful aim with the arrow again, see that the target is well-defined, the decision for directness made, and the bow strung to the right degree of tension, not too much, not too little, to hit the target. The ego must not be allowed to distort the aim.

The control of the energies of this cakra will close the circle of perfection. The physical surrender as in the corpse āsana (Savāsana) means that the balance of body, mind and speech, as represented in the trident, is nearing completion – the awareness of the body and the awareness of the mind and its manifestation in speech. Having become spine conscious, the interplay of the forces on a tamasic, rajasic and sattvic level can now be observed. Straight thinking, straight actions and directness are the results that are expressed in the physical composure and in the manner of mind and speech. There is no longer the need to divide up and set out the exercises because at this point the aspirant will understand the blending of the senses and their manifestation, thereby perceiving the adjustments necessary for perfect balance.

Thoughts on Ego and Responsibility

Habitual thinking patterns are interconnected with emotions and are never questioned by the average person. They are symptoms of anxious protection of unproven beliefs and result in questionable word games. One of the traps is exaggeration, which the ego uses as a trick (consciously or unconsciously) to achieve a more favorable position, to defend its beliefs. The aspirant who has learned to keep emotions under control will observe that wild statements are intended to trick the opponent for the satisfaction of the ego. Irrelevant objections, minor details in discussions, may be the manifestation of a certain type of ego, revealing an aggressive, dishonest trickery, sometimes in an attempt to ridicule, sometimes in a desire to win at all costs. The aspirant is warned not to be caught in word games of this kind, which are deadly games. To admit ignorance is to be strong, while to pretend to know is weakness.

The aspirant, at this point, is also warned that to be convinced for emotional reasons is dangerous. That applies to general life as well as to spiritual life. Aspirants who are not secure through proper reasoning and personal experience can be too easily manipulated either by someone of magnetic personality, or by their own inverted ego. There must be control of emotions expressed in speech and thought. Debating points in our own mind is not wrong necessarily, but it should be watched for dishonesty. Listening to the still, small voice (the Devī) brings clarification quickly and changes old thinking patterns and habitual mental conversations.

Audible sound (the spoken word) and inaudible sound (the spoken word in the mind) are both vibrations that will give rise to creation. What creation comes into being is the responsibility of the originator of that sound.

Thoughts on Kuṇḍalinī

Fire of awareness, fire of wisdom

The snake around the neck of Sadāśiva and the trident in His hand indicate for the first time the possible stirring of the Kuṇḍalinī energy. The fire He holds, which is also symbolic of Kuṇḍalinī, reminds us that "ignorance is burned in the fire of wisdom." Such, then, is the Kuṇḍalinī Fire. It is a fire of awareness that burns ignorance so that life takes on a new meaning and all previous concepts are burned up. It turns the individual upside-down, into a new being. Some Scriptures speak of being clothed with a new garment. Others speak of being touched by the Divine Light, or having Divine Mother reveal Herself in splendor. This experience may be of minutely detailed intricacy or it may suddenly sweep the aspirant to a panoramic Vision of Light, leaving him or her humbled and awed. There are no words.

It now becomes evident why the character building of the previous cakras is so important. In the early stages, the aspirant's development is a matter of awareness and of dumping those concepts that can be let go without any emotional upset. This first state of awareness may have allowed the aspirant to recognize and deal with more complicated and deep-seated beliefs, which might bring such a feeling of release that certain psychic manifestations may result. This is not Kuṇḍalinī. What it means is that we have become more skillful in dealing with the sensations that exist in daily life. As an illustration, if I drive a little Volkswagen and then I buy a Lincoln, even though I have felt very comfortable with my little Volkswagen, I will now have to make adjustments for the steering, parking, speed, size, etc., of the big new car. But when I have learned to maneuver it, I will be in control of a vehicle of much greater power and quality.

To assure this kind of control, clarification of the mind is necessary. By accepting the exercises in this book, skill and awareness will be built up that will enable the aspirant to handle any experiences that come without anxiety.

In the pursuit of Kuṇḍalinī, a true guru will warn against developing exclusively in one area. In other words, if intellect has been developed at the cost of the senses and particularly the emotions, even the greatest intellect will be unable to handle the impact of the emotions when they strike. It is for that reason that the emphasis is on the equal development of the five senses, with particular attention to the mind, which is the operator at the control station of all sense perception.

The Higher Self may announce or signal this stirring of the Kuṇḍalinī energy ahead of time in dreams. Therefore, it is again stressed to carefully watch dreams and be consistent in noting them down. We may not understand the message of a dream, but the Higher Self derives its energy and wisdom from the Universal Intelligence, and it will find other ways and means of sending the message it intends us to have. We must pay great attention to dreams and all insights so the message will not be missed.

When the Kuṇḍalinī energy stirs there is indeed a change in temperature in the body, but it is not like a high fever or an unnatural body heat, although there have been situations where that was the case. It all depends on the preparations that have been made. The many mental acrobatics, the training of the mind, are necessary to make the mind and the senses, as well as the central nervous system, pliable to deal with those incredible realities.

Is psychic energy Kuṇḍalinī?

The question arises of whether the source of information a psychic receives is Kuṇḍalinī energy. This would only be true if the term "Kuṇḍalinī" were used to mean all life. Then, even functioning on the level of unawareness would be Kuṇḍalinī, which would make it more difficult to understand Kuṇḍalinī as a latent power within each individual or, as the old texts call it, "the coiled-up serpent." The many exercises for the attainment of the manifestation of psychic energy and spiritual experiences show that the psychic can only function within the realm of his own development of the senses and the mind. So, again we conclude, this is not Kuṇḍalinī.

Experiencing lights when in a meditative state is not Kuṇḍalinī, but can be taken as encouragement that we are on the right road. These experiences should be carefully observed as they are indications of the development toward the unfolding of the potential that is within everyone.

The many schools of thought concerning Kuṇḍalinī make for confusion rather than clarification. However, Kuṇḍalinī is the essential energy in each, and the means of reaching that state of consciousness is irrelevant. Once a path is chosen, the process becomes important and the steps laid out must be followed with care.

Any yoga singled out by itself is taking a part out of the whole and, as with any part, it is incomplete. The encouragement to sexual indulgence, alleged to be the purpose of the Kamasūtra by some who teach Kuṇḍalinī Yoga, is to be regretted because it means ripping out from a very beautiful and delicately balanced system some small detail and considering it the whole. It is not indulgence in sex that the Kuṇḍalinī energy encourages. However beautiful sex may be, it does not open the door to a state of higher consciousness. If that were so, the majority of people who believe in sexual excesses would all have achieved enlightenment.

The part that brahmacaryā plays in spiritual development can be more easily understood if we use money as a symbol for spiritual power and its hoped-for manifestation. We often scatter energy in the same way that we scatter money and it is only by holding together a large amount of either one that a large project can be undertaken.

Safe awakening of Kuṇḍalinī

Kuṇḍalinī will have to be pursued according to the aspirant's own natural inclinations. When all the groundwork has been done, when quality has been brought into other aspects of life, which itself is a development of human potential, and when the fringe benefits have been renounced (psychic manifestations), Kuṇḍalinī will begin to stir because it has been safely awakened. In the process of doing the exercises, the control of desires and all sense perceptions has increased, inner security has developed, and therefore the awakening of Kuṇḍalinī will not be a frightening, but a blissful experience.

The mythology of many a culture has strenuously tried to explain not only the purpose of life but what is this God/Energy. Modern scientists continue to question this, and for each the answer is expressed differently. The human mind cannot determine what Cosmic Energy is; it can only study its manifestation. This manifestation can be brought about in oneself and studied there. Whatever the Energy is – It can only reveal Itself.

The light of the sun reveals all things,
but the light of the sun can only reveal itself.

Meditation on the Light

Sit in a comfortable position or in any yogic posture, but with your ankles crossed. Close your eyes, focus them on the space between the eyebrows. Do not start until your body is quiet (perhaps with the help of a little prāṇāyāma).

In previous chapters, you have become aware of the necessity of being spine conscious. Feel your spine and as you straighten it out, putting vertebra on vertebra, see at the base of your spine a Lotus bud slowly open and, like a dewdrop, a tiny pinpoint of Light slowly emerging from it . . . floating in the very center of the spine, in that hollow part, up and up and up, passing through the respective places of the other Lotuses, finally floating to the place where the spine joins the head . . . and in a gentle curve (like a shepherd's crook) this tiny pinpoint of Light floats over the pituitary and pineal. In your mind's eye, see a flash of Light illuminating the brain matter, becoming again the pinpoint of Light and traveling back the same way, making the gentle curve, meeting the spine and floating gently and slowly in the very center of the hollow of the spine, passing through all the Lotuses, down to the very first one. When it has touched the center of that Lotus, the four petals close as if to protect something very precious. Stay quiet and allow to come to you whatever delicate intuitive perception may want to arise. Let it happen. If nothing specific happens, that is fine too. Let yourself be absorbed in that beautiful feeling, deep peace and harmony.

Do this exercise not more than once a day. This will prevent the forcing open of the Lotuses. The experience of the arising of the Kuṇḍalinī energy can take place in such small steps, so gently, as never to upset or jar you into any anxiety. Also, it takes time to reach the ability to concentrate, and to be so alert and yet so relaxed at the same time. Patience and perseverence will lead to an unfolding that can be, if the instructions are followed as given, a very beautiful experience that gives a sense of knowing of the Divine. In terms of religion, let us remember that all saints tell us that man cannot command God. To pursue the Most High we may have to learn to wait in humility.

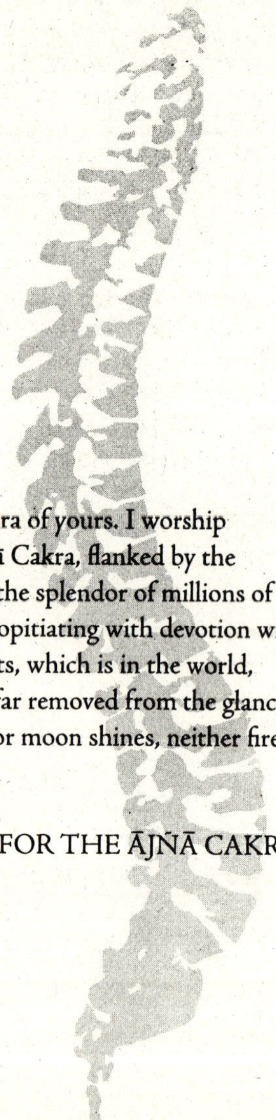

I venerate Him who is residing in the Ājñā Cakra of yours. I worship (revere) the highest Śambhu in your Ājñā Cakra, flanked by the highest intelligence (She), Him who has the splendor of millions of suns and moons. He who worships by propitiating with devotion will reside in the world of the Light of all lights, which is in the world, which no earthly glance can reach and is far removed from the glance of ordinary mortals. There neither sun nor moon shines, neither fire nor the other heavenly bodies.

MANTRA FOR THE ĀJÑĀ CAKRA

9. ĀJÑĀ

THE SIXTH CAKRA

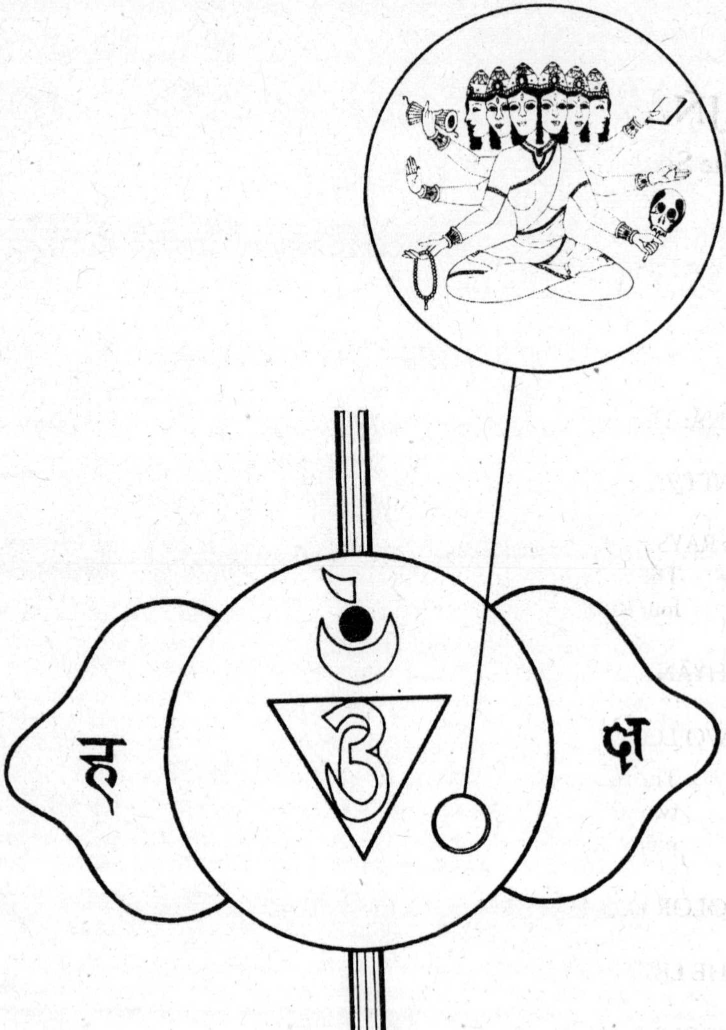
ॐ
ह
क्ष

ĀJÑĀ

The Sixth Cakra and Its Symbols

ĀJÑĀ: The Sixth Cakra or Lotus

TATTVA: Differentiating faculty

64 RAYS: Relate to the region of the mind, ether (akasha)

The six senses, including the mind, are now like rays penetrating the four corners of the world.

DHYĀNA: Meditation, expressed at the Ājñā Cakra

TWO LOTUS PETALS: The Lotus is sacred

The two petals are symbolic for the functioning of the mind (manas) in two worlds of reality, the manifest and the unmanifest, but also for the pineal and pituitary and for Īḍā and Piṅgalā, which unite at this point.

COLOR OF THE PETALS: White

THE LETTERS ON THE PETALS: Ksaṃ, Haṃ

CIRCLE: Perfection at its highest level

TRIANGLE: Golden; within the triangle is the Yoni with a śivaliṅga called Itara, white with streaks of lightning – Power, Energy

The triangle is symbolic of the workings of the Energy in its pure state and in its manifested state, for which sex is the expression commonly known to man. Reproduction is no longer of a child, not even a Divine Child, but of the cosmic nature.

QUARTER MOON: Vortex of Energy, consciousness manifests most subtly

BĪJA: Oṃ (Prāṇava), the Seed Sound; Mahānāda, supreme sound

BINDU: Golden dot, essence of Energy

The bindu symbolizes complete detachment from the body by either the male or female, a precondition to be able to use mind in other than habitual or known ways.

PRESIDING DEITY: Paramaśiva (Śambhu), Śiva in His highest aspect

PIṄGALĀ: The Nāḍī on the right side of the body

ĪḌĀ: The Nāḍī on the left side of the body

SUṢUMNĀ: The central channel of the spine

CITRIṆĪ: Three in one (sattva, rajas, tamas), body, mind and speech; concentration, meditation and contemplation

GODDESS AND HER OBJECTS:

Śakti Hākinī: The aspect of the union of Energy manifest and unmanifest

The intelligence on this level is symbolized in unity. Śakti Hākinī has six faces and six arms. Mind has increased in power and subtlety, as symbolized by the six faces, while the six arms indicate high efficiency level. The yogi or yoginī, having reached this level, becomes a siddha, one who has acquired the power that goes with these experiences.

Vidyā: Book

The book is symbolic for knowledge retained.

Gesture: Vara(da), granting boons; Abhayamudrā, dispelling fears

More spiritual gifts and granting boons, intuitive insights or perception by the various senses are possible. Fears are dispelled through the increased knowledge from personal experience. The control of imagination allows the discovery by the aspirant that all experiences are the creation of the mind.

Ḍamaru: Drum

The drum indicates that the beat, the rhythm, of life must go on and the yogi or siddha must remain on Earth long enough to show the path to others.

Khaṭvāṅga: Staff with skull on top

The skull, previously symbolic for the empty mind, is now symbolic for the attainment of a mind with awesome powers, never before anticipated. If intuitive perception is retained, these powers will be used for the benefit and the blessings of others.

Mālā: Rosary, mantra is becoming a self-generating power

The mantra's self-generating power has to be maintained. Each bead on the rosary is symbolic for the past lives as they have been strung together, exerting their influence to a small or large degree, painfully or joyfully, to bring about the present state. Again, sound is brought to its highest expression, as in Prāṇava Oṃ.

Ājñā Cakra

In the Sixth Cakra, if the highest level within the cakra is reached, one can speak of a "point of no return." Imagine what it means when there is nothing left to enjoy – no food, sex, success or power, but simply a feeling of neutrality about everything. What does life hold after all pleasures have gone? A new choice comes at that point. One may leave the Earth by allowing the body to die or, as some yogins have done, withdrawing the life force consciously, at will. Or one may stay on and help others to reach the same state by encouraging nonattachment to the pleasures that keep people bound to the wheel of life, which goes round and round. But if one stays on, or takes on another incarnation, it is with the decided purpose of helping others to become free from the entanglements and the pursuing of the wrong goals, to help others to see that even success exists only in the minds of those who need to feed their self-importance. It is like the artificially high price of the diamond, decided by those in power, and thereby not being the true worth. What value has this in comparison with freedom from all limitations, inner harmony and peace of mind?

Mental energy through the practice of self-mastery is now observed in many areas and on different levels. The daily reflecting has increased awareness and will still be the guide for deciding where one's energy is wasted or locked up. Knowledge has been gained by personal experience. Here in the Sixth Cakra that knowledge may include the knowing of the time of death by inner perception. Death is understood now as the physical returning to the vortex of Energy until some other time when it decides to manifest again. The physical body, then, is a tool for what by now we can truly term spiritual life, a tool that is used in each lifetime for spiritual evolution.

By inner perception also comes the knowledge of the

Truth that has been voiced by all saints. Yoga, being the path of Liberation, brings freedom from the merry-go-round activity of the ego-mind, strength to listen to the inner being with intuition, and perception of the finer forces and their expression, of which the ether is only a symbol. Śakti, the Devī of Speech, is now understood in terms of the language of the Gods and makes Herself known through this inner communication, intuitive perception and increased awareness.

The First and Sixth Cakras, linked by the Suṣumnā and the two nāḍīs, will now be recognized as the areas where the interplay of forces takes place. The understanding of this interplay of forces is a knowing from experience instead of just an intellectualization. The Suṣumnā is the path in which the Energy can move freely. Self-mastery gives control of the Light, the ability to increase or decrease its brightness.

During meditation, which by now is the natural outgrowth of daily reflection, all colors and all images will slowly disappear and the mind will perceive only the colorless White Light, the White Light that indicates formlessness. The mind, which in the beginning created in a compulsive manner and not for one's benefit, has learned to focus itself and has taken on only one direction, toward the White Light that is symbolic for the Great Void. The mind now is resting in IT.

So the door to the Seventh Cakra, the exit, is opened. The physical body may become weakened, or illness may be the reason for death. When the yogin withdraws the life force, the prāṇa is placed into the Abode. The body passes away peacefully. There is neither joy nor sorrow. It is all finished and there is no need to be born again.

The drop has returned to the ocean.

Concentration: Exercise

Concentration exercises are to be done in an alert yet relaxed manner for maximum results.

If the Divine Light Invocation has been practiced with attention, the aspirant will have achieved a degree of concentration and noticeable benefits from this exercise. A further step is the concentration on one's physical form by limiting the perception of the eyes (sight) and seeing beyond the form.

Filling the spine with Light

1. Sit in meditation posture (alternate to standing).

2. Focus on the space between the eyebrows.

3. Imagine the spine being a hollow tube.

4. See this tube as being of glass. You can see through it.

5. Fill this tube with brilliant White Light.

6. Fill the bottom first.

7. Hold this image as long as you comfortably can.

8. Repeat often till it becomes easy.

Check after each practice the notes of your well-being. When all is absolutely satisfactory, add attention to your breath.

The following procedure will prove helpful.

1. Imagine that with every inhalation you take in White Light.

2. With every exhalation, you focus on the "level" of that Light.

Synthesis of Ājñā Cakra

Here in the Sixth Cakra it is time for the aspirant to make a reassessment. The circle is complete, perfection is almost achieved. Mind has increased in subtlety and power, its mysteries becoming more comprehensible because of the foundation that has been laid. It was an arduous task and it is not ended. The foundation has been laid for the next phase, like learning the alphabet and grammar necessary to write the poetry that you feel is somewhere inside. There is a feeling of exhilaration in the knowing from experience – a feeling of independence. So do not give up. Keep going, keep going! Remember . . . only the gods can walk the rainbow. Reach for a little more of the god and a little less of the human! *Circle of perfection*

The sexual self has come into focus, and the cosmic unity, which stands in contrast to the overindividualization of sex in today's world, is no longer felt to be lost but possible. Ideas of reincarnation and the changes of sexes may still be unclear, but no longer rejected. Judgment is suspended on that point.

The Serpent, which has been "speechless," gently makes its presence known and, through the Devī of Speech, the aspirant has now acquired inner communication, intuitive perception and an increased awareness. Many little things seem to fall into place, or drop away. They are just gone with no struggle, no special discipline. Yet, there is a strong feeling that is not entirely comfortable, a sort of fearful respect. Let that be so. Call it a holy fear. Do not slip back into old ways; always remember that your own sincerity protects you. Trust the Greater Power. Allow emotions of humility, reverence and surrender to emerge. The Serpent closes the circle. Let your intuition guide you in this thought.

The Ājñā-Guru communicates mind to mind. There may have been a preparation for this by hearing somebody speak in a dream while you were asleep, or by seeing images, landscapes, people or pictures in a dream. Then the ability comes to see and hear in the waking state through the same kind of perception without speech. This can happen only when speech is under control. Being in communication with the Higher Self is not the same as mental conversation, although it is a similar process. The response comes from your own Higher Self, or it might also come from a bodiless consciousness (a vortex of energy). When consciousness leaves the body, it can see what is going on in a particular place. It can even project an image to someone in that place so that person knows and recognizes its presence.

The human eye can serve as a helpful illustration for this mental process. The eye has to make adjustments to focus on something close or far away. Let us assume that mind can do the same, that it can focus on something right in front and adjust to something in the far distance. In this way, communicating mind to mind between the guru and disciple is very common. If the disciple's mind is fixed on the guru, an imperceptible switchover of consciousness takes place.

The symbol for nectar and ambrosia, the amṛta, being cool and white, means that these Divine insights no longer excite the emotions, but you can now suspend judgment and wait for conclusions. You are better able to care, be responsive and have gratitude; the cool and white mean that greediness and emotional indulgence no longer interfere with the feelings of pure joy now emerging from the Heart Center. These feelings are an expression of gratitude that your Higher Self has taken care of your needs.

At this stage, love takes on a new quality that is so foreign and so unbelievable that the tendency is to think, "I cannot love anybody anymore." It takes awhile to recognize that the new love is indeed pure and has become free from all self-indulgence, all possessiveness. This really means that you are slowly becoming master of yourself in some areas and have added more stones to this mosaic that you are trying to complete.

It is said at this point that one becomes all-knowing and all-seeing. You become all-knowing not by an undeserved act of grace, but because you have laid the foundation. You now know how much has had to be done to understand yourself, so it should be no surprise that in the Ājñā Cakra you do become all-knowing within your own life.

You will have knowledge of the time of death by a dream, by receiving a message, or by seeing your own body dead. Death can be a conscious decision: "I have no particular attachments and I have nothing else to do. I will withdraw the life force."

You will begin to understand that reincarnation is a chain of cause and effect in the same way as you have observed in many other areas. What you call life is a day, and what you call death is a night. Each night is a waiting period in which you may pursue and embroider the desires that you brought from a previous life. If at the time of death you think, "I am not ready to die. I still haven't done this, and this, and this," these desires and hopes will propel you back into those circumstances in which you can fulfill them. If one life is not enough, it will be a hundred or a hundred thousand. Now is the time to incorporate into your mind and anchor firmly the idea, "I am ever growing into the Light."

Having become all-knowing within your own life allows you to understand others because human nature is not so different. Everyone has six senses, and human bodies all operate under the same law, so of course you are all-knowing. You can also develop one part of your mind to tap others, which allows you access to the knowledge in other people's minds.

Jyotir means Light, having visions of a high order. You can see other people's obstacles to realization by means of the Light. Looking at a dream, the whole life path of the dreamer will be revealed to you. It is Jyotir, the Light, that is all-seeing. This Light, emanating from the Mūlādhāra Cakra, has reached the Ājñā Cakra and now illuminates the mind. By becoming sensitive to the perception of the formless and colorless Supreme Light, the aspirant has been able to destroy the personality aspects so the energy can now go to the spiritual growth.

The communication between guru and disciple, mind to mind, is through this Light. Practice of the Divine Light Invocation has helped to bring you to this point. You become a yati, an advanced student, whose mind is resting intently on the guru. The physical guru is the stepping-stone to the guru within.

The Bīja, or seed sound, of this cakra, Oṃ (A-U-Ṃ), is the thirteenth vowel of the Sanskrit alphabet. It represents the life force, the universal sound.

The candra-maṇḍala means insight into nirvāṇa, or the six stages of samādhī. The goddess Śakti grants Divine knowledge, an understanding of the message of the Divine Śāstras (scriptures), symbolized in the book She holds. The creative power of the Mūlādhāra Cakra, then expressed in sex, now in the Ājñā Cakra reaches its highest point. One can create a mantra and imbue it with power. (However, such a mantra will not be as powerful as a mantra which was created, let us say, 50,000 years ago and has many realized consciousnesses keeping it alive, who will come to your rescue if you falter.)

It is said that the Great Void is served by all Devas. The Great Void is not an empty space. There is no empty space. Even in what we call space in the universe, there are all sorts of forces, attractions and rays, besides the galaxies. So this means that the Devas (gods and goddesses) will serve the aspirant on all levels of consciousness, beyond the three dimensions we have filled with names and forms.

The Great Void within the Triangle means that there is no manifestation perceptible to the senses. Creativity is no longer physical or artistic, but purely spiritual.

The goddess Hākinī of this cakra is the creator and destroyer. This means that all personality aspects have to be killed in order that the Higher Self may live. Without destroying the old person, a new one cannot be born.

Divine Mother Śakti has to keep the world going

to allow rebirth for the lessons that have not yet been learned. When you have learned all lessons, you become indeed Her child and will do Her bidding. You may also be Her special servant and offer all Energy for use as She sees fit.

If you can create Divine Mother in your mind, this is creativity of the mind at its highest. But it must also be kept alive and allowed to take its own course. You create Divine Mother in everything that is most beautiful, most perfect, most forgiving – everything that you desire to become yourself. Having created Her in your mind, you allow Her to give you energy to destroy the personality aspects that are not in keeping with this Most High creation. This makes the energy from these personality aspects available, and you put it all back into your creation of Divine Mother so that it becomes bigger, more beautiful, and, strangely enough, more real. At one point, it takes on a life of its own. Therefore, you must be extremely careful what you create and allow to take on life.

For this reason, never criticize your guru because your guru becomes embroidered by the creation of your mind. The guru, on the other hand, in the process of becoming a guru, has developed the habitual attitude of seeing only the Divine in others and disregards the negative interferences. The process of nurturing the spiritual potential of an aspirant is the height of the creative powers, using that same energy that originates in the Mūlādhāra Cakra.

The two Lotus petals represent powers that work together. They are likened to two grains of rice in which the power is compressed, but mostly unused. The lesson to be learned here is in the form of an exercise. Take a grain of rice in your hand and look at it, keeping your eyes open until they almost water. Through this process you will begin to see auras, not colored auras, but the white aura of Light. Then, recalling the exercise in the Maṇipūra Cakra in which you projected your own image against the sky, now you hold the rice between two fingers and hold it up to the sky.

Look at a grain of rice

The single-pointed mind should be directed to Śiva

(now properly known as Śākta) and Śakti as power. Śākta/Śakti is the source of Brahmā, to whom flows constantly a stream of nectar and ambrosia, of which He is the perfect receptacle. Śakti is power and Śākta is the source of power – the source of Light, the Light itself. But the source will never be discovered if nothing emanates. If Light emanates, then there has to be a source from which that Energy flows. These two have to be seen together. So with the grain of rice. Without the Energy, it will not sprout. You might be able to see the Energy as an aura of life force; see the life force and the grain at the same time. This is not really any longer symbolic, but can be seen directly as the one Power, Śākta/Śakti.

Śākta/Śakti is the constant stream of life energy and also amṛta (nectar and ambrosia), which flow to the disciple who is seeking to understand.

When Śakti wishes to create, She divides Herself in two. On the right, Bindu, male – Haṃ; on the left, Visarga, female – Sa. She divides Herself into many. Therefore, as creator, I am also She. Haṃsa, the combination of male and female, can be translated not as "I am He" or "I am She," but "I am That. That I am," Power manifest and Power unmanifest in one.

Śakti Hākinī has six heads and six arms. The power of the mind is so great it is like six minds put together, mental power at its highest state. Also, with the power of six arms, your practical efficiency has increased beyond normal limitations.

One of the objects She holds is the ḍamaru, the drum. The pulse, the beat of life is going on. Persuasion and temptation are always possible, so do not fool yourself.

The skull, reappearing, maintains the same message – emptiness of the mind. To continue the mind's habit of interpreting would be a big mistake. The need is not to learn new things, but to a-b-s-o-r b Divine nectar, as the body absorbs what it needs from food. Nectar and ambrosia are the spiritual food (the intuitive insights) that need to be absorbed, not analyzed or prejudged.

The mālā that is held, again associated with mantra, shows that now the mantra has been practiced to a degree where its power has become self-generating. What is that mantra power that is self-generating? Turn your gaze toward the vara(da) gesture, the gesture of granting boons. Make that silent request . . . keep that thought alive. Then wait. The goddess promises that you will receive boons in proportion to the extent you practice Kuṇḍalinī Yoga.

The gesture abhaya of Śakti Hākinī means that all fears are now dispelled because of perfect knowledge. Having reached the level of consciousness of the Sixth Cakra, one need never be born again, one moves ever toward the Light. Excellence is now achieved with control of the mind.

The two petals of the Ājñā Cakra are sometimes compared to the pituitary and the pineal, which each have a specific purpose. Such a comparison, if helpful, should only be used temporarily and not be thought of in medical terms.

According to some schools of thought, the pineal is the seat of memory, which can be a curse or a blessing – a blessing when we can remember past mistakes, a curse when the memory stands in the way of learning something new. Everything is interpreted by the mind on the basis of what has already been stored in the memory of the pineal. At this particular level of intelligence and control, the pineal allows past lives to be brought into focus, if that is important, or even past events on a world scale.

The pituitary, in contrast, is called "the master gland" because, old yogis say, it is capable of recharging the entire body and the mind on all its levels. It is here that Divine Mother Śakti has poured the greatest amount of Energy and Power for use in the daily life of the aspirant. If we want to understand this in familiar language, we can say that the pineal functions like the register. It has an enormous filing cabinet, but it is without the power of discrimination. Its purpose is simply to file and when commanded to do so, to recall and produce what has been filed. That part of the mind we could call the "subjective" mind, being incapable of inductive reasoning, while the pituitary can perhaps be likened to the "objective" mind that takes concepts of the objective world. The objective mind has under its control the five senses and is capable of reason.

Functioning from my center

In the center that connects these two petals is the complete, beautiful circle. Here again the balance of the two is that neither overrides the other, and so the control can be given to the Self, perfect in itself. The yogi calls it "resting in your own Ātman." You can call it in a more familiar term, "functioning from my true Center." The male and female aspects are shown as one. The golden dot represents the essence of all energy that will, when understood properly, hold together the two petals and let them function in perfect conjunction with each other. Here is the region of the mind most powerful, the mind being like the center of the spheres, the indicator.

To achieve that perfect balance is not easy. The objective mind needs a lot of training to discriminate what the subjective mind absorbs and collects into its own filing cabinet. Because of its capacity to surrender, the job that it is given will be simply that of the clerk in the court of all lives, to register correctly, not allowing any interpretation by the objective mind. This is a most difficult thing to do, because here, in the region of the mind, we have to investigate the mind to understand its functioning and purpose. And so the mind has to turn on itself. To hold the mind at bay, when it has been allowed to be the interpreter of all that passes through it for all of our lives, makes such investigation extremely difficult.

If the pituitary is considered to have the power of reasoning, but in the early stages is not considered to have the wisdom to use and discriminate between reason or logic, and intuition, perhaps we can say that the objective mind needs to be trained to raise its level of development. One method of this would be laying the foundation and building character. The second stage would be spiritual. And the combination of the two brings wisdom that we may term "celestial." While many theories have been advanced about the mind, limitations are still accepted and numerous interpretations are of no help. As in the area of science, a complete new beginning, a hypothesis that may seem to be outrageous, can be a better start than simply re-interpreting existing ideas.

The subjective mind has an enormous reservoir of collected events, but is restricted in the assessment of what it has been collecting. When it does make itself known, this can result in a frightening experience. The fright comes from the objective mind that does not know what to do with that material. It is exactly this lack of understanding of the functioning of the subjective mind that creates many problems.

Suggestions and hypnosis are possible only when the objective mind has somehow been subdued. That is why it is necessary to achieve that perfect balance, where the objective mind is trained to handle properly, beneficially, the material that can be extracted or recalled by the subjective mind.

Exercises for the Ājñā Cakra

Perfection of prāṇāyāma, having resulted in steadiness of mind, is now combined with Mahāmudrā. The influence of Haṃsa moves all over the body, and the Yonimudrā, honored by all yogis and siddhas, is practiced. Haṃsa is merged with the siddha in prāṇa. The aspirant knows the time of death and joyfully places the prāṇa in the abode of Viṣṇu (Ājñā Cakra) and passes away.

Yonimudrā

The exercise called Closing the House (Yonimudrā) should be practiced with the proper understanding and without the expectation of some sensational happening.

Sit erect, neck and head in a straight line. Place the left heel against the anus, the right heel on the left foot. With the lips form a crow's beak. Draw in air. Tightly close the ears by pushing the earlobes into the openings with the thumbs, cutting out physical sounds. This is a subtle reminder that all mental sounds must also be stilled. Close the eyes with the index fingers, stopping them from moving and forming mental images. By closing the nostrils with the middle fingers, the perception of smell is eliminated. Keeping the lips closed and the little fingers on them means to keep mauna or silence. The doors of perception of the senses are now all closed, the mind set free to become single-pointed – to take one direction toward the Most High. Mentally recite Haṃsa (Ajapa Mantra).

Mahāmudrā

Mahāmudrā, together with Kuṇḍalinī Prāṇāyāma (Kriyā), should be practiced on a regular daily basis. When a guru gives instructions in this type of exercise (including Yonimudrā), they are often called initiations. Each aspirant has to clarify the term "initiation" as well as all other important terms. Initiations take place on many levels and the power derived from an initiation into something depends very much on the person who practices.

Preparation for Performing Mahāmudrā:

1. Make a tube with your hands.
   - Suck air up through your mouth.
   - Feel the cold air move into your spine, all the way down.
   - Then blow warm air through your hands.
   - Feel the warmth in your mouth and again transfer it into your spine.

2. Stand on your shoulders.
   - Tip your legs over your head, touching your toes to the floor above your head.
   - Now by the weight of your body, let it come down slowly, one vertebra at a time, feeling each one touch the floor. See the image of your spine as you repeat the exercise in your mind.

- Think of your spine as you have seen it in anatomical books. See it with an empty central tube.
- Imagine it being made from glass and fill it with Light.

Performing Mahāmudrā:

Sit on the floor erect. Again tuck the left heel against the anus. Stretch the right leg in front. Hook the right forefinger around the big toe of the right foot. In this position there is a bending forward of the body. The left hand is placed on the left thigh. Focus on the space between the eyebrows. Put the tip of the tongue behind the upper teeth. Inhale and let the cool air flow into the spine. A slight sound of aw-aw is barely audible. Exhale the air through clenched teeth. There will be a slight sound of ee-ee. Feel warm air move up the spine.

Now exchange legs and stretch the left one in front. Repeat as given above. Do this 6 times on the left side and 6 times on the right side.

Next sit with both legs stretched out in front. Hook both forefingers around the big toes and repeat the exercise.

The final part of this exercise is to sit in Padmāsana or Siddhāsana and place both hands on the thighs, near the knees. The position is slightly bent, with the chin toward the chest. Do another 6 inhalations and exhalations as before.

Meditation on the Rainbow

This exercise is also known as the Meditation on the Rainbow. It is suggested to help to expand awareness, in conjunction with relaxation. The rainbow is composed of all colors, blending into each other. The meanings to the aspirant of all the colors of the cakras should be clarified so that they can blend together. Now the acceptance of the symbolic meanings has come about. There is a saying among the yogis that only the Great Ones can walk the rainbow.

The Mind

What is this thing called mind, that can keep us prisoner and yet can experience such luminosity? It is like being two selves – one does not share in the experience of the other. Can we leave the part that holds us prisoner? Can we get outside of the old established orbit and stay with the Light? Perhaps we may spiral up into new realms, never before encountered.

What is this thing called mind, that demands with such authority to have everything explained, when there is really nothing to be explained, only to be experienced? Can mind understand the knowing of the heart?

Mind has no form. It is an emanation, like rays from the sun. Like the rays, mind travels in all directions. Mind is without color, without form, beyond all verbalization.

To understand, we have to clarify to ourselves, "What is the mind? How do I use the word?" It is important to have an understanding of the meaning of the words that we use because a word is more than a sound, more than a group of letters – it expresses an idea or even a range of ideas.

Mind and consciousness

As an illustration, are mind and consciousness the same? Do you use these words interchangeably, or do you attach special meanings to each word and give to each different characteristics? Is there only a one-level meaning, or are there many levels of meaning to both words?

The brain, as a physical organ, is the seat of the mind. Can you clearly define what the mind is? Or how it functions? What degree of energy is employed when thinking or transmitting thought into speech?

Consciousness: a bridge between two worlds

What then is consciousness? Consciousness by itself is a phenomenon that has yet to be understood. Look at consciousness as a bridge between the world of daily living and the world of the Absolute. The path of Kuṇḍalinī is one that uncovers the intuitive perception that has been buried by habitually making concrete that which is abstract.

Mind is an expression or characteristic of consciousness. It has access only to the limited consciousness of three dimensions, whereas consciousness itself is unlimited. Extraordinary effort has to be made to enable the mind to experience another dimension without being shattered in its imagined foundation. That is why anything beyond mind cannot be expressed. At that point the yogi keeps silent – there is no other choice.

Mind: the sixth sense

In Eastern thought, mind is considered one of the senses. It is seen as a sixth sense. Like the other senses, the various characteristics of the mind must also be discovered and explored.

Mind the interpreter

Life is perceived through the senses, and mind acts as the interpreter. Therefore, it is necessary to understand the mind's incredible abilities, powers and creativity, and their effect on that interpretation. This is very little understood or thought about in daily life, nor is the power of choice recognized. This fact has a great deal of power and should play an important part in all human interaction.

The need for security and simplicity prevents us from expanding our old limits in order to discover new territory, greater possibilities. Science is "breathless" at the possibility of mind over matter, yet experiences and evidence are rejected because they shatter well-established concepts. As in many other areas of life, there are only a few who are keen to explore the mind, prepared and willing to take risks and rise above their mental-emotional needs for security and reputation. The molding and development of the mind into new areas is a great challenge. If the existence of another dimension has never been intellectually considered, the shock can indeed be devastating when such an experience beyond the ordinary occurs. Each aspirant goes through some incredible "hells," having to let go of all mental, and thereby emotional, security in order to go beyond accepted limits of the mind. The path often seems cruel and unbearable. As time passes, things do not become easier, but increasing insight shows that what has been thrown off has really been an unnecessary burden. In one of the lovely stories of Rādhā and Kṛṣṇa, the Lord says to Rādhā, "You must come to me naked and unafraid," meaning without any artificial "cover" or rigidly held concepts. This stripping of all concepts, that truly "empties" one more and more as persistent work goes on, is really like becoming naked.

So it is sensible in the beginning to travel along well-proven roads. Those who have done so have outlined the path for others to follow. In the process of development ideas are prone to change. What you are thinking now may hold no value in three years, or even three months. You will have grown, you will have developed, your awareness will have increased, your level of understanding will have risen.

There are no final conclusions that can be drawn on any level because, if we look at life, we can see that the classic saying of the Eastern teacher is as correct today as it was in bygone times: "Nothing is permanent." From being a sleepwalker, a hypnotized person, a conditioned person, you want to become a person who is aware. The purpose of the path of Kuṇḍalinī is to wake you up from sleep and ignorance, and to free you from as many limitations as possible in one lifetime in order that you may reach the high goal of Cosmic Consciousness.

The mind is as multilayered as the mountains. It is impossible to even broadly assess all states that the mind can assume. The mind is a miniature universe – the universe is the expansion of the mind.

Mental aspects

The mind operates on conscious, subconscious and superconscious levels. There are the sensational, rational and intuitive aspects; the cosmic, infinite and universal aspects of the mind. The laws of association, continuity and relativity operate within the mind. All these mental characteristics have three guṇas or aspects – sattva (pure), rajas (action, passion) and tamas (inertia, ignorance).

Sattvic mind

In order to grasp the sattvic aspect of the mind, it is necessary to clarify what our concept of a pure mind is, how this relates to life, and in what areas. The sattvic mind is the uncolored mind, possessing the qualities of detachment, desirelessness, dispassion and surrender to what is. The sattvic quality will allow us to consider the happiness or good fortune of others with joy.

Rajasic mind

The rajasic aspect of the mind is connected with the concepts of mental activity, its infinite possibilities to create and destroy, and its passion in regard to daily performance, more intense in some areas than in others. Again, discrimination and new decisions are necessary. The need for "constant entertainment" and self-expression has to be controlled in efforts to raise the mind from the rajasic to the sattvic state.

Tamasic mind

Then there is the tamasic mind, the mind of instinct and desire. The concept of darkness and inertia has to be pondered to be fully understood. The instinctual way of living is the way of ignorance, of darkness. It is our human destiny, being endowed with consciousness, to move from Darkness into Light.

Selfishness clouds understanding. The clear mind is inaccessible to the selfish individual. The elimination of selfishness is essential. Control and discrimination are necessary to achieve the sattvic mind.

Everything starts in the mind. Conscious mental activity is the emergence of unconscious activity. All things are created by the mind and so all concepts are born of mind. While concepts provide the mind with the framework for understanding, the mind may be limited by its own formulations. A mind free of concepts, free of scheming, without the compulsion to interpret, has reached the sattvic state, cleansed, pure and white.

The statement that "everything is created by the mind" must also be carefully pondered. What could it mean? There is the single mind of an individual that creates its own world – as a businessman creates his business the way he perceives it should be. But there is also the collective creation of minds, since minds in contact with each other influence each other. In a collective sense, the world as it is today is the creation of the combined efforts of many minds. Because the creativity of minds is a continuing force, there is constant change in the manifestation of the creative powers of the minds. We are much more masters of our destiny than we may recognize.

Most people function far below the ability of their conscious mind. It needs stimulation and training if it is to grow, for if it does not receive the proper nourishment and care it will stagnate. A healthy, efficient mental attitude is as crucial to human evolution as is physical health.

When its values are clear, the mind has all the energy it needs. A healthy mind has the reasoning power to properly discriminate between pure self-gratification and manifestations that benefit others.

Intelligence

Characteristics are built into the mind over thousands of years. Qualities of the mind, such as intelligence, are developed according to the survival needs of an individual in each life. Intelligence expresses itself in many ways: in the abilities to form concepts, to interpret and generalize, to see relationships and associate thoughts, to differentiate and distinguish, to store and retrieve memory. We owe it to ourselves to make use of all the intellectual abilities of which the mind is capable.

"Know thyself and be free." The mind reacts to the faintest stimulus, which makes its control extremely difficult, but with practice it can be guided and directed. A roaming mind is very inefficient, losing energy and weakening the whole person, physically and mentally. On the other hand, a concentrated mind becomes aware of its own energy and increases it.

The drifting mind is dangerous. The mind can become agitated for no apparent reason. Watching the mind must be carried on at all times. The aspirant must never be in the state of "sleep," but be ever watchful, learning from it, discovering the laws that govern it, gaining control and directing it. This ever increasing awareness gradually liberates the aspirant from mechanical thoughts and actions.

The aspirant becomes aware of the constant "mental background noises," the thousands of thoughts that go unnoticed by the "sleepwalker." Key sentences repeated mechanically have an incredible influence on the life of each person. Key word suggestions are the central controlling factor within ourselves, and we have to take responsibility for all mental activity. When these key suggestions come from a source outside oneself – another person, television, news, etc. – there is a danger, even for very intelligent people, of losing individuality and taking on the concepts of others.

The mind is capable of great trickery. It can create traps and twist memory to suit itself. At first this may be difficult to recognize, but it can be detected with the practice of constant awareness, which is developed through daily reflection. Now we can confront the delay tactics of the mind filled with worldly desires. When desires are strong, their effect has to be recognized. The decision to put off the spiritual work until tomorrow is the best illustration of this. Carried to its extreme, this means "to do the job in the next life" – only a tamasic mind will not recognize that this has happened already in a few hundred lifetimes, or maybe a few thousand, that have been spent unfortunately.

Liberation

That Liberation can be achieved in one lifetime is seen in the life of Tibet's great yogi, Milarepa. The yogis and yoginīs of today stress the possibility also. While the effort is enormous, the result is ecstasy, beyond description.

Powers of the Mind

Daily reflection will have clarified many areas in which the aspirant has been conditioned. Reconditioning is very much bound up with clarification in the major areas of life. The traditional texts tell us how to become free of all conditioning by Concentration, Meditation and Contemplation (Citriṇī, the three-in-one), which are achieved by willpower, the ability to focus, to give attention, to accept and let go. These mental processes have to be understood and applied before they become meaningful and successful.

In the beginning, there is substitution of old ideas for new ones, as this is a process by which people learn. However, excessive substitution will be avoided when individuals become dissatisfied with the way in which they have been conditioned and can see the goal with clarity. Clouded thinking is then replaced by clear thinking (clairvoyance, clairaudience).

Hypnosis

Hypnosis is a state of mind that needs to be understood. Although views differ with each school of thought, here are a few points to be considered.

1. Hypnosis can be effected without a trance state.

2. In hypnosis there is no flow of any type of magnetic "fluid" from the hypnotist to the subject.

3. Body contact or stroking is unnecessary to induce hypnosis.

4. Rapport between the hypnotist and the subject is not necessary. Hypnotism takes place all the time.

5. The subject induces it without any help from another person and can also give post-hypnotic suggestion to himself or herself.

6. No type of magic paraphernalia is necessary to induce a state of hypnosis. Loaded words or questions have a hypnotic effect, as do silent thoughts simply by their repetition.

7. Surprisingly, unwillingness of the subject is no obstacle. A sudden authoritarian approach can have a strong hypnotic effect. Many people are sleepwalkers – they let themselves lapse into a state of semi-trance and this is very conducive to hypnosis. Repetition is most effective during waking hours and before or just after going into a deep sleep. Almost anyone can be hypnotized by another person in this way.

8. Hypnosis cannot lead to a state of samādhī or higher consciousness, as the goal of yoga is Liberation, a state in which consciousness is free.

9. Hypnosis, although not a cure-all, can be a helpful tool under certain circumstances.

Self-hypnosis

Self-hypnosis cannot lead to Liberation, also, because of the absence of a high state of awareness. The old texts assure us that pure consciousness (puruṣa) is uncontaminated, which means it is unresponsive to stimuli. Talking to oneself aloud or mentally, which is habitual in many people, is also a form of autosuggestion or self-hypnosis. Even the very first series of exercises on the five senses will have proven the power of mental suggestion. For example, the smell of something particularly pleasant and appealing makes the mouth water. Or if you look at the back of your hand and imagine a mosquito biting you, if pursued long enough, this may bring about the typical reaction of itching and swelling as if a mosquito had really bitten.

The body, because of its own consciousness, puts ideas into the mind. When pain is experienced in some part of the body, a disorder is suggested. Yoga has made conscious use of this type of physical suggestion through the mudrās. Mahāmudrā, the largest and most powerful, uses the subtle suggestion of postures of the body as well as certain positions of the fingers. The meaning of the mudrā, position or gesture is a subtle influence, a constant reminder of yogic aspirations.

Life as a whole, with all its many influences from birth, may be seen as a flow of constant suggestion. Even the toilet training of a child is much more vigorous than that of a yogi or yoginī holding the thumb and forefinger together with the attached thought, "I want to unite myself with the Most High."

Certain colors are conceived of as being warm or cold. This is not a fact, but an association with the way in which they were at some time presented. The suggested meaning stays with us, which is another form of hypnosis. The way one's name is pronounced can signal a wide range of emotions from fear to enthusiastic anticipation. The natural environment – a gray sky, a rainy day, warm sunshine, glistening white snow, dry desert – all these stimulations create desires and have associations with their own hypnotic effect.

What we perceive through our eyes or ears is a particularly powerful suggestion, as is known in certain areas of business (radio, television, newspaper advertising). The power of suggestion can swing millions of people into a war or against a war, depending on the skill and manipulative ability of those who exercise it. This kind of exploitation by directing suggestions to others or to oneself can create karmic debts which have to be paid for at some time. All teachers have expressed the same warning that one has to account for everything that has been said or done. Anyone who gives a suggestion has to understand that some minds are weak, untrained or simply ignorant and therefore can be easily influenced by a stronger and more powerful mind.

Trance, which is a sort of sleep by suggestion, is a condition that is sought after by mediums so that other forces called entities can take over their physical apparatus to function for the required reasons. This, from a yogic point of view, is at variance with the pursuit of Liberation or Self-realization. The apparent lack of conscious awareness in the trance state is an inability to "recall." The conscious mind takes the liberty of selecting from presented material, but this selection is mostly done in a state of ignorance, without the wisdom and discrimination to make proper evaluations.

Predictions have been made ever since the emergence of the human race. How are they possible and why are they sometimes true and at other times not? The aspirant must realize that space and time are understood only in an oversimplified way. To determine if and when a prediction is fulfilled is difficult, because of our distorted sense of time and space.

Predictions are possible when the mind can hold a state of deep reflection for a long period of time. They take place on many levels and in various degrees. On a general basis, predictions can have a powerful suggestive influence bordering on hypnosis and can, therefore, create the fulfillment of the prediction. The teachers of old have all issued warnings against the attainment of power as a goal when the student is in the early stages of development and may not understand the possible disastrous mental and emotional repercussions from lack of foresight or an irresponsible attitude.

Many sincere seekers (swamis, rabbis, priests, etc.) can suddenly turn in the opposite direction from their spiritual goal because of great disappointment in unfulfilled hopes of spiritual power. They may vent their disappointment in cynical remarks, unjust attacks on others and sometimes even resort to dangerous manipulation of others to meet their own needs. The yogi or yoginī must be prepared for the tremendous fight the ego can put up through fear of being dethroned.

The major objective is to achieve control of all the lower forces. In one of the earlier exercises, the aspirant focuses the gaze on an object for three minutes. This may have shown that one may become drawn into the object; in the same way, staying with one particular idea, one becomes drawn into it.

Awareness, discrimination, freedom

Therefore, the most important powers for any aspirant on the spiritual path are awareness and discrimination: "What do I open myself to and why? Who and what is it that I invite (by my interest) into the house of my mind?" Discrimination is necessary to avoid the introduction of useless, even disastrous ideas. The aspirant again is referred to the practice of the Divine Light Invocation to keep the mind alert and aware. Where there is Light there cannot be darkness and the desires can be focused on the idea of growing into the Light. Or, the yogic method of relaxation may be practiced, which uses the voice as a guiding thread, but emphasizes over and over that with every inhalation awareness should be expanded. Whenever there is awareness, freedom of the mind is preserved.

Consciousness, subconsciousness and superconsciousness are the result of active prāṇa, and any manipulation of its working, on an ignorant level, can bring serious injury to the central nervous system. It is necessary for the aspirant to understand the awesome power of the mind. Sincerity by itself is not enough protection. The aspirant is expected to apply what has been learned.

The mind, which is the vehicle of the Self's expression, is as precious as the body. Care is exercised in any surgery on the body, but psychological scars bear evidence that much more care is necessary when dealing with the mind. Remember, the Power is neutral and it is the application that counts. Make haste slowly. Be courageous, but do not gamble. Yoga is a process of dehypnotizing by the constant invoking of awareness. To escape any power of suggestion means the achievement of an incredibly high level of awareness. Even great yogis can be caught in a moment of unawareness and suffer the consequences. Ambition that lacks dedication, commitment and devotion causes problems that can be avoided with prudence and awareness.

One possible problem may be misdirected enthusiasm and emotional involvement with the controlling forces of mediums. The records prove that these forces have little or no concern for the medium. Some profound and wise information may come through, but let us not forget that many people, before they die, have learned their creed, slokas, verses, proverbs, etc., by heart and this could be the source of such information. It is a good decision for the aspirant to make at this point, to be involved only with forces of the Most High origin and not become a victim of forceful energies that seek expression for their own glorification. What use would there be if it were not the Most High?

Psychic

Another word of caution is necessary at this point. Many psychic manifestations can be the creation of one's own mind, which are picked up by the psychic. True manifestations of psychic energy demand great control of mind in a relaxed state on the part of the psychic. The aim of yoga is to be always in control of the power of any kind of energy manifestation.

Spiritual

In contrast to the manifestation of psychic energy stands the spiritual experience that is of such magnitude that it indeed transforms the individual. No other event in human life has such an impact as a true spiritual experience. It creates a state of awareness in which many other happenings become insignificant, however much importance had been given to them at one time. These are the boons that the Devī has promised in her gesture Vara(da).

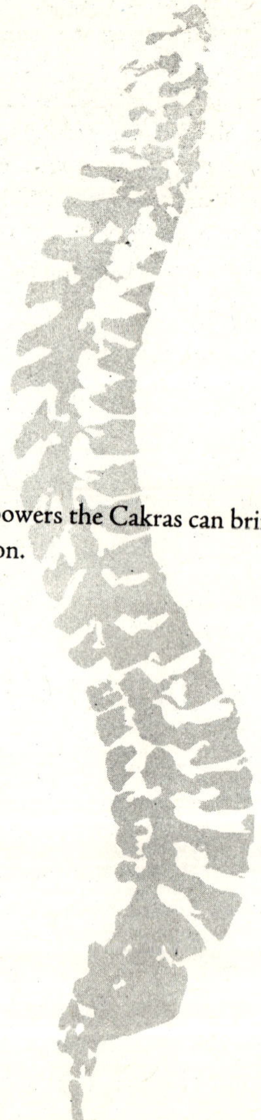

Awareness and discrimination are the greatest powers the Cakras can bring,
but they must be crowned with compassion.

10. POWERS OF THE CAKRAS

POWERS OF THE CAKRAS

Developing the Powers of the Cakras

It is a mistake to assume that Kuṇḍalinī power can be developed easily by one single activity or through one single sense. Although one sense can override the others, a balancing must be maintained. The interplay of forces from the other senses can influence one sense quite unexpectedly at any given moment.

All powers that are mentioned in the texts can be acquired, although it may take many years. Exertion can bring about a premature manifestation and with it the danger of being consumed by these powers. The need for great care is understandable if we remember how many an inventor has been injured in the process of discovery of such powers as X-ray or the various forms of electricity.

While each cakra promises the faithful and persistent aspirant certain powers, they must first be understood from one's present position. It must also be recognized that it is not possible to develop just one cakra, in the same way that one cannot develop just one of the five senses. The senses develop together; if one develops faster or at the cost of the others, the ensuing imbalance results in many problems.

Each of the cakras is in control of one of the senses, therefore each cakra is and should be affected by what is going on in the others. The powers already acquired must first be perfected and brought under control before others can be achieved. When the sattvic stage has been reached, the powers come by themselves, without any danger to the aspirant. This is the safest and most desirable way.

Attaining the powers of the Cakras is humanity's potential.

Mantra for the Mūlādhāra Cakra

In the Mūlādhāra of yours I worship Him who has nine natures, dancing the great Tāṇḍava, having nine sentiments, together with (His Śakti) Samaya, the quintessence of Lāsya. It is from these two, each having its own presiding form, looking in compassion on the disposition of the origination (of the world) that this world has come into existence, having you as father and mother.

Commentary:

His cosmic dance, the great Tāṇḍava.
Supreme Intelligence dances in the Self.
Śiva and Śakti dance together, delicately blended.
Rasa, the final awareness within.
The center of being is touched, free from competition.
The great Tāṇḍava, the dramatic, the cosmic activity, sometimes violent like a storm;
Lāsya, the luring, the sweet, a whisper;
move together in bliss, delight and timelessness,
in perfect rhythm.
Through this dance the world comes into being.

In the play of the Goddess (the Devī), whose substance is consciousness, the dual principle of Śiva/Śakti is presented as a male and female form, pointing to the polarity of the mind. Masculine and feminine principles are not narrowly limited, but are inseparable elements of energy giving birth to whirling worlds, from the tiny atom to millions of galaxies. Nothing fixed, nothing rigid. Richness in mystical variations expressing life itself.

The powers of mind and matter, creation and destruction, birth and death, are an interplay of forces embodied in the dance of Tāṇḍava-Lāsya. In birth death is hidden, as heat is hidden in fire. Illusion and desire dance together. Life is a cosmic wave; dazzling creation. All forms come into existence upon the manifestation of consciousness.

Powers of the Mūlādhāra Cakra

Power of speech

In this cakra, we are dealing with the powerful effect of verbal and mental speech and its results on the individual mind. Self-suggestion and self-programming must be recognized to counteract their negative influence. The First Cakra is pure energy. It is the beginning of speech, which means formulating what the childlike mind understands. And as the childlike mind goes through a process of maturing, not only through each cakra, but through all the cakras at various times, it is possible to see how the power of a later cakra to create and destroy worlds is already present. We have seen that each world has its own realities, but it is now increasingly important to understand what is meant by this and how this Kuṇḍalinī power can suddenly leap into another dimension before control has been achieved.

Learning is a process that goes step by step. The most intelligent level of learning is achieved when the awareness is greatest, when pride is under control, and when we can learn from our mistakes of the past, as well as from the mistakes of others, without having to repeat them. Sometimes we catch ourselves when we are just about to make a mistake, and often the awareness is there, but pride refuses to admit that the decision or action is faulty.

Eternal knowledge

It is stated in the texts that knowledge is eternal. This also needs to be understood at a deeper level. In all ages there have lived some men and women of high intelligence and great awareness. They were able to tap the source of knowledge in themselves and by way of intuition understand the meaning of that knowledge, which they put into the language of their own time for the benefit of others. Eternal Knowledge is therefore omnipotent.

One of the promised powers of the First Cakra is Eternal Knowledge. This all-powerful knowledge is of a different type from knowledge as we have discussed it so far, and an unusually high degree of intuitive perception is necessary to understand such messages.

People all over the world have the feeling that there is a Power greater than themselves. The Power is often personified but, when understood properly, the personification only applies to the vessel or the instrument through which that Power and all-powerful knowledge emanate.

Freedom from sin

Freedom from all sin is achieved at the first stage by recognizing mistakes, by controlling impulses, by learning through reflection, and by making the simultaneous connection between learning and knowledge. Sin, from a yogic point of view, is the intentional repetition of mistakes that are well-known. Mistakes that come through the process of learning are not sin. Human beings can only learn by trial and error. So again it falls to the aspirant to develop a high level of awareness and discrimination. It is within our own power to become free of sin.

Greed and ambition can deprive the mind of its wonderful potential for creativity and quality in all aspects of living. Quality in living is the first step to bliss. The joy of life is our inherited right. To be always living in the spirit of gladness comes when we are free of selfishness and all that it entails. This process of self-mastery is indeed an experience of bliss that comes once the early stages of learning are past.

Mantra for the Svādhiṣṭhāna Cakra

In the Svādhiṣṭhāna of yours I praise Him as Saṃvarta forever happy in the form of fire, O mother and also Samaya, the great one. When His glance filled with great anger consumes the worlds, it is Her glance dripping with compassion that makes this cool (soothing) service.

Commentary:

Śiva/Śakti: I am the glow of the fire,
the birth of all things,
all-consuming death,
memory and wisdom,
grace and firmness,
speed and patience,
silence and sound.

The Divine appears terrible only when the dark cloud of ignorance screens the seeker from consciousness. Like a child, the ignorant seeker is attracted to the toys (gadgets, money, success) of the world. In its consuming anger Śiva's powerful glance indicates that ignorance is to be burned in the fire of wisdom. It is Divine Mother's compassion that allows the truant to return and try again. This is Her most soothing service. The old ego, in spite of its struggles, has to die. The dark cloud of self-will has to be dispersed so that the Light will no longer be obscured.

Powers of the Svādhiṣṭhāna Cakra

Ability of well-reasoned discourse, prose or verse

The ability of well-reasoned discourse or the writing of prose or verse leads to the power of imagination, which can be the basis of beautiful and inspiring words or of monster and horror stories. Writers of horror stories have often lost their minds because they did not know how to control their self-created world. The Power is neutral and it is the responsibility of the individual how to use the imagination.

It is not possible to fully separate the powers of one cakra from another. Imagination and emotions work hand in hand, creating desires that can make almost everything possible. The image that emerges from the Second Cakra can move with lightning speed to the Third Cakra and can become a victim of the emotional impact made there. The creation of the imagination is reinforced by the emotions. Most of our fears are caused by uncultivated imagination based on ignorance. Only increased awareness can remove ignorance.

Freedom from enemies

The scriptural texts also say that we will be free from all enemies. It would be a mistake to personalize this and see them in the setting of the family or work situations. Rather, it is the enemies we have within ourselves, the evil inclinations driven by exerted self-will that kindle self-importance and self-absorption. Self-control is the first step, in conjunction with obedience to one's choice of the path, toward the attainment of mastery. The control of those enemies, or their destruction, will make the aspirant a sovereign among yogis and yoginīs.

When one is free of all enemies and the mind dwells more steadily on the beauty of the Most High, the most ideal, that which one would like to cultivate in oneself, speech expands and another level of poetry is reached. The highest level is perhaps the poet who is also a prophet.

Mantra for the Maṇipūra Cakra

In the Maṇipūra of yours I serve Him as a dark cloud, which is the only refuge (of the world) raining down the rain on the three worlds scorched by the sun that is Hara. (This cloud which) carries the rainbow, Indra's bow, bedecked with ornaments of various glittering jewels, and which has flashes of lightnings due to His Śakti bursting forth from the enveloping darkness (of the cloud).

Commentary:

The rainbow has no substance, it is intangible and cannot be grasped.
The rainbow is an optical illusion which becomes perceptible to the sense of sight under certain conditions.
Sometimes the mind builds a rainbow to another dimension.
Sometimes flashes of lightning (insights) glitter with jewels of intuition.
Who can gaze at the sun when it is at the zenith?
The light, too great, too blinding, will scorch the mind.
The dark cloud offers much-needed rest, time to gather new strength.

Powers of the Maṇipūra Cakra

Power to create and destroy worlds

The power to create and destroy worlds is signified in the power of speech. How ideas are expressed, the intonation of the voice, can create an environment of blissful happiness. Self-gratification and self-glorification, with their resultant impatience, greed or pride, can destroy a harmonious relationship.

Wealth of Knowledge

The practice of awareness by itself creates a great wealth of Knowledge. In contrast to the Eternal Knowledge of the First Cakra, knowledge is now beginning to have meaning on the personal level. This is the knowledge and discrimination applied to daily events as they happen.

Appreciation of the harmonious aspects of life is personified in Sarasvatī, the goddess of speech, of art, of music. When we can speak words of inspiration that touch an inner chord in another person, we can say that this is the worship of the Goddess Sarasvatī. We thereby have created our own world of harmony in which we function.

A saintly person, by simply entering the room, can bring a sense of quiet and stillness into a tumultuous group, opening the senses of those present to higher perceptions. It is on a much higher level, and through much more training, that the worlds created by the mind can be put into words and this inner knowing of the heart can be expressed.

We have many spiritual tools that would enable us to help ourselves to a higher state of consciousness, but we allow these tools to be forgotten, the practices to become routine, and thereby never attain to those other worlds of power. The spiritual practices are too precious to be degraded to a level of routine, and in the performing of the exercises it is important to guard against mechanicalness if we wish to increase consciousness and attain any degree of realization.

Mantra for the Anāhata Cakra

I venerate (revere, render devotional service) this pair of swans which swim in the mind of the great, feeding on the unique honey of the Lotus (heart) that is the opening of understanding. From their chatter comes the development of the eighteen kinds of knowledge, and by using them one acquires all qualities out of defects, just like taking the milk from water.

Commentary:

Devotion is the antidote to all self-glorification. The devotional approach includes reverence, as well as the knowing and recognizing of the Greater Power.
Being devoted to Śiva/Śakti, symbolized as a pair of swans in the lake of the mind, the mind becomes saturated with the milk of Divine wisdom.
Through devotion the devotee opens up like the Lotus in the light of the sun.
Thereby one becomes receptive to Divine knowledge, manifest in many ways.
By application of this knowledge to living one is like a bee collecting honey from the flower.
One emulates the swan learning to take the Divine milk from the water of illusion.

Powers of the Anāhata Cakra

The Cosmic Auṃ

Anāhata implies the sound of Śabdabrahman. The Anāhata Cakra promises the hearing with the inner ear of the cosmic Auṃ. This cosmic sound is the sound that can be heard without the striking of two objects together. It can be heard only if listening has been practiced and if all the internal noises of the mind can be stopped.

The text tells us that Divine Mother Śakti dispels all fears and grants boons of the three worlds: past, present, future. If the aspirant has learned from past mistakes, the increased understanding and discrimination will mean there will be fewer mistakes in the present. The characteristics of sincerity and devotion, humility and honesty, which the aspirant will now possess from the past and the present, will somewhat determine the future, a future of harmony and happiness.

Protect and destroy the three worlds

The aspirant will be able to protect this newly created environment and destroy those negative aspects that may still remain from the past. The application of what has been learned in all situations increases awareness, which takes on the soft, gentle glow of a first glimpse of what illumination could be.

By living wisely, doing noble deeds, keeping the senses under control, and having an extraordinary ability and power of concentration, the devotee or aspirant is able to render himself invisible and to enter another's body. Both of these promises need further elaboration. If I eliminate all my self-will and remove all self-protective screens, I can put myself in another's shoes and, while not identifying with the other person, I can have an understanding of that person.

Entering another's body

If we consider an actual physical body, then very highly developed practices are necessary in order to put on, like a garment, the discarded body of another person. Ernest Wood, in his book *Practical Yoga: Ancient and Modern*, gives a description of meeting an old yogi who, because his body had grown old and he felt that the work of his life was not finished, entered the body of a youth who had just died.

Invisibility

To render oneself invisible, it is first necessary to overcome the desire to be in the center of a group or to be the focus of the attention of another person. The desire for closeness to another and all the emotional needs that go with it have to be overcome first. Another person's preoccupation can create our invisibility.

Today there are people who use the energy field around a human body to detect disturbances and to analyze and pinpoint defective organs that are not visible to the eye. Those energy fields can be charged. The power of concentration of one's own mind allows for the renunciation of the desire to be seen or noticed. The energy field around the body can keep the mind of a passerby suspended and make one invisible at that moment. No image of oneself is leaving the orbit of one's own energy field.

The practice of the Divine Light Invocation is one of those exercises that will aid in reaching a different type of visibility. It can increase one's energy field by one's own efforts. If one's brain matter is lit up properly, one can be invisible and one can also project an image of oneself to some distance. That happens naturally with practice of the Divine Light Invocation and takes place on its own account, without any frightening experiences.

Persistent study and the practice of awareness and discrimination will aid in acquiring these powers, but the aspirant should be warned that the results may come after many years, even lifetimes.

Mantra for the Viśuddha Cakra

In your Viśuddhi I serve Śiva, the progenitor of the sky, transparent like a pure crystal, and also the Devī who is like Śiva and attached to Him. It is through their beauty and graceful movements, shimmering like the rays of the moon, the world shines, its internal darkness having been dispelled, like the Cakọra. (The world is feminine.)

Commentary:

Selfless service makes one Divine.
To be a servant demands that one renounce self-will and thus become pure and transparent like the blue sky so the Divine may shine through.
As the color that gives form to the crystal cannot be separated from it, so Śiva and the Devī are joined together.
The graceful movements of their cosmic dance are only perceptible in those mystical moments when the ethereal inspirations are perceived like the shimmering rays of the moon, in that act of complete surrender.
The Cakora bird subsists on the moonbeams.
Just as it rejoices by drinking the rays of the moon, so also the sādhaka drinks the Brahmic bliss by meditating on Śiva and Devī.
The sādhaka's ignorance is thus dispelled.

Powers of the Viśuddha Cakra

Freedom from worldly desires

This cakra promises that one becomes free of worldly desires. At this stage of one's life, they have served their purpose. The desires have created ambition, perfection, skills, efficiency and helped one to see and develop strengths. The energy that is no longer locked up in

The Gateway of Liberation

the pursuit of worldly desires raises the aspirant now to a higher plane, to the Gateway of Liberation. But at the Gateway of Liberation, self-will must be surrendered to the Higher Self, no longer to the ego-mind.

Complete Knowledge is obtained

All that has been learned to this point contributes to the aspirant's wealth of yoga. In the First Cakra, Eternal Knowledge has been promised and in the Third, wealth of Knowledge may be acquired. Now in the Fifth Cakra, the subjective and the objective are united in the Complete Knowledge and the aspirant comes closer to the meaning of yoga, the union.

Knowledge of the past, present and future

At a later stage of development, the Complete Knowledge is all powers that can be known, or even those that are unknown except to highly developed yogis and yoginis. Complete Knowledge can only be achieved by increased concentration. The key to all powers is control of the mind. Understanding this on a deeper than intellectual level brings peace of mind that enables one to see the three worlds, the past, the present and the future, as already discussed in the Fourth Cakra. One can with greater clarity look back, see the present and anticipate the future; see what one must avoid doing, what one has to do, and perhaps what one should expand to do.

Destruction of dangers

The first step in destroying danger is taken by careful thinking, the removal of all false ambition, and no longer rushing emotionally into decisions. Simply by increased awareness, greater discrimination, and more care in all actions and reactions, no longer mechanically responding to events, we understand how danger can be destroyed. This awareness creates an attitude of heart and mind that will make one merciful to all. We begin to understand that we are all a product of our environment and the victim of our own ignorance. When ignorance is removed much danger is removed. But to become more knowing takes courage as well as a willingness to accept greater responsibility.

Mantra for the Ājñā Cakra

I venerate Him who is residing in the Ājñā Cakra of yours. I worship (revere) the highest Śambhu in your Ājñā Cakra, flanked by the highest intelligence (She), Him who has the splendor of millions of suns and moons. He who worships by propitiating with devotion will reside in the world of the Light of all lights, which is in the world, which no Earthly glance can reach and is far removed from the glance of ordinary mortals. There neither sun nor moon shines, neither fire nor the other heavenly bodies.

Commentary:

When mind looks at the Supreme Intelligence it stands in awe of its splendor and its power.
The comparison of millions of suns and moons is insufficient to describe their brilliance.
Even the galaxies of stars and suns and moons can only reflect the Light that comes from the source of all light.
The Power that has created the eye can see.
The Power that created the mind is beyond mind.
Śiva/Śakti is neither male nor female (nor neuter) but existence, consciousness, bliss – Sat-cit-ānanda.

Powers of the Ājñā Cakra

Creator, preserver, destroyer of the three worlds

At this point, the aspirant understands how one has created one's own life, all of one's pains, problems and difficulties, as a process of learning. That which has been gained needs to be preserved, and what is no longer necessary must be destroyed. In order to fulfill the Divine union, even this perfect state in which one finds oneself, with the wisdom, the excellent powers, the pure intellect – even this state has to go as well, before the last and final plunge can be taken. Some yogis have told me that when this final decision is taken, the body drops off in between nine and twenty-one days. The yogi usually chooses the time of death and the method.

Leave the body at will

Proper identity is achieved by indeed knowing that one is created by Divine Light, or by the Cosmic Intelligence, the Absolute or God, whatever word is most desirable.

Identification with the Supreme

Nothing specific can be said of the "excellent unknown powers," but the indication I can give is that there is the knowing of more than three dimensions or even four, a conception that can only be described in nebulous terms, because language has not expanded far enough for a more precise description.

Excellent unknown powers

Pure intellect means intellect free of selfish desires. The Śakti aspect of intellect creates. All the world is Mother Śakti's creation.

Pure intellect

We have been talking throughout these pages about the necessity for balance. Here is, perhaps, the most crucial point where balance is needed. If the foundation has been carefully laid and all the practice done, the aspirant will have control over the powers and not be consumed by them. There will be the Divine union of the individual Self, or the individual intelligence, with the Supreme Cosmic Intelligence, by becoming half and half, male and female, intellect and intuition.

Divine union

Powers of the Cakras

Contact with a guru is necessary to perform and persevere in all the exercises and practices that will bring about the true realization of the powers mentioned in the text. No exercise must be excluded. It is necessary to go through the whole process. Advanced exercises for the attainment of the powers of the cakras can only be given after the foundation has been laid and through personal instruction.

The practice of yoga means to transform ourselves from sleepwalkers into people who are wide awake and responsive to the needs of others. Without compassion, all the powers and the techniques mean nothing. One could become more self-centered, almost narcissistic, which is not the aim of yoga. We cannot realize Oneness if we isolate ourselves from others.

The desire to grow is like a beautiful flower. It must root in the world and it must grow, piercing through the surface of the earth and unfolding into the Light. We do not think that roots are bad – without them, the flower could never be. Discrimination and a greater understanding grow from the limited concepts we have held.

The discovery of so many negative aspects in ourselves and the limitations should not be seen as something evil. They are part of the perfection of Life, one half of the unit. Without knowing the darkness of night, the light of day is not enjoyed. Even illness is perfect when the individual needs to develop a sense of gratitude for health. By being cut off from the "busy-ness" of the pursuit of life, the individual is forced to think, to realize the balance of life.

Although healing is possible even over long distance, we must ask if the reason we wish to heal is for our own ambition. The plight of another person is your opportunity to develop compassion to an almost Divine degree. Compassion can be seen in three stages: at first, it is expressed only to friends and loved ones; then you are moved by the suffering of an unknown but worthy individual whose plight is brought to your attention; finally, when your concern can extend to include the violent, the drunken, the downtrodden, your compassion approaches the Divine.

You will reach a point when you will even be grateful for those who criticize you and make you feel miserable. You must not waver, even when it seems that the rug is pulled from under your feet. Liberation is always worth the price, whatever it may be.

Temptations continue to come even in the life of the greatest yogi, or most saintly person. The temptations just become more subtle. Therefore, put your guru – a priest, a minister, or whoever you choose – into the Light too.

Criticism by followers can undermine the guru. Too much adoration will do the same, but only to a guru who still has much ego left, who does not have sufficient discrimination, perhaps not even the intellectual understanding of what it means to be a guru. The guru can make a mistake but, like a good parent, without intent.

Do not undermine other seekers who, in your opinion, are following the wrong path. Put them into the Light. Let the Light take care of it. How can we know what is in the Divine plan?

Awareness and discrimination are the greatest powers that the cakras can bring, but they must be crowned with compassion.

"The Divine in me salutes and recognizes the Divine in you" – this is the attitude of the Higher Self, of which the ego has no part.

Am I willing to travel uncharted seas of the mind?

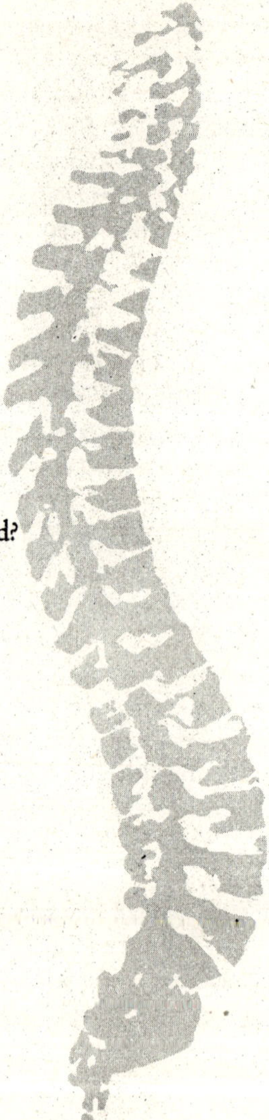

11. BRAINSTORMING

MIND, CONSCIOUSNESS, ENERGY

BRAINSTORMING: MIND, CONSCIOUSNESS, ENERGY

Enormous power is required to lift heavy material beyond the gravitational field of the Earth. Consider also that it takes a substantial increase of power for the ordinary mind to lift itself through the accepted barriers. The exploration of mind and consciousness needs to be carried out by all who wish to go beyond those barriers. This must include all segments of human society, as then only will a wide range of mental powers surface. It would be wise to discard all racial prejudices and see people in terms of "time-space-circumstances." The cultural conditions of each social group determines the life of its people, whose minds develop differently and achieve varying potentials. This can be recognized from the accounts of Kuṇḍalinī and its powers written by people of different cultural backgrounds.

The practice of brainstorming applied to investigating mind and consciousness would help to overcome the power of preconceived ideas that sets firm limitations and thereby undercuts true research. Many questions have to be asked of oneself in this exploration. "Can I bring myself to keep all judgment suspended? Am I willing to travel uncharted seas of the mind? How will I deal with my anxieties? If, for the moment, I anticipate that some 'phenomena' have a basis of reality, how much will it alter my mental perception, interfere with my mental and emotional security? How will I have to change my familiar and comfortable picture of the world?"

Consider first being able to move objects by thought only. Or, what would it do to your ideas of your world if you could watch the seed of a violet, resting in the palm of your hand, grow and flower in ten minutes? Did the walls of Jericho fall because somebody knew which key to blow on the trumpets? Were the massive granite blocks of the pyramids moved by sound? Have you spent "your time off the Earth" in space, and by what decision did you return, for what reasons?

We must not hesitate to do this kind of brainstorming if we wish to expand our understanding of mind and consciousness. These are only a few of the many questions that must be asked. Once again, the need for mental and emotional discipline becomes evident. Fears and anxieties that are the result of lack of discipline must be dealt with. However, those that come from other unknown sources should be seen as a protection in disguise as they prevent premature exploration. The aspirant should not force the mind for any reason, because an overload may cause a breakdown.

Aspirants who are well-grounded in themselves, enriched by the innumerable experiences that have resulted from their practice, have had their minds stretched sufficiently to handle non-ordinary experiences. Similarly, newly invented machines are first big and cumbersome, but they finally become miniaturized as technical and psychological obstacles are overcome. What at first may seem difficult becomes more acceptable as limitations diminish.

Mind is different from consciousness. In small children, clairvoyance or clairaudience is often observable, although such a child is not conscious of it nor aware that there are children who do not share the same capacity. Consciousness is a manifestation of prāṇa (energy). How prāṇic energy produces consciousness is not known. There are no hints in the ancient texts because the most profound knowledge was only handed down in a very direct, personal manner from guru to disciple. If gurus are still alive who have that knowledge, it will be difficult to find them, more difficult to obtain that knowledge. The reason is obvious – abuse of power. Even Ramakrishna told Vivekananda, after giving him an out-of-body experience, that he had been shown but now would have to do it by himself.

The study of Kuṇḍalinī indicates that higher states of consciousness apply to dimensions beyond the first three. It is difficult for the mind to imagine what a fourth, fifth, sixth, seventh, or maybe even an eighth dimension, or the state of consciousness known as samādhī, could mean. There is no text translated into English that really clarifies what samādhī is, or that sufficiently explains the difference of the six stages called samādhī. Maybe the true meaning of samādhī has not been handed down because of loss of that knowledge. It stands to reason that the sixth stage of samādhī is really nothing more than the first glimpse of the fourth dimension, simply because humans, with the possible exception of mathematicians and physicists, cannot conceive of other dimensions.

The statement that everything is created in the mind can be seen in psychological terms and from a viewpoint of imagination. Although there is no text available that would state that there is anything in existence that is not created by human intelligence, it is important to consider to what degree that all-embracing phrase "everything is the mind" can really be useful. Yet, Patañjali, in

Sūtras III-27, 28 and 29, respectively, said that we can have knowledge from the sun, the moon and the pole star. The implication is that those heavenly bodies have not been created by the ordinary human mind.

Consciousness that operates on a fifth or eighth dimension cannot be anticipated on the third. Even if it could be vaguely understood, language has limitations and anything beyond the third dimension can only be expressed with great difficulty. It is a well-known fact that all realized persons have kept silent about these dimensions because there are no words with which to communicate. What has been created outside human consciousness by other intelligent forces is a question that at the moment no one can answer. It is my understanding that all definitions of samādhī exclude this point.

We have said previously that the Power that created the eye can see and the Power that created the ear can hear. If this Power is not in need of a physical eye to be able to see, or a physical ear to hear, it is reasonable to assume that this Power or Energy would not need a vehicle as human beings do at the present stage of evolution.

We must take our hypothesis a step further. If consciousness is energy and energy is indestructible, what happens to that vortex of energy-consciousness when its vehicle of expression, the body, is gone? Will we have bodiless consciousness? What can those forces do? Will they affect anyone? If so, in what way? What happens to those forces and where do they "reside"? What power can such bodiless consciousness exercise? Is that power inexhaustible? Does it generate itself by itself, or through something else? If we assume that there are bodiless mind-consciousnesses (forces) and if the energy of these forces is limited, where and how might such regeneration take place? Could these bodiless consciousnesses be termed "extraterrestrial" consciousness, being outside the orbit of the Earth? Can they influence those forces that are still in a body, or use a body as a vehicle, and therefore also use emotional energy? Can the human mind and its emotional energy become the fuel or recharger of the bodiless consciousness?

These thoughts are not as outrageous as they will first appear. Physically, humans feed on the vegetable and animal kingdoms. Emotionally and mentally, people feed on each other. There is no reason to assume that there is not something that would feed on us.

People may have wondered thousands of years ago if there was life on other planets and what form that life would have. How else would Patañjali have made the statements referred to above? Astronomers today speculate about the same question. Perhaps we can consider that such a bodiless consciousness finds a place of rest or further learning, or just waits to take on a body once again to keep the process of birth and death going. Such bodiless consciousness is difficult to imagine and perhaps the ideas of angels, spirits and great masters have been needed to indicate the existence of intelligence that is able to communicate, but by different means from what is possible in a three-dimensional world.

The power of belief of millions of people can itself become a vortex of energy. Consider a great being, that for simple communication we will call "Umā." Let us assume that at one time Umā was intended to be a great savior or liberator for mankind. If 500 million people believed in the power of Umā, as 500 million Catholics believe in Jesus, we must accept that we are dealing with an enormous power of those millions of minds.

All illustrations are insufficient to explain something that is beyond sense perception, but this power will be more easily understood by thinking of the incredibly active force that is generated in all mass hypnosis, where the individuality of consciousness is lost and becomes part of the mass. If this can happen on the physical level, there is no reason to think that it cannot happen on other levels also.

The aspirant should now read the two excerpts at the end of the Further Thoughts chapter, pp. 332–33, about the young gods from mid-heaven and the descent of the soul. How are we to understand the workings of the power of the mind when we are told that Brahmā created His first four "mind-born" sons? Is this connected with the young gods from mid-heaven? Is it possible that the mind at one point could reproduce itself and, after losing that power, had to resort to the method of reproduction now known? By the power of imagination, a woman who intensely desires to have a child can produce every symptom of pregnancy except the child.

Can this be taken a step further? What is behind the saying, "Ye are gods"? It might indeed be that the accumulation of intelligences makes a demand of enlarging consciousness and that this evolution of humankind is still going on. Perhaps this process was somewhat immature when curiosity brought these young gods down to Earth. Their bodies are described as being ethereal, which means of such fine stuff that it is invisible to sight. Obviously these young gods who stayed around on the Earth for too long lost some of that quality. We are told that their bodies hardened. We must conclude, therefore, that living on Earth would depend on the use of a body, while a center of consciousness that is unencumbered by the heaviness of the body might be able to spend some time on other stars or planets for development, or for the purpose of increasing energy from those who do not care to have it.

Energy is available for anyone who wants to make use of it. Pursuing higher consciousness, or increasing our level of consciousness, is like going after the yellow or black gold that is buried in the bowels of the earth. In either case, only those who are willing to put in the effort will achieve results. In the same way that the explorer for gold makes use of the intelligence of others, so we can also attract the intelligence of others for nonordinary ends.

What we have been talking about is energy. God is a personified idea of Energy – Cosmic Energy, Cosmic Intelligence, the Absolute. Unless you have gone through the kind of mental acrobatics that I have just presented, the words "Cosmic Intelligence" have little meaning. To overcome the personified idea of God is only possible through gradual development of individual consciousness.

The belief held for centuries that only by suffering and poverty can a person become a saint is not valid and has been rejected by the intellectual and the scientist. But the arrogance and pride in the intellect must also be rejected because they block the road to higher consciousness. The saint is, in fact, a different type of genius and it is in the acceleration in the growth of intelligence and awareness, by cooperation with the process of evolution, that the future of the human being lies. The evolution of human intelligence is therefore not only inevitable, but is the thrust of each being endowed with consciousness.

The evolution of intelligence has been the destiny of all human beings ever since their appearance on the Earth. Each life experience is part of that evolution – the more intense, the more dramatic, the greater the lesson. One not learned will be repeated. Some lessons are learned by being taught by another person, or by reading and studying. Some knowledge is transmitted from mind to mind (guru to disciple), but there is also evidence that transmissions are possible through a massive group of minds that may or may not be embodied. Transmission of knowledge also takes place by radiating from a source of knowledge as yet unknown.

The mind's most intriguing quality is intelligence, at present mainly used for scientific discoveries and inventions. There are still undiscovered possibilities of the functioning of the brain, which was created for the evolution of consciousness and as a receptacle for radiation of knowledge from other dimensions.

Maybe now you will look for your guru!

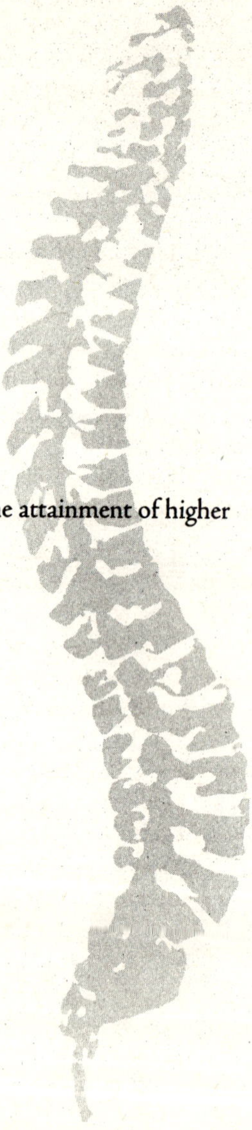

The course of evolution, the purpose of life, is the attainment of higher consciousness.

12. FURTHER THOUGHTS

FURTHER THOUGHTS

Different Paths for the Aspirant

The purpose of this book is to provide tools for the development of greater potential to those who wish to give the time and effort to discover the latent power inherent within them and who are willing to cooperate with the law of evolution as it pertains to each aspirant. In writing, I have tried to steer a middle course for the aspirant who is a householder or a career person: those individuals who want to pursue higher values in life without abandoning the pursuit of worldly interests. This path is different from that of the renunciate, who gives up many worldly activities and interests in order to devote more time and energy to the goal of Liberation.

The word "renunciate" has a wide range of meaning in different religions and perhaps can be understood in part through the example of marriage, where each partner has to renounce some desires, will and freedom of choice in consideration for the other. When lived in the strictest sense, renunciates depend totally on every life situation for the fulfillment of their human needs, believing that the Power that created the human being in the first place is capable of looking after them. This statement has little meaning unless it has been experienced. The experience of renunciation clarifies many of one's own personality aspects that would be difficult, if not impossible, to know in any other way. The degree of renunciation, the desire and stamina to experience it, is a decision that must rest with the individual.

Another aspect in the life of the yogic aspirant that is frequently misunderstood is brahmacaryā or celibacy. The vow of celibacy is not given because of a religious belief or vocation, but is an accepted choice enabling the aspirant to more quickly ascend the spiral of evolution through conscious cooperation. Another popular misconception concerns the life of the ascetic. It does not mean starvation or self-torture. The true ascetic is a person who is living a self-controlled and ordered life with the purpose of directing maximum energies into the search for Liberation.

The Power of Speech

Throughout the book, there has been a major emphasis upon the power of speech and its development. Many scriptural texts contain commands or utterances that show a common recognition of the power of the Word. For example, Jesus in Matthew XII: 36, 37, says: "But I say unto you, that every idle word that men shall speak, they shall give account thereof in the day of judgment. For by thy words thou shalt be justified, and by thy words thou shalt be condemned." This quotation refers to cause and effect as it is expressed in the idea of karma. It points to scrutiny of all actions, including speech, and implies a depth of responsibility that we rarely consider. Similarly, the concept of ahiṃsā, or non-injury, means that all actions, speech and deeds have to be performed without injury to anyone else or to oneself. That is a simple expression of a complex formula and therefore needs to be pursued in depth.

In the ancient texts, the power of speech is spoken of as the Devī or Goddess of Speech. Some texts speak of the Devī in the Mūlādhāra Cakra and later change to the Lord of Speech. In this book, the term "Devī" of Speech has been used consistently because speech is an expression of creation that has a female or mother aspect. It also means power of speech, persuasion, hypnosis or luring by song.

When the meaning of the power of speech is comprehended, then the importance of "key sentences" in the mind can be understood and used to effect changes. The key sentence is a short command phrase that is used, most of the time without awareness, in a repetitive way: "I can't do this" or "I have never done such a thing" – thereby undermining willingness to try (and avoiding success). Key sentences can be counteracted in a positive manner. There is room for a great deal of experimentation by the individual aspirant. Key sentences have to be short to be effective. Their formulation should be clear and positive, and can be compared to autosuggestion.

Mantra

The practice of Mantra Yoga will increase the individual's sensitivity to the vibrations. The mind uses both sound and vibration as a focal point for concentration in order to achieve a state that leads to meditation and beyond.

As sound can stir water in a glass, so the vibrations of the mantra stir the subconscious.

Emotions can only be controlled; they are not meant to be overcome. They serve a definite purpose in our lives, but to control one's emotions is far easier said than done. The chanting of mantras is a means of expressing any kind of emotion, from the most ugly to the most exalted. In chanting out these feelings, we learn to accept both parts of ourselves; we do not hide behind the illusion that we are only good, or pure, or ugly. We are attempting to transcend the pairs of opposites, which we must do if we are to be free.

Repetition of a mantra gradually awakens the higher faculties in us. This repetition may be carried on by verbal, whispered or mental recitation. The mental repetition can be alternated with voiced repetition to help keep the mind from wandering.

Extended mantra chanting brings the aspirant in touch with the Self and brings release from emotional imbalance. We can bring ourselves into harmony within our own being. But, although all this is true, none of the above-mentioned benefits will come unless the efforts are completely serious. The chanting of mantra for hours a day or even one or two hours a day is not easily done by the Westerner who has been entertained by external input since infancy. It can seem boring, dull, pointless. But with perseverance it can prove to be of profound benefit for those who take the time to do it.

A Further Note on Sex and Celibacy

In order to further understand why some aspirants renounce sex, it is necessary to expand our understanding of "feeding." All forms of life must feed upon other life in some way. The human body feeds on the various kingdoms of nature: vegetable, mineral and animal. But the emotions also feed on the needs, minds and imaginations of other people as well as on our own. Think about the effects of all those activities, particularly as they relate to sex. When this has been done, celibacy can be more easily understood as a free choice of action occurring at a certain stage of development of the human being. A generally accepted scheme of evolution is seen by the yogi as: mineral-human, vegetable-human, animal-human, human-human or being truly human, and god-human or the perfectly liberated.

Celibacy can invoke hallucination and some of the stories of the gods and goddesses are certainly the result of that. A study of mythology can be a source for research in this area. It must, however, be considered that the human mind cannot think of anything that is nonexistent. Celibacy, examined from the view of mind over matter, can lead to some useful speculations. These may at some time take a different turn, toward space travel or the planned occupation of planets. It is clear not only to the scientist, but also to the average intelligent thinker, that there cannot be life on other planets as it is known here on Earth. But fertility of the mind will, when needed and when the time comes, give birth to manifestations presently not considered.

Mind and Consciousness

While assumptions can be useful, in the case of learning about the mind and consciousness they can be disastrous. It is safer to assume that consciousness is energy and that the process of its manifestation is not known yet. Mind can then be seen as a screen on which the pictures emerge. Consciousness is omnipresent. Mind and matter are interrelated by the one unifying force of consciousness making all knowledge possible.

The course of evolution, the purpose of life, is the attainment of higher consciousness. Liberation from ignorance leads to higher consciousness, which is knowledge by personal experience. The future of humanity depends on that knowledge and its application.

Worship

For many people in the West, worship is not understood and they may think that it does not play a part in their lives. However, it might be helpful to remember that the first rock group, the Beatles, was such a hit that *Life* magazine showed a picture of people scraping up the earth and saying: "The Beatles walked here," as if these young musicians were Jesus Christ Himself. In such circumstances, worship springs from a deep desire that needs to be fulfilled and will find its outlet in these ways if traditional worship has not been developed or has been undermined.

Anyone who can claim exclusiveness in knowledge or position of power has the adoration of those who are impressed. This also applies to a person of a different race, and many of the pseudo-gurus of the present time are successful simply because of their outer attire, which agrees with the imagination of the ignorant. Worship when positive is a very helpful factor, contributing to personal development. However, discrimination must be applied.

In one's personal worship, a spiritual image may be created and visualized by the power of imagination. This imagery serves a certain purpose only. It is an appearance. The practice of the Divine Light Invocation will make it transitory. Intuitive perception will take proper care of the transition. The image is therefore a provisional concept of three levels of power: self-mastery; concentration-contemplation; and pure consciousness. Meditation on Light is one of the most subtle ways to start. It sets some seekers free from religious aspects that may be undesirable. At the same time, substitutions of various gods and goddesses is avoided, once the practice of concentration has been mastered.

Worship is a process of self-awareness and the seat of what is reflected is somewhere else. It cannot be touched or taken away. Like the fragrance of a flower traveling on the airwaves, it cannot be picked up and placed elsewhere. It is intangible and yet it has a reality of its own. It has a presence.

Secret Powers of the Mind

The aspirant who looks for clearcut answers must realize that the achievement of certain mental powers is kept secret. Government's power is dependent on the support of the masses who have little understanding. History has shown that when there is fear of someone rebelling against the system in which the majority feels secure, harassment or even imprisonment is the result. Jesus was such a rebel of His time and paid dearly for it. However, the observations of great yogis can be pursued by deep thought.

One such tightly kept secret is mystical Haṭha Yoga as symbolized in the upside-down tree. It is up to the individual to practice the āsanas to the point where that secret can be unlocked. However, it is my understanding that without some study of scriptural texts and mythology, such secrets will yield little gain.

Another exercise – filling the spine with Light – is much more than a concentration exercise. It involves a change of the atomic structure of the brain, eliminates unnecessary fear, and thereby prepares the student for experiences that are beyond the ordinary. Therefore, it is not possible to give instructions for advanced levels.

Another secret power is withdrawing the life force. I have met the son of a yogi who, although he was at first angry and disappointed that his father had deserted the family for the yogic path, was himself in the process of doing the same thing when I knew him. His father had allowed him to observe the procedure when he withdrew the life force, consciously and at will, after explaining in detail what he was going to do and how long it would take. Although this young man had decided to also follow the yogic path, he was making preparations to ensure that his family would not suffer from his actions.

Prāṇa is translated as life force. While this is not the best translation, it has to suffice for now. The Egyptians used the symbol of the ankh residing in the spine for the life force. An interesting wall hanging depicts the spine of Osiris, from which the ankh emerges with two outstretched arms and the sun above. The sun is symbolic for that particular life force and a dot indicates that the actual sun is not meant. The meaning of prāṇa has to be deeply contemplated to discover various levels, as all the powers have their origin in prāṇa. The explanation of prāṇa as the life force is only the first stepping-stone to discovery by the aspirant.

In the introduction to his book, *Light on Yoga,* B.K.S. Iyengar cautions the aspirant in the practice of prāṇāyāma by quoting from Haṭha Yoga Pradīpikā, chapter 2, verse 16 as follows: "As lions, elephants and tigers are tamed very slowly and cautiously, so should prāṇa be brought under control very slowly in gradation measured according to one's capacity and physical limitations. Otherwise it will kill the practitioner." Those who understand that yoga is more than a passing fad will know that the warning given in this book is well-founded.

Misunderstandings about Kuṇḍalinī and Sex

Because tradition emphasized the direct teaching from guru to disciple, Kuṇḍalinī has remained mysterious and thereby created much speculation and confusion. It is unfortunate that today when there is a great deal of interest and discussion about Kuṇḍalinī energy it is mainly linked to only one aspect – sex. Particularly in the West, it has now become a word and a concept that serves as an excuse for many things. Attributing events to Kuṇḍalinī energy and its overwhelming power, men and women throw aside sexual inhibitions and indulge in all sorts of illicit sexual activity. This lack of real understanding of the nature and purpose of Kuṇḍalinī is leading not only to confusion and disaster in human relationships, but also to mental imbalance. This happens because the path of Kuṇḍalinī has not been sufficiently understood and the groundwork has not been laid. This emphasis, which invites greater freedom and enjoyment of sexual pleasure, has been taken out of context from an ancient Eastern culture that was vastly different from the one now existing in the West.

There are two principal schools of thought in Kuṇḍalinī Yoga. Both acknowledge the pure Energy in the Mūlādhāra Cakra. One school applies this Energy in a concrete way by an emphasis on sex. The other does not concretize the direction of the Energy but seeks to transcend all attachment, including sex, through the development of the mental powers. If this difference in the application of the Energy is not understood, problems will arise. Even in the case of concrete application, which means the inclusion of the sexual experience, it has to be recognized that all the statements of the ancient texts have been made from a man's point of view. Sex does not burden the male with responsibility for the possible offspring because that has traditionally been viewed as the female's responsibility. Neither in the ancient texts nor in the stories is there any clarification of what happens to the female and her offspring when the male aspirant is geared to the attainment of the goal he has set for himself – using sex for his liberation and to attain higher consciousness. In this case, the woman is taken as an object of practice. Because of the biological result that makes her a mother, she and her child become an obstacle to the attainment of his goal. Is that not, in the very end, self-defeating? One cannot help but wonder if a high state of awareness and bliss can be achieved at the cost of the rejection of the mother and child.

If the male and female are indeed complementary to each other and if a higher level of bliss can be achieved through sexual union, then the possible result of that bliss, the child, should also be accepted and revered. The West is a throwaway society – we do not mend things – and this is also reflected in the relationships between men and women. Without due consideration of the partner involved and without the acceptance of responsibility for the consequences of action, how could there be the achievement of a higher state of consciousness?

In the Kuṇḍalinī symbolism, the union of Śiva and Śakti is presented in one body, not as two bodies united. Lord Śiva ultimately becomes half-man and half-woman, indicating that power and its manifestation are inseparable. The meaning of this symbolism is lost today. True oneness is only achieved in a particular state of mind for which the sex act is not essential. The pleasure from the sexual act, which is often misinterpreted as spiritual union, is in fact only the registration of stimulation in the pleasure center of the brain. The experience of union has many levels, beginning with that of the male and female united in oneself. This has nothing to do with sex. The last union of the individual consciousness with Cosmic Consciousness is the final experience, which is beyond the limitations of language to describe.

We can go a step farther and say that whatever is felt on the physical level is a stimulation and sensation that is interpreted by the mind. In the Second Cakra it is stated that the yogi can destroy worlds. These are the worlds of the mind whose creative power has an awesome reach. While the intense practice of Kuṇḍalinī Yoga includes a recognition of one's needs, these needs are more often projected onto another person. By doing this, the projector does not realize it, but in reality he is seeing his needs through the other.

Sexual instinct has almost the power of gravitational pull. Emotional and sexual dependency are much more than just a hang-up created by social upbringing. As long as the emphasis is on the "I" and everything is related to this little word, we have to see that there is a whole chain of construction behind it, which has been created for the purpose of serving the "I." As the individual progresses in awareness, it becomes clear that the overemphasis or priority given to sex has no place in the other cakras. In the same way, the joy of self-gratification attained through acquiring a lot of material goods and comforts is short-lived, and the list of desires keeps increasing. But at some point in their development, aspirants experience joy for the happiness of another person which has nothing to do with themselves. This is pure joy that echoes back to the aspirant.

The other school of thought seeks to transcend the application of the Energy in a concrete way by realizing that for thousands of lifetimes human beings have applied and experienced sex. It recognizes that at some time it is necessary to loosen all attachments and especially the attachment to the sexual experience. The dhyāna yogi (the meditative yogi) wants to preserve energy to pursue the arduous path toward Liberation. This is really very easy to understand when we consider that in everyday life certain demanding executive jobs are not open to the young person, who is still giving too much time and energy to physical interaction with the opposite sex. Only a beginner would assume that while focusing on the fulfillment of his desires he can at the same time pursue his development for Liberation. When there is attachment to sex, then Liberation cannot be achieved.

It must be understood that the Kuṇḍalinī system is for the man and woman who, by their own choice, have gratified sexual impulses in many lifetimes. Every human being goes through different stages of development. A child plays with colorful toys. A young person has different attractions, and the adult seeks again very different gratification, generally shifting into the pursuit of success and achievements of various kinds. On the spiritual path, and particularly on the path of Kuṇḍalinī, it needs to be understood that Kuṇḍalinī is not for the person for whom life is the continuous seeking of pleasures or the achievements of success in name and fame. All the Scriptures point out the same truth.

Each individual makes the decision how far he or she wants to go. The pursuit of Kuṇḍalinī is not necessarily only for the attainment of its highest goal. For most, this is far in the distance and there is the need for intermediate goals – goals such as the development of the five senses, as well as bringing more quality into all aspects of life. Only when a certain development toward our true potential has been achieved can we truly speak of entering upon the path of Kuṇḍalinī.

Symptoms of Kuṇḍalinī

The effects of Kuṇḍalinī are negative if rethinking has not been done and if the conscious mind (the interpreter) has not been sufficiently trained to accept changes, such as a wider acceptance of greater brainpower, which had been previously rejected as impossible. Many experiences are claimed as Kuṇḍalinī when there has been only the removal of inhibitions, including inhibitions toward sex. All inhibitions are learned to a large degree and are not consciously controlled. Inhibitions as well as discrimination are necessary to balance instinctual desires and drives that could hurt others.

Manipulation of the mind through such means as hypnosis can produce startling or bizarre actions. The question arises of how many of the bodily experiences now described are a fabrication of the mind, the result of information fed into the mind through the publicity given to Kuṇḍalinī by lectures or publications.

Another significant question is why the Cosmic Intelligence allows a Kuṇḍalinī awakening to occur in an unprepared person. Before attempting to answer this, each person must first define what is meant by Cosmic Intelligence, by Kuṇḍalinī, and by "awakening." A comparison from nature may help to clarify this question. When branches from a fruit tree are placed in water in the spring after pruning, there is enough energy in the branch to produce flowers. However, these flowers will not produce fruit. In the same way, manifestations of what is claimed to be Kuṇḍalinī energy may be produced from the existing energy in the mind and body. The fruit of full enlightenment, though, is not produced by the creative ability of the mind.

Spontaneous Kuṇḍalinī may cause problems. Some of the symptoms are:

- lapsing easily into meditation (an indication is people who take a long time to awaken)
- dizziness (if there is poor blood circulation)
- sudden crying spells (this is just a release of pent-up emotions)
- pressure or pain along the spine
- pain along the right or left side of the chest
- pressure in the eyes – visual aberrations
- pressure in the forehead
- pressure in the top of the head
- spasmodic breathing
- a feeling of energy
- sounds inside the head
- respiration slowed dangerously low
- heat and cold in various parts of the body
- cold body, warm fontanella
- the feeling of a pulsating leaf around the pelvis area, the abdomen or head
- a sense of emptiness, of not being "here"
- irritability

Weakness in the back is present only when the karmic situation is bound up with emotions. If strong emotions have ruled in past lives, the problem may now recur in the physical for the purpose of eliminating the obstacle. Feelings of revenge and abuse arising from uncultivated imagination or very ordinary physical conditions can also be the reason.

Psychic energy is not something unusual, limited to gifted people. Small happenings, which are usually neglected, must be given continued observation in order to increase this faculty. Such things as the body-timer (being able to awake at a time decided upon), mother and child communication, hunches or uneasy feelings of warning should be observed.

Intense practice can create enormous pressure in the beginning, bringing to the surface weaknesses and causing mental-emotional pain when selfishness, false modesty, vanity and all sorts of pride are encountered. Depressions are normally the result of not meeting one's abilities.

The Potential of Mind

Human beings live in the world of three dimensions. This includes the world of thought and all mental creativity and bringing this under control is the gateway to the fourth dimension.

Since the time of Aristotle, the West has subscribed to the linear method of thinking, which allows only for logic and reasoning. However, we know by experience that life is not linear but a wave, and intuitive thinking is needed for balance.

It has been stated in the Mūlādhāra Cakra that the two nāḍīs cannot be properly defined to the satisfaction of linear thinking, but as a starting point they can be *temporarily* compared to the two vagus nerves. The two nāḍīs, joining in the Ājñā Cakra, are also symbolic for a practical as well as intuitive way of thinking. The practical includes, of course, logic and reason.

The Eastern mind does not make the clear distinction between intuition and intellect that the Western mind tends to do. The difficulty comes for the Westerner when there is an overemphasis upon the intellect at the cost of the intuition. The simple person who is unencumbered by intellectual concepts is more receptive. What can be done to remain receptive and not to have the intellect continually interfering? Stop intellectualizing and just receive.

Intelligence is assumed to be related to the speed of energy transmission between thought connections. This rate of transmission is closer to the speed of sound than to that of light. If the brain could increase the number of connections and develop the speed of, let us say, a computer, then it should be possible for the brain at some time in its development to outperform the computer and maybe even perceive communications from unknown sources.

The old mammalian brain seems to be functioning in only a limited way in the human being. However, when brought back to its full power, it allows for much greater expression. In other words, while individuals have gained in one way, they have lost in others. If we could recover the full potential of the mammalian brain, it would mean increased mindpower. It is possible through yogic practices to regain control over areas of the brain that have been left behind for lack of use. However, there are no "gifts" available only to a privileged few. The yogi and yoginī have their attainment as a result of effort.

There are many provocative questions that can be asked concerning the usually untapped potential of mind over matter. For example, how is it possible to move objects by mental power alone? Is there such a phenomenon as virgin birth? The ancient texts speak about the "four mind-born sons of Brahmā." What does this mean? Is it possible to ascend into more subtle ways of creation than those now open to us?

Another series of questions concerns the destiny of the mental-emotional thought patterns. What happens to them? Do they continue in existence? Is it possible that patterns created millions of years ago are still in existence? Are they traveling through space and is it possible that they can be retrieved? These are all thought-provoking possibilities.

The Gods on Earth

Excerpt from *Ekottara-Āgama XXXIV*, J. Takakusu, trans.

After the floods receded and the earth came back into being, there was upon the face of the earth a film more sweet-smelling than ambrosia. Do you want to know what was the taste of that film? It was like the taste of grapewine in the mouth. And at this time the gods of the Central Heaven said to one another, "Let us go and see what it looks like . . . now that there is earth again." So the young gods of that Heaven came down into the world and saw that over the earth was spread this film. They put their fingers into the earth and sucked them. Some put their fingers into the earth many times and ate a great deal of the film, and these at once lost all their majesty and brightness. Their bodies grew heavy and their substance became flesh and bone. They lost their magic and could no longer fly, and cried out to one another in dismay "Now we are in sad case. We have lost our magic. There is nothing for it but to stay here on Earth, for we cannot get back to Heaven." So they stayed and fed upon the film that covered the earth, and gazed at one another's beauty.

Then those among them that were most passionate became women, and these gods and goddesses fulfilled their desires and pleasure in one another. And this was how it was, Brethren, that when the world began, love-making first spread throughout the world; it is an old and constant thing . . .

And the gods who had returned to Heaven looked down and saw the young gods that had fallen, and they came down and reproached them, saying, "Why are you behaving in this unclean way?" Then the gods on Earth thought to themselves, "We must find some way to be together without being seen by others." So they made houses that would cover and hide them. Brethren, that was how houses first began.

Now the people . . . hated and despised such couples and . . . hit them or pelted them with sticks, clods of earth, tiles or stones . . . That is why today, when a girl is married, she is pelted with flowers or gold or silver . . . and the people, as they pelt her, say, "May peace and happiness, new bride, be yours!" Brethren, in former times ill was meant by these things that were done, but nowadays good is meant.

The Descent of the Soul

From a description of the Sabian doctrines by El-Khatibi, quoted by Jean Doresse in *The Secret Books of the Egyptian Gnostics,* reprinted with permission of the publisher: Viking Press, New York, © 1958, 1959 by Librairie Plon, Paris, p. 316.

"The Soul turned at one time toward matter. She fell in love with it and burned with desire to experience bodily pleasures, wished no more to be separated from it, thus the world was born. From that moment the Soul forgot Herself. She forgot Her original dwelling, Her true center, Her everlasting life. But God, unwilling to abandon the Soul to its degradation with Matter, endowed Her with understanding and the faculty of perception, precious gifts which would remind Her of Her high origin, the spiritual world which would restore Her consciousness of Herself, teach Her that She was a stranger here below . . . as soon as the Soul has just been taught by perception and understanding, as soon as She has regained self-consciousness She longs for the spiritual world, as a man exiled in a strange land sighs for his distant homestead. She is convinced that to regain Her original state She must loose Herself from the ties of this world, from carnal concupiscences, from all material things." Thus El-Khatibi describes the descent of the Soul and then its return to the spiritual world.

RECOMMENDED READING

ACKERMAN, DIANE. *The Natural History of the Senses.* New York: Vintage Books, 1991. A poetic, idiosyncratic exploration of the senses, ranging across cultures.

AVALON, ARTHUR. (Sir John Woodroffe). *Garland of Letters.* Nesma Books India, 2001.

———*Shakti and Shakta.* Madras, India: Ganesh & Co., 1998.

———*The Serpent Power.* Madras, India: Ganesh & Co., 2000.

AVALON, ARTHUR & ELLEN. *Hymns to the Goddess and Hymn to Kali.* Madras, India: Ganesh & Co. 2001.

The above books by Arthur Avalon have been the source of much of the theoretical material underlying the presentation in this book. They are recommended for study by the serious student. Other recommended books by Arthur Avalon are:

Principles of Tantra. Kessinger, 2003.
Kama-Kala-Vilasa. Ganesh & Co., 1961.
The Greatness of Shiva. Ganesh & Co., 1953.
The Great Liberation. Ganesh and Co., 2001.
Tantraraja Tantra. Motilal Banarsidas 1997.
Introduction to Tantra S'astra. Ganesh & Co. 2001.
Kalacudamani Nigama. Ganesh & Co., 1956.

BERENDT, JOACHIM-ERNST. *The World Is Sound: Nada Brahma.* Rochester, VT: Destiny Books, 1991. An inspiring exploration of the sense of hearing that encourages listening in new ways both in daily life and in spiritual development.

BLACKMORE, SUSAN. *Consciousness, An Introduction.* New York: Oxford University Press, 2004. An undergraduate-level textbook that pulls together current avenues of research and hypotheses about consciousness.

BROWN CHEEVER MACKENZIE. *God as Mother.* Hartford, VT: Claude Stark, 1974. A detailed examination of Radha's evolution to the stature of goddess during the late medieval period in India, as portrayed in the Brahmavaivarta Purana.

———. *The Devi Gita: The Song of the Goddess.* Albany, NY: SUNY Press, 1998. This "song" to Divine Mother is a truly inspiring presentation of the Kuṇḍalinī System in poetry. The whole eight-limbed path of Kuṇḍalinī is presented as a mystical Gita (song), including meditation on the Light.

CAPRA, FRITJOF. *The Tao of Physics.* Boston: Shambhala Publications, 1999. Emphasizing the value of experiential knowledge, Capra looks at the world through the lenses of modern physics and Eastern mystical traditions.

DAMASIO, ANTONIO R. *The Feeling of What Happens: Body and Emotion in the Making of Consciousness.* Fort Washington, PA: Harvest Books, 2000. Using scientific research, medical cases and introspection a neuroscientist explores the role of emotions and feelings in consciousness.

DOUGLAS-KOLTZ, NEIL. *Prayers of the Cosmos.* San Francisco: Harper Collins, 1994. A mystical interpretation of the Aramaic version of the Lord's Prayer and Beatitudes. Complete with the Aramaic text, translation and notes on the translation, it reveals the radical, feminist and meditative side of Christ's teaching.

DOWMAN, KEITH. *Skydancer: The Secret Life and Songs of Yeshe Tsogyal.* Ithaca, NY: Snow Lion, 1996. An excellent translation of the life story, songs and teachings of Yeshe Tsogyal. Consort of the renowned guru Padma Sambhava, Yeshe Tsogyal taught in 8th - century Tibet and became known as the Guru Dākinī, an embodiment of the female Buddha.

DYCZKOWSKI, MARK. *The Doctrine of Vibration.* Albany, NY: SUNY Press, 1987. A presentation of the Kashmiri Śaivist view that consciousness is an active, pulsating energy, and that the world is a manifestation of this conscious energy. A scholarly work that offers much food for thought.

EDOU, JEROME. *Machig Labrong and the Foundations of Chod*. Ithaca, NY: Snow Lion, 1996. Based on the teachings of the Prajnaparamita, Chod was studied and practiced by the Tibetan Yogini, Machig, and eventually returned to India in an advanced form of practice based on her teachings. Machig was the first woman to be recognized as a purveyor of authentic Buddhist teaching in the land of its origin, India.

EVANS-WENTZ, W.Y. *Tibet's Great Yogi: Milarepa*. Whitefish, MT: Kessinger Publishing, 2003. This classic biography of a yogi who achieves liberation in one lifetime offers insights into the guru-disciple relationship, the importance of dreams in spiritual development, and the necessity for devotion and commitment on the spiritual path.

FEUERSTEIN, GEORG. *Tantra: The Path of Ecstasy*. Boston: Shambhala Publications, 1998. Feuerstein's clear introduction to the Tantric tradition includes a brief history of Tantra, an explanation of the philosophical principles and practices, and extensive quotes from original Tantric scriptures.

FORMAN, ROBERT, K.C. *Mysticism, Mind, Consciousness*. Albany, NY: SUNY Press, 1999. A popular account of what mystical *experience* "feels like." Includes examples from a variety of traditions, and concludes with an exploration of mind and consciousness.

GALLAGHER, WINIFRED. *Spiritual Genius: The Mastery of Life's Meaning*. New York: Random House, 2001. A profile of ten contemporary spiritual leaders. The hard work and dedication needed on any spiritual path, reflected by the lives of these leaders, dispels the fantasy that spiritual life is easy and blissful.

GOVINDA, ANAGARIKA. *Foundations of Tibetan Mysticism*. York Beach, ME: Samuel Weiser 1989. A Tibetan mystic's account of the esoteric principles and practices – including mantra and the nature of the cakras – upon which Tibetan Yoga is based.

GROF, STANISLAV. *The Cosmic Game: Explorations in the Frontiers of Human Consciousness*. Albany, NY: SUNY Press, 1998. A readable summary of the spiritual insights the author has gained from a lifetime of personal exploration and as a leading practitioner of Transpersonal Psychology.

GUENTHER, HERBERT V. *The Tantric View of Life.* Boston: Shambhala Publications, 1976. One of the clearest expositions of Buddhist Tantra available. Concerned with existence or being-as-such, Tantra is founded on the knowledge gained from intimate personal experience of body and mind as interdependent and interpenetrating organisms.

HARDING, SARAH, trans. and ed. *Machik's Complete Explanation: Clarifying the Meaning of Chod.* Ithaca, NY: Snow Lion, 2003. The first complete English translation of the central teachings of Machik Labdron, the great yogini of 11th - to 12th - century Tibet. Her teachings focus on practical ways to direct the energy that arises in the form of fear, anger and negativity to cut through ("chod") whatever stands in the way of compassion and love.

HAYWARD, JEREMY W. & FRANCISCO J. VARELA. *Gentle Bridges: Conversations with the Dalai Lama on the Sciences of Mind.* Boston: Shambhala Publications, 1992. This dialogue between the Dalai Lama and several Western scientists explores the nature of the mind in the light of both recent scientific discoveries and Tibetan Buddhist philosophy and practice.

IYENGAR, B.K.S. *Light on Yoga.* London: Harper Collins, 2001. A thorough presentation of Haṭha Yoga. Speaking from his personal experience, Mr. Iyengar stresses the necessity for the student to be persistent in practice in order to obtain results.

IYENGAR, GEETA. *Yoga: A Gem for Women.* Spokane, WA: Timeless Books, 1990. A detailed guide to the practice of Haṭha Yoga, including specific āsana instruction for women. Includes photos, description of the health and healing benefits of the poses, plus instruction in relaxation, breathing techniques and the practice of meditation.

JOHNSON, WILLIAM. *Mystical Theology, Science of Love.* Maryknoll, NY: Orbis Books,1998. Written by a Jesuit author who lived in Japan for 40 years, this exploration of Eastern and Western mystical traditions also encourages dialogue between science and Eastern traditions. Includes experiences ranging from Padre Pio and Gandhi, to Ramakrishna and Theresa of Avila.

KRISHNA, GOPI. *Kuṇḍalinī, The Evolutionary Energy in Man.* Boston: Shambhala Publications, 1970. Gopi Krishna presents a first-person account of the symptoms of Kuṇḍalinī.

LERNER, GERDA. *The Creation of Patriarchy.* New York: Oxford University Press, 1986. Using exceptional academic standards of objectivity and methodology, Lerner summarizes the cultural/historical foundation of patriarchy throughout the last five millennia.

MARGULIS, LYNN and DORIAN SAGAN. *Mystery Dance.* New York: Summit Books, 1991. Two biologists look at the evolution of sex from the beginning of time as the primary procreative force in all forms of life. The facts of life are presented with a practical and often humorous perspective.

MISHRA, KAMALAKAR. *Kashmir Saivism: The Central Philosophy of Tantrism.* Portland: Rudra Press, 1993. Deciphers Tantric texts and their rich symbolism to reveal a philosophy that is not abstract, but practical and relevant to modern life.

MOOKERJEE, AJIT. *Kali: The Feminine Force.* New York: Destiny Books, 1988. The powerful symbol of Kālī as the Divine Feminine is explored through images, poetry and artistic prose.

MULLER-ORTEGA, PAUL EDUARDO. *Triadic Heart of Śiva.* New York: SUNY, 1985. Muller-Ortega describes the non-dual Śaivism of Kashmir as the unitive vision of the heart, a vision that appears to end all separation in a truly transformative way. Based on the teachings of the Kaula Tantra of Kashmir with commentary by Abhinavagupta, a 12th - century master.

NARBY, JEREMY. *The Cosmic Serpent.* New York: J.P. Tarcher, 1999. The personal story of an anthropologist's journey to the Amazon, his experiences with Amazonian Shamanism and its connection to DNA, consciousness and serpent symbolism.

PAGELS, ELAINE. *Gnostic Gospels.* New York: Random House, 2004. Continues to rank as one of the most thorough and insightful analyses of the Gnostic influence on Christianity, and why the Gnostics were a political liability in the institutionalization of the early church.

PEAT, F. DAVID. *Blackfoot Physics: A Journey into the Native American Universe.* Grand Rapids, MI: Phanes Press, 2002. A physicist's tantalizing perspective on Native American cosmology and its startling similarity to insights currently emerging from modern Western science.

PENROSE, ROGER. *The Emperor's New Mind: Concerning Computers, Minds, and the Laws of Physics.* Oxford: Oxford Press, 2002. One of the most brilliant and eclectic physicists of our times explores the mysteries at the frontiers of physics, and speculates on the connection with the mind.

RADHA, SWAMI SIVANANDA. *The Divine Light Invocation: A Healing Meditation.* 4th ed. Spokane, WA: Timeless Books, 2001. Complete instructions as well as preliminary exercises are given for this standing meditation practice. Also included are the history and helpful directions for directing the Light.

———. *From the Mating Dance to the Cosmic Dance.* Spokane, WA: Timeless Books, 1992. A yogic viewpoint that draws on a model of evolutionary psychology. Offers practical guidance on how the pursuit of Higher Consciousness can be understood in the context of sex, love and marriage.

———. *Hatha Yoga: The Hidden Language.* Spokane, WA: Timeless Books, 1987. Haṭha Yoga is presented as an integral part of the Kuṇḍalinī system, with instructions on how to deepen personal understanding through accessing the symbolic language of the āsanas.

———. *In the Company of the Wise.* Spokane, WA: Timeless Books, 1991. Swami Radha describes her meetings with many of the world's great gurus, and offers advice on how to choose a guru as well as common illusions to be aware of.

———. *Mantras: Words of Power.* Spokane, WA: Timeless Books, 1980. A classic guide to the practice of Mantra Yoga, including the musical notations and meanings of various mantras, their benefits, and advice on establishing a personal practice.

———. *Realities of the Dreaming Mind.* Spokane, WA: Timeless Books, 2004. An introduction to yogic dream analysis, offering practices and techniques for translating dream symbols in a personal way and applying dream messages to daily life.

RANK, OTTO. *Beyond Psychology.* New York: Dover Publications, 1958. A contemporary of Sigmund Freud, the author seeks to go beyond Freud's gender-based psychology to a new psychology of self, beyond male and female. Forerunner of the transpersonal movement.

ROSEN, RICHARD. *The Yoga of Breath: A Step-by-Step Guide to Prāṇāyāma.* Boston: Shambhala Publications, 2002. Rosen offers exercises and tips on how to incorporate prāṇayama into existing āsana or spiritual practices and stresses the necessity for commitment and persistence in practice.

SHANKARANARAYANAN, S. *Glory of the Divine Mother.* Veyangoda: Prabha Publishers, 2001. Written in classical Indian poetic form, this universal story depicts the battle between good and evil, light and darkness. Includes commentary explaining the symbolism of the goddesses wielding weapons against evil demons and instructions on how to use this scripture as a devotional practice.

SILBURN, LILIAN. *Kuṇḍalinī: The Energy of the Depths.* Albany, NY: SUNY Press, 1988. Silburn studies the underlying purpose of Kuṇḍalinī Yoga based on the ancient scriptures of Kashmir.

SIVANANDA, SWAMI. *Concentration and Meditation.* Shivanandanagar, India: Divine Life Society, 1997. What is often called meditation in the West is usually nothing more than creating spiritual movies with the imagination. This book leaves no doubt about what is required to build a mental foundation for true concentration and meditation.

———. *Kuṇḍalinī Yoga.* Shivanandanagar, India: Divine Life Society, 1994. Swami Sivananda covers all aspects of Kuṇḍalinī Yoga in a clear, straightforward manner. Includes detailed instruction in the various yogas that make up the Kuṇḍalinī system, such as prāṇāyāma, Haṭha Yoga and Mantra Yoga.

———. *Mind: Its Mysteries and Control.* Shivanandanagar, India: Divine Life Society, 2001. A discourse on the functions of mind as well as instincts, emotions and imagination and how to control them. Language is dated but still a useful reference.

———. *The Science of Prāṇāyāma.* Shivanandanagar, India: Divine Life Society, 1997. Inspiring and practical, this text removes the mystery and misconceptions that so often arise in the West about prāṇāyāma and breath control. First published in 1935 and now in its 16th edition, it is as good a reference and guide as is available.

TYBERG, JUDITH. *Language of the Gods.* Los Angeles: East-West Cultural Center, 1970. Dr. Tyberg has put together an excellent book on the Sanskrit language based on her studies at the Sanskrit University in Benares.

WHITE, JOHN, ed. *Kuṇḍalinī: Evolution and Enlightenment.* New York: Paragon House, 1990. This cross-cultural, cross-disciplinary review presents Eastern and Western, traditional and contemporary views on Kuṇḍalinī and its place in the development of consciousness.

WOOD, ERNEST E. *Practical Yoga: Ancient and Modern.* New York: Wilshire Book Co., 1948. The text focuses on the Yoga Sutras of Patanjali. The practices described are based on 40 years of the author's personal experience.

———. *Concentration: An Approach to Meditation.* Wheaton: Theosophical Publishing House, 2001. A practical manual containing 36 mental and physical exercises aimed at developing concentration, powers of thought and awareness.

YOGANANDA. *Autobiography of a Yogi.* Los Angeles: Self-Realization Fellowship, 1994. The autobiography of Paramahamsa Yogananda, one of the first yogis to bring the teachings to North America, is helpful reading to ease the mind into the Eastern way of thought and perception.

SANSKRIT PRONUNCIATION GUIDE

a	like *a* in *organ* or the *u* in *but*
ā	like *a* in *far* but held twice as long
i	like *i* in *pique*
ī	same as *i* but twice as long
u	like *u* in *rule*
ū	same as *u* but twice as long
ṛi	like *ri* in *Rita*
ṛī	same as *ri* but twice as long
lri	pronounced *lree*
lrī	same as *lri* but twice as long
e	like *e* in *they*
ai	like *ai* in *aisle*
o	like *o* in *go*
au	like *ow* in *how*
ṃ	anuswara is a resonant nasal pronounced with an open mouth.
ḥ	Visarga is an h followed by the sound of its preceding vowel: thus kaviḥ is pronounced *kavihi*, etc.
k	as in *kite*
kh	as in *Ekhart*
g	as in *give*
gh	as in *dig-hard*
ṅ	as in *sing*
ch	as in *chair*
c	as in *match*
j	as in *joy*
jh	as in *hedgehog*

ñ	as in *señor*
ṭ	as in *tub* with the tongue to the roof of the mouth
ṭh	as in *light-heart* with the tongue to the roof of the mouth
ḍ	as in *dub* with the tongue to the roof of the mouth
ḍh	as in *red-head* with the tongue to the roof of the mouth
ṇ	as in *nut* with the tongue to the roof of the mouth
t	as in *tub* with the tongue against the teeth
th	as in *light-heart* with the tongue against the teeth
d	as in *dub* with the tongue against the teeth
dh	as in *red-head* with the tongue against the teeth
n	as in *nut* with the tongue against the teeth
p	as in *pine*
ph	as in *up-hill*
b	as in *bird*
bh	as in *scrub-hard*
m	as in *mother*
y	as in *yes*
r	as in *run*
l	as in *light*
v	as in *vine*
ś	as in *shine*
ṣ	an s, but with the tip of the tongue curled up towards the roof of the mouth
s	as in *sun*
h	as in *home*

Note on aspirated sounds kh, gh,ch, jh, ṭh, th, dh, ḍh, ph, bh: these sounds are produced with a puff of air (represented by the h). Contrast the *p* sound in *option* with the *p* sound in *pair*.

Courtesy of Judith Tyberg, PhD, East West Cultural Center

INDEX

RESOURCES

Yasodhara Ashram

Workshops and courses based on the teachings of Swami Sivananda Radha are available through Yasodhara Ashram in British Columbia, Canada, and worldwide through Radha Yoga Centres.

Yasodhara Ashram
Box 9, Kootenay Bay, BC, Canada, V0B 1X0
(800) 661-8711
yashram@netidea.com
www.yasodhara.org
Radha Yoga Centres: **www.radha.org**

ascent magazine

For previously unpublished articles by Swami Sivananda Radha and a fresh perspective on yoga and spiritual life, explore *ascent* magazine.

ascent magazine
837 Rue Gilford, Montréal, QC, Canada, H2J 1P1
(888) 825-0228
info@ascentmagazine.com
www.ascentmagazine.com

timeless books

Since 1978, *timeless* has been publishing print, audio and video media that bring alive an ancient lineage of yogic teachings. *timeless* presents a variety of practical spiritual tools for daily living. For a free catalogue contact:

in Canada: (800) 661-8711
contact@timeless.org
in the US: (800) 251-9273
info@timeless.org
www.timeless.org

ABOUT THE AUTHOR

Swami Sivananda Radha (1911–1995) was one of the foremost spiritual leaders of our time. Her knowledge of the Kundalini system was based on personal experience and direct teachings from Indian and Tibetan masters. She later verified and broadened her understanding through research into the original texts. Her own foundation in yoga was based on character building, courage and awareness, and her special gift was to convey the teachings in a concise, expansive form – providing a flexible structure for aspirants to discover their own path to awakening their potential.

Swami Radha was born in Germany in 1911, moved to Canada after World War II, and traveled to India in the mid-fifties to meet her spiritual teacher, Swami Sivananda. Initiated into sanyas in 1956, she then returned to Canada and spent the next forty years passionately committed to teaching, living the ideals of yoga, and updating the ancient texts. Swami Radha wrote ten books and founded Yasodhara Ashram, a thriving yoga retreat and study center in British Columbia. She established *ascent* magazine, *timeless books*, and a number of urban centers called Radha Yoga Centers. These centres and publications continue to present her work in the spirit it was created, maintaining the quality and integrity that were the essence of her life.

THE CAKRAS

COLOR ILLUSTRATIONS

The First Cakra

Mūlādhāra

PLATE I

The First Cakra • Mūlādhāra

Child Brahmā

PLATE II

The First Cakra • Mūlādhāra

Śakti Ḍākinī

PLATE III

The Second Cakra

Svādhiṣṭhāna

PLATE IV

The Second Cakra · Svādhiṣṭhāna

Viṣṇu

PLATE V

The Second Cakra • Svādhiṣṭhāna

Śakti Rākinī

PLATE VI

The Third Cakra

Maṇipūra

PLATE VII

The Third Cakra • Maṇipūra

Viṣṇu (Rudra)

PLATE VIII

The Third Cakra • Maṇipūra

Śakti Lākinī (Lakṣmī)

PLATE IX

The Fourth Cakra

Anāhata

PLATE X

The Fourth Cakra • Anāhata

Īśa

PLATE XI

The Fourth Cakra • Anāhata

Śakti Kākinī

PLATE XII

The Fifth Cakra

Viśuddha

PLATE XIII

The Fifth Cakra • Viśuddha

Sadāśiva

PLATE XIV

The Fifth Cakra • Viśuddha

Gaurī

PLATE XV

The Sixth Cakra

Ājñā

PLATE XVI

The Sixth Cakra • Ājñā

Śakti Hākinī

PLATE XVII